The Great(er) Delaware Sports Book

I0150416

Second Edition

Doug Gelbert

CRUDEN BAY BOOKS

THE GREAT(ER) DELAWARE SPORTS BOOK
Second Edition

Cruden Bay Books
184 Kanuga Heights Lane
Hendersonville NC 28739

International Standard Book Number 978-1-935771-32-6

THE LINE-UP

INTRODUCTION

Almost twenty-five years have passed since the research for the original *Great Delaware Sports Book* was completed in the early 1990s. Since the history of organized sports in Delaware only spans about six quarter-centuries that means an additional 16% of First State sports heritage is now missing from that book. So let's see what has happened in that time...

But first, one must grapple with that nagging question - "Who is a Delawarean?" Of course, there are those athletes of the first order, the native Delwareans, born and raised. Your Porky Olivers, your Chris Shorts, your Elena Delle Donnes. The lucky ones, if you will.

And there are those who arrived early and accomplished much - Vic Willis, Judy Johnson, Randy White, et al. Or those who arrived later, stayed awhile and left an indelible mark such as Pete Oakley or Tubby Raymond.

No one would confuse Rich Gannon or Joe Flacco with a "Native Delawarean" but the feats of athletes of their ilk demand inclusion. A thornier question concerns those who were born in Delaware but left before their careers blossomed. Or even started. No one wants to deny Paul Goldschmidt his birthright as a First State native but is he a Delawarean athlete having never perfomed on athletic fields here? Like in his Delaware life, he gets a cameo in here, too.

This edition is organized much like the original. Section I looks at Delaware sporting life through the decades. What was the Delaware sporting scene like? What games were Delawareans playing? Section II is a history of specific sports in Delaware.

One difference is found in Section III - the Record Book. It is mostly gone. The *Great Delware Sports Book* was compiled before there was a widespread Internet. Many of the statistics and team and player records put in that book were assembled in one convenient place for the first time. These days everybody carries around a Delaware sports record book in their pocket so, in deference to the digital age, only biographical capsules of Delaware's Athlete of the Year are included in Section III.

Enough. Let's get started and learn about the Delaware athletes who have brought recognition and glory to the First State through the years...

Delaware Sporting Life Through The Decades

1870s

Prior to the Civil War sporting events were manifestations of everyday life: marksmen toted their hunting rifles to the shooting range, teamsters raced their wagons along dusty country roads and even fire departments dueled in city streets for recognition as the fastest rescue squad in town.

By the 1870s leisure activities began to evolve for their own sake. In Delaware baseball was the first team sport to come to the fore. Every town fielded its own nine: the Tammany Club of New Castle, the Newark Agiles, the Milford Academic, the Bumble Bee Club of Laurel, the Odessa Mutuals. By mid-decade the *Every Evening* in Wilmington was calling baseball the national game and reported, "the fever for this game is becoming more prevalent than for several seasons. Practice games are constantly going on in lots about town."

While First Staters up and down the peninsula were picking up bats and balls, trotting races reigned as the premier spectator sport in the state. Trotting horses were America's first sports super-stars and Delawareans turned out by the thousands to cheer - and bet - on some of the country's top trotters at tracks in Wilmington, Middletown and Dover. Local horses also raced around ovals in Felton, Christiana and Hares Corner. When a 1/2-mile dirt track was leveled in Newark local residents expressed relief that "we will now know who has the fastest horse without endangering the lives of our people."

By all accounts sports were booming in Delaware by the 1870s. On September 25, 1871 the state's first sporting grounds opened at Scheutzen Park as the home of the Wilmington Rifle Club. The Park would soon be hosting wheeling matches, running matches, walking matches, foot and sack races and trotting races. In July of 1873 Scheutzen Park witnessed the birth of women's sports in Delaware.

In reporting on the running races it was recorded by *Every Evening* that "perhaps the crowning feature in the afternoon sport was the race between Mr. and Mrs. Moulton, 100 yards, this being the first opportunity of witnessing female pedestrianism. All eyes were centered on her. We are pleased to say that she proved that ladies could enjoy athletic sports and yet not be coarse and vulgar. Her lady-like deportment excited considerable comment. Mrs. Moulton is a fine-looking, fluty formed lady and judged from the time she made (13 3/4 seconds) she bids to be the fastest runner in America."

Elsewhere croquet was sweeping the state; there were reports of playing even by moonshine. On the waters of the Christina and Delaware Rivers boatmen raced their yachts and skiffs. Crow merchants in Delaware City enjoyed a brisk business supplying birds for shooting matches. Indoors there was bowling at the Atlantic Garden on 224 King Street in Wilmington. Across the street at 104 Market Street were team and single-handed shuffleboard matches between Wilmington and neighboring cities. Down the street in the Hardings Billiard Room at 6th & Market billiards and finger

First State Sports Hero of the Decade: Bachelors Boat Club

Undoubtedly the greatest sporting venue in Delaware in the 1870s was the Christiana River, as the Wilmington stream was known until 1937. Large crowds gathered on wharves and bridges and lined her banks to view crew races. The first big race occurred in 1873 when the *Falcon* of the Undine Club tangled with the *Thistle* of the Pioneer Club. The course stretched from the 3rd Street Bridge to the Wilmington & Western railroad bridge and back, about 1 1/4 miles. *Falcon* reached the finish line first in the opening heat, winning 20 minutes to 20:20 and took the second heat more decisively, 19:30 to 20:30.

The next year a third club joined the Christiana regatta to race before a crowd estimated at 8000. The Bachelors Boat Club was only together one month and using a hastily acquired boat from Philadelphia. The new crew was lightly regarded among the bettors. They entered the 5-man gig class with *Idalia* and, averaging less than 140 pounds a man, thumped the Pioneer Club by 26 seconds in the 3-mile feature. Undine, the heavy betting favorite, was more than a minute back. In the 7-man barge class *Falcon* once again ruled over *Thistle*.

The Bachelors performance excited Wilmington boatmen. Their time was competitive with prominent crews around the country. A rematch was arranged for the fall of 1874 to further showcase the three boats. Bachelors raced to a three-length lead early but collided with Undine making the turn at the buoy, allowing the Pioneer Club to reach the finish line first. After great deliberations over many days a re-row was ordered and Bachelors prevailed by ten open lengths.

It was the end of the heyday of rowing on the Christiana. In 1876 Undine and Pioneer merged to form the Delaware Rowing Club but their challenge to Bachelors was not accepted. In 1879 the barges from the defunct rowing clubs were sold to the University of Virginia where they were quite successful again, this time on the James River.

billiards were extremely popular.

Delaware hotels staged many a sporting exhibition; there were boxing and wrestling matches in the Dobbinville Hotel in New Castle; the Washington Hotel in Wilmington hosted an international checkers match won by Wilmington's Matthew Priest - 9 games to 3 with 33 draws - at $100 a side; and the National Hotel in Middletown witnessed the first visit to Delaware of the famed billiards players Joseph and Cyrille Dion. The Dions spotted some crack Delaware amateurs 90 out of 100 points and beat them routinely. If not overwhelmed by the quality of local billiard playing the invaders were said, however, to be much impressed with Delaware's magnificent peach orchards.

But as the decade drew to a close the novelty of sport was tattered. Attendance at the Scheutzen Park trotting races was dwindling and its Wheel of Fortune was doing the lion's share of the business. Several meets had to be cancelled. The Quickstep Baseball Club, the darlings of Wilmington, was disbanded. In desperation, with the prospect of no games to bet on in 1880, the *Every Evening* re-printed an account of a Quicksteps glory game from 1876 explaining that "sport is at such a low ebb in Wilmington that raking over the old ashes is found more satisfactory than doing nothing."

The Battle For The Lady Fayre

Jousting began in 11th century France as a military exercise and soon spread throughout Europe. Despite church opposition for its savagery and occasional state banishments jousting continued through the Middle Ages until the death of King Henry II of France from jousting injuries in 1599.

Its revival, in a decidedly more humane form, occurred in Mount Solon, Virginia in 1821. Surely no sport in America has more romantic origins than jousting. A young Virginia maiden could not choose between the affections of two ardent suitors. So she decided to bestow her favor on the winner of a jousting contest.

The site chosen for the joust was the the Natural Chimneys, a rock formation in the Shendandoah Valley that resmebled medieval castles. The two contestants were to ride at three rings suspended from arches 30 yards apart. The young "knights" practiced for weeks and on the day of the event a large crowd turned out to view the spectacle.

Such a good time was had that it was decided to make the joust an annual event. From that day to this, on the third Saturday in August, the winning knight has earned the right to name and crown his "Queen of Love and Beauty," making the Mount Solon jousting tournament the oldest continually held sporting event in America.

In Delaware riding tournaments were staged at St. Georges, Hares Corner, and elsewhere. Carriages bearing hundreds of spectators streamed to the tracks and fans would line the long, straight course behind fences. Near one end of the course, where the horse and rider would start, stood a stand where a man was at the ready with the starting flag.

Riders, competing under colorful jousting titles, lanced the three successively smaller rings - some as small as 1/4" in diameter - from iron hooks suspended below wooden arches while riding their charging mounts down the 90-yard course in not more than eight seconds. A single ride was known as a tilt and a tournament typically would feature five tilts per rider before lunch and five afterwards. As many as three dozen knights would compete with the one capturing the most total rings being declared the winner.

The hand of a fair maiden was soon ignored; by the 1870s the top prize at a Delaware riding tournament could be a $300 buggy. Perhaps it was this loss of tradition that sounded the death knell of big-time jousting in Delaware but with the advent of more modern sports riding tournaments began being supplanted as sporting entertainment in the last decades of the century.

Oh, and the fate of that first winning modern day knight and his "Lady Fayre"? Alas, it is lost to history.

1880s

If the post-Civil War years witnessed the birth of spectator games in Delaware, the 1880s must be acknowledged as the decade of participation. In 1880 one observer noted that, "the prospects for tennis and archery will come into general use this year, with much improved equipment in these games." Gymnastics became so popular by 1882 that *Every Evening* editorialized that, "we should have a first-rate gymnasium here and we could if young men would take hold of the thing in popular spirit. If the time that well-dressed loafers spend in ogling women on Market Street were spent in healthful exercise it would be pleasanter for the women and better for their overbold admirers."

Such athletic spirit indeed swept over Delaware. Young men banded into clubs to indulge in their favorite sports. Soon in existence were the Delaware Cricket Club, the Wilmington Bicycle Club and the Wilmington Camping Club. The oldest gun club in the state, the Wawaset Gun Club started in 1883. The Wilmington Croquet Club organized in 1888 and rented a plot of ground at the corner of 7th and Franklin for competition. The historic athletic clubs, the Delaware Field Club and the Warren Athletic Club, both organized in this decade.

July 4th was the greatest sports day of the year with bicycling, cricket, baseball, shooting matches and horse racing all available throughout the state. Indoors, in addition to gymnastics, there were two seasons: the roller skating season which started on October 1 and the swimming season which opened on May 1.

The Wilmington Natatorium opened at 4th and Jefferson in 1885 and the aquatics were instantly said to exceed even roller skating for "pure, unrestricted enjoyment." Women were especially enamored with swimming. Whereas the women of the Delaware Field Club held their tennis tournaments in secrecy away from the critical male eye, women swimmers were much in evidence at the Natatorium. The services of a woman instructor were retained and she quickly had 35 ladies in her class. When an observer dropped in one day he reported, "Four or five ladies, one a swimmer, the other learners, took a dip at the Natatorium this morning. They enjoyed the clear water and, under the instruction of Madam Pagenstecher the neophytes made satisfactory progress. The swimming lady of the party was bold enough to essay the high dive, a feat many of the males prefer to avoid."

In the manner of all converts, promoters of the new athletic fervor oft times took their passion to extremes. Thus the odd marathons of the day. Milford's Dorsey Hall hosted a 12-hour pedestrian contest open to all for $100 in gold. In Wilmington, the sports halls featured days-long, go-as-you-please walking matches.

The greatest such event occurred in the Wilmington Rink in 1888. A track of tan bark and sawdust was laid out for the 75-hour marathon, refereed by world champion James Albert. Albert was the first man to run over 1000 kilometers in a six-day race, logging 621.75 miles earlier that year. Albert gave exhibitions

FIRST STATE SPORTS HERO OF THE DECADE:
WARREN ATHLETIC CLUB

For five years during the 1880s the Warren Athletic Club staged track and field exhibitions that were the envy of cities ten times again the size of Wilmington. In the five-year run of the games, despite persistent bad weather that became the hallmark of the event, a slew of American and world records were toppled. Nationally prominent athletes paid their own way to Wilmington, with only the lure of gold and silver medals and the hospitality of the Warrens.

The first exhibition, in the spring of 1885, featured dashes of 100 and 220 yards, runs of 1/4 and 1/2 mile, a hitch-and-kick, a tug-of-war, and a 2-mile bicycle race for the championship of Delaware. The races were handicapped with lesser competitors granted either a head start or a reduction in distance.

In 1886 the Warren Games began attracting national athletes and a spring and fall meet were held. By 1887 the only Delaware winners remaining were in "Delaware state championship" events. That year Wilson Coudon, the North East, Maryland strongman, shattered the American record in the hammer throw with a toss of 102' 7" and in the high jump William Byrd of the University of Pennsylvania soared 6' 3/4" for a new national mark. Byrd narrowly missed a world record and the spring 1887 edition of the games was widely acclaimed as one of the finest meets ever staged anywhere.

The next year Coudon made 28 throws with different hammer weights, establishing 13 world records at the Warren games. In 1889 he again favored Delaware with a world record toss. Despite the excellence of the athletic performances and the first class accommodations provided by the Warren Athletic Club the games were never a financial success. Once again Delaware sports fans were chastised by the local press: "There was a fair attendance (roughly 750) of spectators filling the grandstand but not so large as the character of the sports and contestants merited or is due from the public of Wilmington."

Unable and unwilling to shoulder the monetary burden of first-class national track meets the Warren Athletic Club stopped the games in 1889. It was the last time the track and field world would ever take notice of Wilmington.

and expounded on his diet necessary to triumph in such a contest: no solid food, not even bread; calves foot jelly; ten quarts of milk daily; beef extract; ice cream to keep his stomach cool; 30-40 bottles of ginger ale and daily raw oysters.

Five runners competed and 500 fans, many spending the night, looked on. The contestants averaged about two hours of sleep a day and Frank "Black Dan" Hart, led the entire way, winning by less than a mile before an enthusiastic crowd of 1300 on the final night. Hart, a superstar "pedestrian" who had set the world record by covering 565 miles in Madison Square Garden in a six-day race in 1880, covered just over 216 miles for the three-plus days in Wilmington.

At the Natatorium on June 7, 1887 Wilmington favorite John Pierson and United States champion Dennis Butler of Philadelphia met in a much-publicized marathon swim. Butler and Pierson were lifeguards together in Atlantic City in the early 1880s when both were credited with more than 80 ocean saves. Since then each had often engaged in lengthy river and ocean swims.

Now the game was to swim for two hours each night for six days with the winner taking $200 of the $250 purse. Butler entered the water first on opening night and entertained the crowd with feats of eating and smoking underwater, imitating a number of fish and demonstrating different styles of swimming. Predictably, perhaps, he battled through cramps much of the first night and Pierson swam to a half-mile lead. The national champion made up the advantage the next night and by the end had won handily.

With the demise of the Middletown Fair in 1883, Dover was the indisputable capital of Delaware horse racing throughout the decade. But the horsemen were now sharing their tracks and roadways with a new contraption that was rapidly eclipsing some of their popularity: the bicycle. Wheel clubs formed in Smyrna and Middletown and the Wilmington Wheel Club members were so successful on a national scale that Wilmington became a mecca for top riders.

The Delaware sports fan continued to greet tries at professional baseball with an impassioned indifference. In 1889 Wilmington baseball talent was consolidated into a single team which took on all comers. The club started by winning its first seven games but attendance was "distinctively Wilmingtonian - small." Fans countered with complaints that the park was the most dreary place imaginable, littered with broken seats and

Frank Hart was the biggest national sports hero Delaware had seen when he came to race in the 1880s.

filthy walls in need of paint. Professional baseball again fizzled in Wilmington.

Amateur baseball, on the other hand, was booming in other Delaware towns in the 1880s. Newark was "infested with the baseball epidemic" and it replaced horse racing as the prominent topic of conversation at the agricultural fairs. The Kent County teams in Dover, Smyrna, Milford and Camden engaged one another with nothing short of open hostility. During the State Fair upwards of 6000 would attend these spirited games with thousands of dollars changing hands among the spectators.

Finally, as the decade drew to a close, on October 26, 1889 a little event took place that was destined to become the most enduring sporting passion in Delaware: Delaware College, with all of 68 students, was demolished by the Delaware Field Club 74-0. The University of Delaware had played its first football game.

Delaware Bicycle Racing in the 1800s

The first high-wheeled bicycles began appearing in Delaware in the 1870s. These unwieldy contraptions could only be urged with great exertion to speeds approaching 10 miles per hour, slower than a good distance runner. By 1880, however, the sport had gained enough enthusiasts to form the Wilmington Bicycle Club. The Club rented out the Old Foundry at 10th & Orange streets and built a bicycle track 10 feet wide and 210 feet around, making 25 laps to the mile.

Still, when the first Championship of Delaware bicycle race was staged later that year at Scheutzen Park no Delawareans were as yet accomplished enough riders to enter. A New York invader took home the title. By 1885 when the 2-Mile Bicycle Championship of Delaware, now part of the Warren Games, was open to only Delawareans there was only one entry. Harlow H. Curtis pedaled the solitary distance in 11 minutes and 52 seconds. In 1885 there were but 42 members in the Wilmington Bicycle Club.

Then, the mania hit. Wheel clubs sprang up throughout the state. The riders of the Wilmington Wheel Club were acknowledged as some of the country's best. Wheelmen strove to cover each of America's major roads in record times. Frank Dampman of the Wilmington Wheel Club set the 20-mile record on the Lancaster Pike in 1888 in 74:50.3 and won the prestigious 100-mile Buffalo to Erie road race against many strong entries from around the world. Also in 1888 B. Frank McDaniel recorded over 5000 miles on his bike, comparing with the best totals recognized in the country. And neither of these men was the top rider in Delaware; that honor belonged to Wallis Merrihew. McDaniel and Merrihew would trade championship honors for several years before establishing a cycle shop together on Market Street.

In 1889 Delawareans took five of the first 20 places in the nation's biggest race in Newark, New Jersey and plans were made for Delaware to host its own 25-mile road race. The course was planned for the main road between Wilmington and Middletown and offered the most prize money in the country's history, mostly in the form of new bikes, athletic equipment and even cigars.

Attendance was estimated at between 5000 and 8000. So many fans crowded the route in some spots that the 23 riders were forced to navigate single file through a small aisleway of humanity. The roads were sandy and pitted with stones and every rider tumbled at least once. There were several reports of collisions with racing fans as well on the road. William Van Wagoner, the United States Champion from Rhode Island was in 8th place at the mid-way point but overtook the leaders with four miles to go and beat Dampman to the finish line. Van Wagoner was carried off his wheel by the enthusiastic crowd; eventually he would join the Wilmington Bicycle Club.

The next year Van Wagoner repeated his triumph in the greatest bicycle race yet seen in this part of the country. To accommodate the eager crowds the 25-mile route ran from Wilmington to New Castle and back, beginning and ending on the track at Hazel Dell in South Wilmington. For most of the race Van Wagoner and Washington Seeds of Wilmington raced in tandem. They reached the Hazel Dell track together for two final trips around the oval. They traded slight advantages to the deafening screams of fans until Van Wagoner out-sprinted Seeds in the final 15 yards as the

Wilmingtonian hit a puddle.

Seeds was relatively unknown in Delaware sporting circles before this performance but within a year he would be the state champion cyclist and establish a record time between Wilmington and Dover of 3 hours and 32 minutes. By this time bicycle racing was the dominant sport in Delaware. Thousands would turn out for the big races to cheer the colors of their favorite club.

In addition to the great road races regular events were held on the horse tracks. Although not suited for the "silent steeds" some impressive records were set by top riders from across the country. At the kite track in Kirkwood Carroll B. Jack of Wilmington set the state record for the mile in 2 minutes and 22 seconds, averaging over 25 mph.

Indoors the Old Foundry had evolved into the Pyle Cycle Academy with indoor races and training facilities. Starting in 1896 the Academy sponsored the first great Delaware exhibition for bicycles, the modern-day car shows of the 1800s. "Come see 10,000 wheels," gushed the promotional flyers. Proceeds went to the construction of a first class banked, cinder track at the Riverview grounds. That year 2000 fans packed the new track for regular Friday night races under the lights. Delaware sports fans were enjoying the best cycling in America.

But just like that it was over. Even without competition from the automobile bicycle racing died out in Delaware before the turn of the century. It would be nearly another 100 years before sporting America would cast its eye back to Delaware for bicycle racing.

Out for a ride on a penny-farthing in the 1880s.
When the riding got serious, Delawareans were at the
first rank in the nation's bicycle racing.

The First Delaware Thanksgiving Football Game

Traditional Thanksgiving football kicked off in Delaware in 1889 when the top athletic clubs, the Warren Club and the Delaware Field Club, tangled on the Union Street grounds. Both teams were about equal in weight but the Warrens had not even known how to play football until two weeks before the game. Despite the impending mismatch 700 people turned out for the contest, played through a steady downpour.

Out in the quagmire the more experienced Delaware Field Club did not hesitate to take advantage of their opponents' ignorance of some of the technicalities of the game. An impressive winning margin, it was thought, would inspire terror in upcoming opponents. Even the umpire was woefully lacking in the rules and occasionally turned to the Field Club for help with some calls. All told, Warren was lucky to get out of the first half trailing only 40-0.

After the ten-minute intermission the game Warren Club, dressed in canvas suits with blue stockings and caps, grew accustomed to the game. They tackled better and even gained some yards with their primitive offensive thrusts. Delaware's first Thanksgiving game ended with the final score 68-0.

Roller Skating Mania

With the introduction of the ball-bearing wheel in 1884 the popularity of roller skating zoomed. An indoor rink was hastily built in Wilmington at 11th and Madison and the enterprise paid for itself inside of three months. Flushed with optimism, investors established the Citizens Skating Rink at 4th and Washington before the winter was out.

Roller skating races and rink polo matches, in addition to the recreational skates, were well-patronized. But the skating craze, which lasted two or three years in most cities, didn't even grip Wilmington for one season. Skating was all but dead in Delaware by the spring of 1885. The town could support one rink but not two. The flashy Citizens Skating Rink was razed in 1888.

America - and Delaware - was gripped by a roller skating craze in the 1880s.

1890s

Late in 1889 an *Every Evening* reporter observed that, "athletics has taken a wonderful, and it is to be hoped, permanent hold on this community." Indeed it had. And the sport that had the strongest hold on Delawareans in the Gay Nineties was football. Prior to football, baseball in Delaware had been played well into November; now the baseball playing season wound down in mid-September so area elevens could commence practice.

Football, first played in 1869, was slow to gain a foothold in the First State. Delaware College had received challenges to the gridiron as early as 1883 but didn't play their first scrimmage until 1889. The Delaware Field Club played the earliest football and dominated state teams for several years. Primitive football produced either total mismatches with lopsided shutouts or, if the teams were evenly skilled, low-scoring exchanges of territory. There was no such thing as the 35-31 shootout popular today. Of Delaware College's first 75 games there were only four in which both teams scored in double figures.

In Newark when news leaked out in 1889 that the college boys were going to play football Sheriff Bill Simmons swore up and down Main Street that the first corpse carried off the field would mean the end of the game. Sheriff Simmons was on the sidelines but there were no incidents and by the early 1890s Delaware College was the state championship football club.

In 1891 the Newark school completed a shutout sweep of the three Delaware teams: YMCA, 58-0; Warren Club, 30-0; Delaware Field Club, 6-0. It was common practice in those days for schools to welcome any nearby resident to the team, regardless of whether he happened to be a student or not. In 1894 Delaware College announced that future football squads would comprise only matriculated students and the school would no longer engage non-academic institutions in battle. The banner of football supremacy for the rest of the decade passed to the Warren Club.

If football was king of Delaware sports in the 1890s, it reigned over the most diverse kingdom yet seen in the state. Basketball made its first appearance in the Wilmington YMCA in 1894 and the YMCA also began playing the first lacrosse in the state. Over at the Delaware Field Club golf was being played for the first time and was soon seen on the expansive private residences of several Delawareans.

Cricket was as popular as baseball for several years and the Delaware Field Club enjoyed its best year ever at the wicket in 1891, going 5-3-2 against the strong Pennsylvania clubs. New smokeless powder and clay pigeons sparked a revival in shooting - in 1892 there were 60,000 gun clubs across the country. Several marksmen from the Wilmington Rod & Gun Club gained national recognition during the decade.

Croquet was as popular as ever and bowling was coming into its own, the state record game being raised to 256. It was a Golden Age for Delaware boxing with regular weekly exhibitions being fought. Even pigeon racing enjoyed a flurry of popularity. Homing pigeons were shipped

FIRST STATE SPORTS HERO OF THE DECADE:
SALADIN

On his farm in Kirkwood about ten miles south of Wilmington medical entrepreneur and sportsman James McCoy constructed a so-called "kite" track that was pinched at one end - a configuration that produced some of the fastest harness racing in the country.

McCoy offered big purses to attract the nation's finest equine talent. Many of America's top horsemen sent their top pacers to the McCoy Farm. For Independence Day 1893 he put together his greatest day of racing when he lured Mascot, the world record pacer with a 2:04 mark, to Kirkwood with an offer of $5000 for a new record.

Mascot would face the Delaware champion, Saladin, who had set a world record of his own with a 2:09 mark on a half-mile track. In the hyperbolic journalistic style of the day it was said that, "if the race had taken place in New York or Philadelphia it would attract a million spectators."

Saladin, foaled in California in 1886, was very sickly at his yearling sale in New York and owner James Green was able to claim him for only $500. Many observers doubted the brown colt would even survive the train ride from New York to Wilmington. He debuted in Philadelphia as a 4-year old, finishing second in a 2:30 pace. By 1893, as a 7- year old, Saladin had performed in several big meets around the country and claimed 8 wins in 27 starts.

Some 7000 fans paid 50 cents each to see the two great horses battle. Saladin, with Green handling the reins, broke twice in the early going and trailed Mascot by two lengths at the half-mile pole when he found his stride. Saladin caught Mascot at the 3/4 pole and raced to the wire five lengths the best. His time was recorded at 2:05 and 3/4 seconds.

Fans raced to surround and pet Saladin while others lifted Green to their shoulders and carried him around the track as they yelled themselves hoarse. His feats at Kirkwood thrust Saladin into the class of world-class pacers but he was so fast he soon had no owners willing to test their stock against him and his racing career faded to a close.

On the track at Kirkwood racetrack operated by the Maple Valley Trotting Association.

500 miles by rail and released for the race home to the loft. Wilmington birds typically made fine showings in these events. In 1899, 11 of 123 Wilmington birds returned from South Carolina in a single day; only 19 of 720 Philadelphia birds accomplished the same feat.

Baseball, amateur style, could still lay claim as the national pastime in the smaller communities but in Wilmington, as usual, interest ran hot and cold. In 1896 there was just enough enthusiasm to carry Wilmington through its first minor league season from first pitch to final out - but not enough support for a second season in 1897.

On the race track Delaware produced its first superhorse - Saladin, a record-breaking brown colt. For two years Delaware even sported the world's fastest race track, Dr. James McCoy's innovative kite track near Kirkwood. Moving almost as fast in the early 1890s were Delaware's wheelmen, who became recognized as some of the finest cyclists in America.

But as the decade ended Delaware's sporting grounds were not nearly as fertile as the rest of the Gay Nineties. There was no pro baseball and the semi-pro Brownson club was so reticent about committing money to the sport they did not even don uniforms. The Warren Club had suffered severe economic reversals, lost their gymnasium which was the finest in the state, and were disappearing altogether. A game of basketball was still not much to look at and bicycle racing was gone. Delaware sports slipped quietly into a new century.

Off-Track Betting Comes to Delaware

Without any advance notice a new establishment opened at 612 Market Street in Wilmington in the winter of 1895. Despite the lack of publicity the Electric News and Money Transfer Company was doing a thriving business within days. It was Delaware's first off-track betting parlor.

Large blackboards lined the walls of the spacious room listing all sorts of sporting information, mostly for horse racing. Typically ten races, five from New Orleans and five from Arlington, Maryland, were available to Delaware sportsmen. Given the communications of the day, the handicapping information on the horses in the races must have been virtually nil, making the wagering little more than betting on numbers.

Clerks behind frosted windows collected bets and telegraphed the money to the main office in New Jersey where it was played on any race selected. Bulletins provided updates during the races and any winning monies was telegraphed back to the parlor. The Electric News and Money Transfer Company took a 25-cent commission on each play; the minimum bet was $1.00.

Business was brisk with crowds of 150-200 hovering around the parlor during business hours from 2:00 p.m. to 5:00 p.m. Well-known businessmen mingled with the assorted shady characters expected around the fringes of gambling. The operation was perfectly legal but alarmed politicians rushed laws through the legislature banning the gambling parlor. Delaware has not seen legal betting on horse races away from the racetrack since.

Delaware Gets A National Champion

General Manager Thomas Kane of Wilmington's Institute Hall had taken special pains to present his building for the occasion. The platform was placed as close to the center of the main floor as possible and raised some four feet. Chairs were meticulously arranged at suitable intervals on all four sides to afford the most convenient and comfortable viewing of the evening's proceedings. Yes, even the Opera House could not stage a better event, thought Kane.

There was no way Mr. Kane could anticipate the pandemonium that would soon convert his orderly hall into chaos even a New Castle County conventioneer wouldn't recognize. The Warren Athletic Club's wrestling program on May 12, 1892 was particularly strong, with the main attraction featuring the American champion, Weiss, of Brooklyn.

After several preliminary boxing and wrestling bouts Warren Club member John Cooper appeared to face Weiss. For a full five minutes the 700 partisan fans roared and pounded on chairs in anticipation of the 125-pound match. Officials called for order but could not harness the Warren enthusiasm. Only the referee's wave to wrestle brought silence in the hall.

Cooper sprang to the offensive throwing his opponent in the opening moments, although the referee failed to award the bout to the Wilmington man. Cooper tackled Weiss again but in the flailing arms and legs the referee was kicked and refused to render judgement on the second fall. The crowd was frothing as Cooper pinned the champion for a third time and was awarded the match. The great victory was achieved in one minute 29 seconds.

Cooper's hand was not even raised before he was hoisted to the shoulders of Warren men and paraded around the hall. The din of shouts and cries shook the building as the audience rose en masse on top of chairs to salute the new champion. The enthusiasm on the street almost equalled that in the hall. Cooper was shouldered up and down Market Street and feted in celebrations until well past midnight. But Mr. Kane had one more chore. The fallen ex-champ, literally dazed by his beating, had to be carried off the platform and through the crowd to the dressing room by the ubiquitous manager.

Cooper left active competition that year and began an association with the Wilmington YMCA that would stretch into the 1940s. He turned out numerous championship teams and wrestlers, the best being 135-pound Hubert Williams who won the collegiate title with the Naval Academy in 1935. He would one day be the earliest Delaware athlete recognized by the Delaware Sports Hall of Fame.

When it was constructed in 1871 the French Second Empire-styled Grand Opera House replaced the Wilmington Institute Hall, built in 1850, as the sporting venue of choice in Wilmington.

The First Night Baseball in Delaware

Seeking any way to draw apathetic Wilmington fans to his minor league baseball team manager Denny Long arranged to play the first night baseball game in this part of the country at the Union Street grounds on July 4, 1896. Night baseball was no longer a novelty on the Pacific Coast and a game under the lights in Indianapolis had attracted 10,000 curious onlookers. But Wilmingtonians proved less enthusiastic.

After his regular Atlantic League doubleheader against Paterson Long strung electric arc lights on the ground and up high around the field for a third game. In addition to the ballgame the stands at Union Street afforded an excellent view of the Delaware Field Club's fireworks down the street.

An oversized, bright white ball was used and the likely apocryphal story has been passed down from that night that Wilmington hurler Morris "Doc" Amole hid a firecracker inside the ball before a pitch to batsman Sam McMackin (some versions of the tale had the immortal Honus Wagner at the plate) in the fourth inning. When McCackin swung and made contact the resulting pyrotechincs caused the bat to shatter and the disgusted umpire ended the game.

If such an incident occurred the Wilmington reporters somehow missed it and did not include the prank in game accounts. As it was, the players couldn't manage well and score was not kept as the contest deteriorated into a "funny exhibition." In the end only 200 people showed up to see an event that was fully 40 years ahead of its time.

Wilmington Peaches pitcher Doc Amole was said to have ended Delaware's first night baseball game by throwing a pitch with a firecracker hidden in the ball.

Live Bird Shoots

With the coming of fancy shooting clubs and better equipment target shooting became a much more humane sport in the 1890s but for some nothing matched the excitement of a live bird shoot. One of the last - and best - of these matches took place in Claymont in 1896. The team of Joseph Cross and George Huber of Wilmington squared off against Robert Miller of Wilmington and Reuben Stout of Magnolia in a 50- bird shoot for $200 a side. The four men were widely regarded as the best marksmen in Delaware.

Several hundred spectators turned out even as rumors spread through the town that Cross, the state champion, was gravely ill and near death on the morning of the match. Cross indeed made it to the shooting grounds and struggled to the shooting line. He managed to record 42 kills in 46 tries before fainting and forfeiting his final four attempts. His partner Huber killed all but one bird but nine of his hits fell out of bounds and he was credited with only 40 kills. Miller and Stout recorded 85 legal hits out of 100 to take the prize 85-82.

1900s

Football in the early 20th century was increasingly coming under attack for its brutality. Harvard and other schools, where the game was played at its highest level, dropped the sport altogether, demanding reforms. At the end of each year newspapers would dutifully print the death count from that season's play. Delaware was not immune. Clarence Pierce, 20, of Claymont Street in Wilmington died after being kicked in the stomach during a football game in 1909. Pierce was one of 30 American men to perish on the gridiron that season.

Worse, for football lovers, than the violence on the field was the boring style of play which gripped the game. Seldom did fans enjoy even a ten-yard run, and following the ball was a nightmare as 22 players dissolved into an amorphous pile on every play. there were many mismatches between teams of disparate abilities and when squads of equal strength engaged a scoreless tie could be expected.

In this environment baseball grew into truly the national - and state - pastime. In Delaware the spring, summer and fall were filled with baseball and the winter was cherished as a time to speculate on future happenings on the diamond. During the season if fans weren't attending a game they could be found gathered around bulletin boards in newspaper offices clamoring for inning-by-inning updates of local and national games. So many teams were clamoring for Wilmington baseball fields that a permit system for use of the diamonds was instituted in 1908.

Baseball was always a business, not a privilege for the Delaware sports fan. Any promoter of a baseball game could expect to incur the following expenses in 1905: rent for the grounds - $55; umpires - $15; balls -$12; ads -$30; grounds man - $10; police - $15; extras -$10. With an admission price of 25 cents an owner needed to attract 600 fans just to cover his fixed expenses. And that didn't begin to cover his biggest costs - player salaries and guarantees to the visiting team.

With professional baseball virtually dormant in Delaware at the turn of the century the Brownson Library Association nursed play-for-pay ball back a game at a time in 1901. Each game that made a profit led to the next one being scheduled. The timing was right. With the game popularized by the consolidation of the best players into two major leagues, baseball was exploding. And by 1902 the best baseball in America outside the major league parks was being played in Wilmington. For the rest of the decade Delawareans could count on professional baseball in Wilmington and topflight amateur ball throughout the state.

Also enjoying a revival in popularity with the new century was horse racing. In 1901 the Wilmington Horse Show Association began leasing the former Wawaset Park grounds at Ninth Street and Woodlawn to stage fancy horse programs. To complement the judging contests the organizers added a few trotting races. Within a few years the races, now known as matinees, supplanted the horse shows. These weekly events became so popular Delaware became recognized as the

First State Sports Hero of the Decade:
Vic Willis

Vic Willis won 248 games in a 13-year career. Every eligible pitcher with a career predominantly in the 20th century who won more than Willis' 248 games is in baseball's Hall of Fame.

Vic Gassaway Willis was born in Cecil County in April 12, 1876, his colorful middle name appended from a character in Buffalo Bill's Wild West troupe who his father had met while a traveling member. Young Willis started playing ball in Newark, competing for the Wilmington YMCA and Newark Academy as a teenager. After one year at Delaware College in Newark Willis left for Harrisburg and pro baseball. He helped Syracuse to a pennant in the Tri-State League in 1897.

Willis gained wide renown for his nasty curve ball, a pitch he called his Grapevine Sinker. He broke into the majors the next year and as a 22-year old rookie helped pitch the Boston team to the National League title with a 24-13 log. In 1899 he went 27-10 with a no-hitter, th elast thrown in the 19th century. After an off-year in 1900 Willis came back to go 20-17 for a fifth place team. The next year the curveballer again won 27 games and set the National League record for complete games in this century with 45, a mark that still stands.

After 1902 the Boston club became an awful team, always a threat to lose 100 games. Willis lost 25 of those games in 1904 despite an ERA of 2.81 and in 1905 he established a modern record for losses in a season with 29. Mercifully, Willis was shipped to Pittsburgh where he regained his winning form, tallying 20 or more victories for the next four years. In a series that matched the immortals Honus Wagner and Ty Cobb the Pirates and Willis won the World Series in 1909.

The next year Willis labored for the St. Louis Cardinals and when he was sold to Chicago before the 1911 season he retired. Willis returned to Delaware where he purchased the Washington House in Newark. He remained the proprietor until his death in 1947 of a stroke at the age of 71.

For many years Willis had more wins - 248 - than any pitcher not in the Baseball Hall of Fame. His eight 20-win seasons, and 50 shutouts were topped by fewer than a score of hurlers. The call from Cooperstown finally came for Vic Willis in 1995.

WILLIS, PITTSBURG

Vic Willis enjoyed his best seasons after being traded to the Pirates in 1906. He went 89-46 in the next four years and won a World Series title.

A golfing group from the early 1900s at Wilmington Country Club.

Matinee Racing Capital of America.

Racing at the matinees was strictly an amateur affair. Expensively bred trotters shared the track with horses unhitched from milk wagons and delivery carts - all in quest of blue ribbons. The working stiffs were especially popular, none more so than William H., who went to the post more often than any other matinee horse. William H., winner of 53 blue ribbons with a lifetime mile mark of 2:38, raced until 1907 when he was knocked down and injured by a Peoples Railway trolley car at 2nd & Madison while on his day job. Meanwhile the best matinee horses from Wilmington were tabbed to compete in intercity races against Philadelphia, Trenton, and Baltimore.

The cream of Delaware society turned out for the matinees not just to watch but to compete. DuPont Company president T. Coleman du Pont was a prominent owner and timer and judge. In a heat in 1905 Howard T. Wallace, president of the Diamond State Steel Company, shattered his collarbone in a sulky accident during a race. Towards the end of the decade horse racing began to wane somewhat as these wealthy men turned their attention from swift horses to fast automobiles. The first auto races were roadability tests by the Delaware Automobile Association in which target times were assigned and each car hauled its full capacity of passengers as stated in the owners manual. Hundreds would turn out in downtown Wilmington to send off the roadsters on their round-trip outings to Kennett Square and Valley Forge and elsewhere.

Other motorsports were sweeping Delaware as well. Nick Charles, a shoemaker in Wilmington, attained a record motorcycle speed of 65 mph and inked a contract with the Indian Motorcycle Company as a professional rider. On the water Harry Richardson of Dover won national races in the Thousand Islands, New York, averaging 21 mph.

For the first time Delaware sports enthusiasts could find as many diversions indoors as out. Professional basketball came to the state for the first time and in its wake strong amateur teams like the Old Swedes and Brownson entertained new converts. Up to 1000 people would cheer on teams on the Grand Opera House stage and more traditional gyms.

Indoor track meets at the Wilmington YMCA featured the standard fare of dashes, jumping events and shot putting but also offered such novelties as rope climbs and potato races. In the window races competitors would strain against the clock as they squeezed through progressively smaller openings. For awhile indoor baseball - with 25-foot bases and a 6" ball - caught the fancy of fans at the Eleventh Street Rink.

Exciting the most fans was roller polo. The fast five-man game had been around since the skating craze of the 1880s but

Bowling was the "prince of winter sports' in Delaware in the early 1900s.

suddenly took Delaware by storm in 1907. That year the Orange Athletic Club travelled to Bridgeton, New Jersey and dispatched their hosts - winner of 31 straight games - for the first time ever on its home rink. Then an all-Wilmington aggregation fell only 3-1 to a Baltimore

team that had never lost even a single game of roller polo.

When the Country Rink opened next to Brandywine Springs an intrastate rivalry began to fester among Wilmington teams and thousands attended the Delaware League matches. In 1909 Wilmington joined the Tri-State Roller Polo League with Baltimore and Atlantic City, skating before crowds of over 4000 when visiting the latter's Steel Pier rink.

In 1904 boxing was re-born with Wednesday night exhibitions in The Casino at 50th and Market Streets. Fighters donned huge gloves so knockouts were rare but the bouts were lively. Boxing season ran from October to May and fans of the sweet science could count on a cleverly-promoted fight card each week. In 1907 the organizers moved the weekly matches out to the Country Rink. Now directly on the train line at Brandywine Springs it was not uncommon to find thousands of fight fans in attendance, especially when a Philadelphia fighter brought Pennsylvanians down in droves.

For those who preferred participating, bowling was the "prince of winter sports." By 1906 there were four bowling leagues and 22 teams in Wilmington. That year the Wilmington Bowling Association sent an all-star team to the national tournament to represent Delaware for the first time. The lanes in Louisville, Kentucky played fast and the Wilmington kegelers suffered through 29 splits and 22 misses for a three-game, five man total of only 2428.

In singles play, however, William "Pop" Roach, the "Grand Old Man" of Wilmington bowling, tallied a 652 series to finish third nationally. Roach, a 190s-average bowler, was proprietor of the Academy Bowling Alley at Fifth and French Streets until ill health forced him to retire to his native San Antonio, Texas in 1907. He left Delaware with five perfect

300 games and a high series of 859 to his credit.

Delawareans could also see the best bowlers in the country when Wilmington was represented in the Eastern Bowling League. Lanes 12 and 13 at the Academy were groomed and reserved for the bowling greats from Philadelphia, Brooklyn, Newark and New York. In this fast competition Wilmington easily proved the equal of any city. In no sport did Delaware offer greater competition than trapshooting. The Delaware Trapshooting League, comprised of clubs from Claymont to Dover, produced several marksmen capable of breaking targets with America's best. The major trapshoots held throughout the state attracted some of the largest sporting crowds in Delaware. In January 1904, when world champion Fred Gilbert competed at the Wawaset Gun Club, the throng was so large that fans had to go into the clubhouse in shifts to warm themselves by the coal stove.

The development of homebred shooting talent reached its apex in 1908 when Captain K.K.V. Casey of Wilmington won a silver medal in the 1000-yard shoot at the London Olympics - the first ever medalist from Delaware. Captain Casey, commanding officer of Company C in the First Delaware Infantry, was joined in the rifle matches at Bisley, England by fellow Delawarean John Hessian. Two days later another Delawarean on the 86-member American team, George Dole, son of Wilmington preacher George Henry Dole, aggressively wrestled through four English opponents to win gold in the 133-pound class - the first Olympic gold for Delaware.

Finally, A Succcessful League

Throughout the 1800s leading Delaware sportsmen had tried to organize state sports teams into leagues. In baseball, in shooting, in football - all attempts failed. There were transportation problems, there were money difficulties, there were competitive disparities, there were petty jealousies.

It was not until 1901 that all dragons were slain and a sports league survived in Delaware from opening day to awards banquet with all members remaining intact to the end. The league that turned the trick was the Wilmington City Bowling League. Even then it stuttered through several false starts. Plans in 1900 were scuttled sending one of the primary movers in the enterprise, the Wilmington Whist Club, off to the Intercity Bowling League with Pennsylvania teams.

Finally in the summer of 1901 the Young Mens Republican Club, the Knights of Columbus, the Wilmington Bicycle Club and the YMCA bonded into an agreement for a wintertime league. The format was recognizable to any bowler of today: five-man teams, total pinfall deciding the winner over three games, every Thursday night. Each club hosted an equal number of matches on their home alleys.

The Republican Club won top honors with 15 wins in 18 weeks. The well-balanced team averaged 151.4 per man, yet anchor Henry Kurtz rolled only 157.4 per game. The Knights of Columbus, the tailender of the list with only five wins, toppled 143 pins per man, only eight pins a man shy of the champs.

The Wilmington City Bowling League was so successful a second team league formed in the middle of the season. Thereafter, leagues binding Delaware athletes became commonplace in many sports.

A Soccer Fantasy

"Followers of the game of soccer declare that it will not be many years before their favorite game becomes a most popular sport. They have visions of great things which are about to come to pass. Visions of great amphitheaters which will hold tens of thousands of cheering soccer rooters. Visions of strongly entrenched professional soccer leagues, as great in scope perhaps as the present leagues of baseball..."

A newspaper article from the 1960s perhaps? The 1970s? The 1980s? The 2000s? No, 1907. For nearly a century it seems soccer aficionados have been waiting for their game to seize the imagination of the American public. Delaware did begin interstate competition in soccer in 1907 with teams from Philadelphia and New Jersey. But, while these contests were greatly enjoyed by the participants, the games were typically private affairs, attracting little interest among Delaware sports fans.

A Hotbed of Roque

For a brief time at the turn of the century there was no better roque being played anywhere in America than the roque being played in Wilmington. Roque? Best described as a sort of scientific croquet, roque players crossed mallets at the private grounds of Dr. Benjamin Veasey at 1502 Franklin Street. Veasey was widely considered one of the top five or six roquers in the country.

As the Wilmington men polished their craft several became factors in national championship matches, mostly held in New England. James Hickman, a leather manufacturer, won laurels as the best Second Level player in American roque. Enough good players developed that the Wilmington Roque Club established permanent grounds at Jackson, Tenth and Adams streets.

The popularity of roque never expanded beyond this tiny enclave of devotees and disappeared from the scene with the passing of the Wilmington Roque Club. But for a fleeting moment Wilmington stood at the pinnacle of the roque world.

Roque was so hot in the early 1900s it was contested at the St. Louis Olympic Games. America was the only country to field a team and there were only four competitors. That was it for roque in the Olympics.

1910s

The 19-teens were a transitional decade in Delaware sports. A time traveler from the 1990s would feel at home with distinct seasons for baseball, football and basketball, albeit in primitive form. His fellow traveler from the 1890s would still recognize these games as well - before the lively ball, the forward pass and the jump shot - and also find the major sports of his century, trotting and trapshooting, going strong.

Baseball dominated the Delaware sports scene. Pro baseball was sporadic but there were more leagues and teams than at any time in the state's history. Downstate, where sporting diversions were fewer, baseball was an absolute passion. Some games between ancient rivals Milford and Dover drew as many as 5000 fans, including many taking the train down from Wilmington.

In Wilmington the biggest sports day of the year was Baseball Booster Day which marked the end of the long winter and Opening Day of the baseball season. All the teams displayed their colors in a great parade through the city. There was seldom any question when Opening Day arrived as newspaper headlines screamed: THIS IS THE DAY! BASEBALL BUMPS OTHER THINGS ASIDE.

In football Wilmington High School emerged as the leading pigskinners in the state. Grudge matches with Chester High School were the most anticipated games of the day. Only two of the sports fields in Delaware - outside of Delaware College's glorious Frazer Field - had stands for football so the games were for real fans only - standing several heads deep and battling the elements.

In women's sports Ursuline and the YWCA played the first field hockey in Delaware in 1914. That first contest was taken by the Ursulines 4-3 in front of a large gathering at Rockford Park. Elsewhere, women could be seen competing in baseball and basketball.

In basketball dribbling was allowed for the first time and standardized rules enabled more games to be played. The Wilmington Amateur Basketball League formed with eight teams but bowling remained far and away the leading indoor winter sport. Any club that had any room at all installed a few lanes for members.

The roller polo craze died out by 1912 but was soon replaced by indoor quoits as the Delaware sports rage. The Wilmington Fraternal Indoor Quoit League organized in 1914 and all games were witnessed by large crowds. The game caught on so quickly that two more leagues formed within a month and stayed popular through the decade.

During this time Wilmington was still known around the east as "Horsetown" but the trotter was slowly losing its hold on the public's imagination. In 1915 automobile and motorcycle races became a feature of the Delaware State Fair on the card with the horse races.

For the one-mile race, drivers had to run 100 yards and enter their machines with engines running and circle the 1/2-mile track twice. The winning mile was raced in a fraction over one minute and 24 seconds. Also on the program were three-

and five-mile runs.

Even more insidious to traditional sports than the automobile to the horse was the spreading of the population. By the end of the decade both Wawaset Park, begun as Scheutzen Park nearly a half-century before, and the grounds at Front & Union Streets, Wilmington's leading 19th century sporting grounds, were sacrificed for housing developments. Downstate the Seaford grounds, the most historic sporting field in southern Delaware, was similarly dispatched for building lots. Not twenty years into the new century, Delaware had severed most of its sporting ties to the 1800s.

The Big Noise

In the first decades of the 20th century the two great sporting passions in America were baseball and trapshooting. Naturally it was only a matter of time before the world's greatest gunpowder concern got into the game. As the dominant supplier of the new smokeless powder E.I. du Pont de Nemours and Company maintained a force of 20 men whose sole responsibility was to build up trapshooting clubs across America. And when the DuPont Gun Club organized on November 14, 1910 it was an enterprise befitting Delaware's leading company.

The clubhouse on the grounds at New Bridge, just beyond Rising Sun, was built at the cost of $3000. President T. Coleman du Pont pledged $200 a year for trophy spoons which became coveted prizes for Delaware marksmen. At the first shoot on December 17 the DuPont Gun Club boasted 100 members; several months later the rolls swelled to over 500.

The first year over 1.3 million targets were broken - more than any trapshooting club in the country. An enterprising young contractor named Harry Carlon reclaimed 23 tons of lead from the DuPont grounds by skimming one inch of soil and putting it through a grinder. He was able to sell his buried treasure for 4.5 cents a pound.

All this shooting produced superior marksmen in Delaware. With Alden "Dal" Richardson, Billy Foord, Eugene du Pont, J.H. Minnick and Wardlaw Hammond the DuPont Gun Club team was one of the strongest in the East.

In 1913 Harriet Hammond organized the Nemours Club for women trapshooters, the first women's shooting club in America. The Nemours Club soon boasted over 100 members, mostly from the agricultural division of the DuPont Company. The Nemours women even toured the country to demonstrate their skill.

Several thousand spectators would arrive for the "Big Noise" on days of important tournaments, which went on year-round. In 1915, to accommodate the huge throng of shooters, lights were installed for night shooting. The popping of guns against the stars pushed area residents past the breaking point. Night shooting was stopped on August 15 but a suit was brought against the DuPont Gun Club complaining that the noise was a nuisance. A court injunction temporarily closed the grounds.

In January 1916 the suit was heard in open court. Over 110 witnesses jammed the courtroom to testify that shot falling into the public road was endangering life and traffic. So many people were on hand to testify that the overflow was sent home. Although the original DuPont Gun Club site was selected for its excellent distance from the city, yet its remoteness from residential areas, the club was disbanded. The former members scattered to the 23 other trapshooting clubs in Delaware, the best forming the Wilmington Trapshooting Association at Old Homestead on the Philadelphia Pike near Bellevue.

FIRST STATE SPORTS HERO OF THE DECADE:
ALDEN B. RICHARDSON

For want of 543 votes Harry Alden Richardson, canner and president of the First National Bank of Dover, would have been governor of Delaware in 1890. He re-emerged in state politics in 1907 when the Kent County Republican stalwart was elected to the United States Senate. While Richardson was attracting attention in the Roosevelt and Taft administrations his son Alden B. "Dal" Richardson was making noise back home on the trapshooting line.

When he wasn't tending to Dover business Richardson won over 30 trapshooting medals, knocking clay targets out of the sky at a rate of over 93% most years. He was the Delaware state champion in 1909, 1910, 1913, 1914, and 1916. He won at the national level as well, taking first place from the 20-yard line in the prestigious Grand American Handicap in Dayton, Ohio in 1913. He was runner-up for the national amateur championship that year and again in 1915.

Richardson was a member of a world-record setting five-man team described by *American Rifleman* as "the fastest moving and fastest shooting squad in the Eastern States." Richardson shot fourth in the potent line-up.

The Dover marksman was enjoying his best year in 1916 at the age of 40 when he was roundly hailed as the top shooter in America. He ran a program of 200 straight in a Philadelphia tournament on Memorial Day - "he nailed every target in the center" - and made a world's record of 99 from 22 yards at the Midsummer Handicap a month later.

But on the evening of July 30 Richardson returned to his Dover home and reached into a pocket in the side of his car to retrieve a Colt revolver when the gun discharged a bullet that punctured his intestines in eight places. Richardson, known for his graceful and perfect positions at the trap, did not survive.

Alden B. Richardson was Delaware's finest shot in the days when trapshooting ranked second only to baseball as a national sporting pursuit.

The Great Shipyard Teams

During World War I the U.S. government issued a "work or fight" edict that sent many major league baseball players scurrying to the safety of the huge shipyards and munition plants that peppered the Atlantic Seaboard. Enough big leaguers came to work for Wilmington's Harlan and Hollingsworth yard to mold two teams, including the nine that captured the Atlantic Coast Shipbuilding League title in 1918. Pusey and Jones of Wilmington also fielded a squad of local stars which, while a good club, was not of the caliber of the galactic Harlan team.

Anchoring the Harlan and Hollingsworths were Rogers Hornsby and Shoeless Joe Jackson, two of only three major leaguers to hit over .350 for their career. The 22-year old Hornsby cemented the inner cordon at shortstop while Jackson, a terrific slugger then in his prime, patrolled the outer perimeter in centerfield. He was heavily criticized as a draft dodger but he had been married ten years at this time and supported his mother and crippled sister as well. He had applied for work in the shipyard even before the 1918 baseball season had begun. Unable to read or write, the other players would drive Jackson crazy, it was said, by pointing to something in the newspaper which they told him was his name on the draft list.

All told there were eight big leaguers on the Harlan and Hollingsworth team. The moundsmen were led by Lefty Williams, a two-time 20-game winner who would compile a .631 winning percentage. Both Jackson and Williams would be thrown out of baseball as members of the Chicago "Black Sox" two years later.

The shipyard ball park was an exceptionally fine playing field and large crowds would turn out for the Saturday afternoon games. When an overflow crowd of 4000 greeted the opener of the Ship League it was observed: "It was a typical Wilmington baseball crowd too, because it 'panned' every player who made a misplay and then made him king when he redeemed himself."

So popular were the contests that the team began playing illegal Sunday games. Police waited patiently until the final out when each player was ceremoniously arrested, escorted to City Hall and assessed a slight fine. Gate proceeds were turned over to the war effort so even strict Blue Law adherents winked at the Sabbath charade.

The Harlan and Hollingsworths met the Staten Island yard of the Standard Ship Company for the league title in September 1918. The five-game series opened in Phillies Park in Philadelphia and although Hornsby was ineligible for the championship the Wilmington team prevailed 3-2 in Game 1. They won another low scoring affair the next afternoon in New York, 2-0.

Williams took the hill for Game 3 back in Philadelphia and shut down the New Yorkers on two scratch singles. But his service in the 4-0 clincher was overlooked in the excitement of Jackson's performance. He doubled and scored in the game's first run in the 4th inning and crushed a long 2-run home run over the right field wall in the 6th. In the 8th inning pandemonium

Shoeless Joe Jackson played ball in Wilmington during World War I.

reigned when Shoeless Joe clouted another circuit blast. When the great outfielder reached home plate he walked around in front of the fan boxes and picked up bank notes which workers, who seemed to entirely disregard them in those days, threw to him. He returned to the dugout clutching a large handful of such notes.

The drives were not hit off a local riveter. Dan Griner took a 2.15 ERA with him that year when he left the Brooklyn Dodgers. Harlan and Hollingsworth thus brought the Coxe Trophy back to Wilmington with a 3-game sweep. The Armistice was signed less than two months later and the greatest baseball team to ever play in Delaware was quickly disbanded.

1920s

The 1920s. Ruth. Dempsey. Jones. Tilden. The Golden Age of American sports. In a poll at mid-century each was named the greatest performer ever to play his sport. For the first time America had national sports stars. Delawareans could listen to their exploits on their new radios and read the first national sports columns in Delaware papers, written by Grantland Rice and Harry Grayson. Non-Delawareans now eclipsed residents as sports heroes. And the legends came a' callin'.

In golf Bobby Jones toured the Wilmington Country Club and the great British golfers Harry Vardon and Ted Ray played a popular exhibition at the Kennett Pike Club in 1920. Walter Hagen, Tommy Armour and Gene Sarazen appeared at Concord Country Club, a satellite of Wilmington Country Club, drawing thousands to their matches. The greatest American woman golfer, Glenna Collett Vare, competed in the annual woman's invitational at the Wilmington course. And Joyce Wethered, who Bobby Jones called the greatest golfer he ever saw, man or woman, appeared in an exhibition before 700 at Wilmington.

For tennis players the Delaware Open was strategically scheduled the week before the national amateur, usually held in Philadelphia. As a tune-up for the big event America's best players competed on the Wilmington Country Club grass courts. Bill Tilden, holder of two Wimbledon and seven United States Open crowns, also had a Delaware Open trophy in his ample showcase. Big Bill was of

Bill Tilden, the first great American tennis player, won two Delaware Open crowns. His father was a Delaware native.

"sturdy Delaware stock," his father being a native of St. Georges. In the 1920s he played several times in Delaware, helping christen the new clay tennis courts at the Du Pont Country Club and staging several charity exhibitions.

Babe Ruth was a frequent visitor to teammate Herb Pennock's farm in Kennett Square for some foxhunting and golf. The Babe even cracked up his car once on Route 1 near Wawa. The greatest star of them all played in Wilmington once, in a barnstorming game at Wilmington's Harlan Field. When the Babe came into Wilmington for some shopping he would invariably be mobbed on his walks down Market Street.

Jack Dempsey teaches his Wilmington bride, Estelle Taylor, a few boxing moves.

The biggest sports hero in Delaware in the 1920s was boxer Jack Dempsey, the Manassas Mauler. The heavyweight champ first visited Wilmington in 1921 as a training break for an upcoming bout in Atlantic City with Georges Carpentier. Wending his way through the adoring crowds Dempsey professed a liking for the town. Three years later he found more reason to love Wilmington. Dempsey married actress Estelle Taylor, a Wilmington girl whose mother and grandparents still lived there, and the champ's visits became more frequent.

Dempsey fights would be broadcast live over loudspeakers set up outside the newspaper offices and crowds of over 8000 would jam city streets for four blocks, listening and cheering to the blow-by-blow radio accounts. When Dempsey met Gene Tunney in Philadelphia it was estimated that more than 3000 Wilmingtonians took the train to join the crowd of 125,735. Jack Dempsey was a magical name in Delaware for years.

Professional sports in Delaware suffered in the shadow of the national sports explosion. In baseball there was minor league action available downstate, albeit by raw rookies, for much of the decade while in Wilmington the best ball was often played by "colored teams" like the Harlan Giants, starring Wilmington's Judy Johnson, and the Wilmington Black Sox. The Hilldale Daisies from Philadelphia, who were the world champions of the Negro Leagues, often played home games in Wilmington. The top amateur leagues were the All-Wilmington and Twilight Leagues.

While there was less baseball to watch there was plenty to play. In 1921 Wilmington sported 15 baseball diamonds, three of which were reserved exclusively for the 6 women's leagues in town. Even winter baseball was common in Delaware throughout the 1920s.

Football was the premier spectator sport of the age. It was not unusual for 20,000 people to see games across Wilmington on any given fall Saturday. Baynard Field, with two gridirons, could host four games on such days. Wilmington High School, which charged no admission, was the most popular eleven and could bring out 8000 rooters on game day.

The best semi-pro football teams were the Defiance Bulldogs and the St. Mary's Cats. In 1925 the battle was joined when St. Mary's broke a three-year Bulldogs' hold on the state title by thrashing them 16-0 on Thanksgiving Day before 6500. St. Marys took advantage of a 75-yard fumble return and a 35-yard interception return for touchdowns to stun Defiance. St. Mary's won on Turkey Day the next year as well to insure the Cats a place among Delaware's best-ever local football teams.

On the whimsical side, casting, fishing-style, became a popular outdoor activity. The Delaware Anglers and Gunners

Babe Ruth was a frequent visitor to Delaware in the 1920s and once even wrecked his car on Route 1 in Wawa across the state line in Delaware County.

Association began staging an annual baitcasting tournament each spring on the Washington Triangle in Wilmington. There were nine accuracy events and six for distance. By the end of the decade the Wilmington Casting Club was hosting invitational tournaments that attracted national distance and accuracy champions.

The Defiance Bulldogs were the state champion footballers of the early 1920s and one of the last great semi-pro teams in the state.

First State Sports Hero of the Decade:
Judy Johnson

In the first half of the 20th century third base was a waste area of sorts in major league baseball. The only three guardians of the hot corner named to the Hall of Fame from this era were Pie Traynor, Frank "Home Run" Baker and Jimmy Collins, hardly among the first rank of baseball immortals. Perhaps the greatest of all third basemen was a player hardly anyone saw - Judy Johnson.

William Julius Johnson was born in Snow Hill, Maryland in the last year of the 19th century. His father was a seaman and licensed boxing coach who brought the family to Wilmington for work in the shipyards when Willie was seven years old. He wore out the dirt playing ball at the field at 2nd and DuPont streets - now named Judy Johnson Park. He attended Howard High School for awhile but played no sports and dropped out as a sophomore to earn money for his family.

In 1918 Johnson began playing on Saturdays for the Chester Giants for $5 a game. In 1919 he was asked to join the Hilldale team from Darby, Pennsylvania. As the Hilldale Daisies became a charter member of the Negro Eastern League in 1922, Johnson became a full-time baseball player, earning $150 a month. With Hilldale his teammates remarked how much he looked like a former manager, Judy Gans, and Johnson became "Judy."

In 1924 Johnson played in the first Negro League World Series, losing to the Kansas City Monarchs. The next year Hilldale and Johnson downed the Monarchs to capture the Negro World Championship, capping off a season when Johnson batted .392.

Johnson - who never weighed more than 150 pounds in his playing career - went on to play with the Homestead Grays and the Derby Daisies of Philadelphia, both of which he also managed.

Judy Johnson, playing for the Hilldale Daisies in the first ever Colored World Series in 1924. Johnson batted .364 in the Series and slugged .614 but the Daisies lost to the Kansas City Monarchs.

In the winter Johnson played in Florida and Cuban leagues - often against the white major leaguers he was excluded from competing against in the regular season.

Johnson discovered Josh Gibson playing on sandlots and mentored the young catcher who would come to be known as the greatest hitter in Negro League ball. Winding down his playing days he joined the Pittsburgh Crawfords - the New York Yankees of the Negro National League. Besides Johnson, who served as captain, the team boasted Hall-of-Famers Gibson, Satchel Paige, Cool Papa Bell and Oscar Charleston. Not surprisingly, Johnson called the Crawfords, "the best team on which I ever played and the best ever I think in Negro baseball." Johnson played until 1937, hitting below .300 only once, as best as sketchy Negro League statistics can reveal. He was a deadly right-handed curve ball hitter with superb bat control, a peerless fielder and a master thief of opponent's signs.

Johnson retired after the 1936 season and returned to Delaware to work for Continental Can and operate a general store in Millside. He took over the reins of the Alco Flashes, a semi-pro basketball team that featured fellow Negro Leaguers Bill Campbell and Bill Yancey, and won a Delaware state championship in 1937.

He was called back to a now-integrated baseball in 1951 as a scout of black players for the Philadelphia Athletics. In 1954 the A's made Johnson the first black coach in major league baseball. Later he scouted off and on for the Phillies for 15 years until he retired in 1972. The National Baseball Hall of Fame opened its doors to the great stars of the Negro Leagues in 1971 and in 1975 Judy Johnson assumed his rightful place in Cooperstown - the sixth Hall of famer inducted from the Negro Leagues.

This came as a complete surprise to most Delawareans, few of whom had any notion a great ballplayer lived in their midst for 70 years. Delaware fell all over itself to rectify this slight. Johnson was the only unanimous choice in the first voting for the Delaware Sports Hall of Fame in 1976. The Wilmington Sportswriters and Broadcasters Association designated him their Athlete of the Year for 1975, an award heretofore reserved only for active athletes. Governor Pierre S. du Pont IV declared a "Judy Johnson Day" in Delaware. Johnson had a standing reservation at the head table of every sports banquet from Delmar to Claymont and many Delawareans came to know what many who knew Judy Johnson realized all along - he was a Hall-of- Famer off the field as well as on.

Judy Johnson was married for over 60 years to his wife Anita, who died in 1985. He followed in 1989 and their house in Marshallton at the junction of Newport Road and Kiamensi Avenue is now listed on the National Register of Historic Places. A statue of Judy Johnson, hands on knees, staring resolutely in anticipation of the next pitch, as imagined by Puerto Rico sculptor Phil Sumpter, greets visitors at Wilmington's Frawley Stadium.

The Marshall Marathon

The Marshall money stemmed from the vulcanized fiber products churned out in the family mill in Yorklyn. T. Clarence Marshall was more interested in the plant's steam power than the paper and he built his first steam automobile when he was 19 years old. Between 1910 and 1920 Marshall sold Stanley Motor Carriage steamers.

In 1921 T.C., an avid trapshooter, gathered some friends on his estate for a little tournament. Marshall set up eight traps on the line, along with two practice launchers. The format was unique; when most shoots consisted of at most 200 targets the Marshall shoot was a true marathon: 500 targets.

Wilmington businessman Isaac Turner won the inaugural Marshall Tournament by breaking 492 out of the 500 clays. The marathon format proved to be an exciting attraction and over the next decade the Marshall Marathon grew into the second largest trapshoot in the country behind only the Grand American. More than 500 shooters from across the country would travel to Delaware to test their skill on the hillside traps at Marshall's estate. In addition to the 500-clay shoot the "Twinkling Star" night shoot proved extremely popular with the target blasters.

With the marathon's exploding growth came a dramatic increase in prize money. The purses offered exceeded $5000 - more than most professional golf tournaments of the day. With the best target shooters in the country on hand many world records fell over the years at the Yorklyn traps.

The Marshall Tournament was suspended during World War II but starting in 1946 two a year were held to "catch up." But after 30 years the trapshoot just stopped. Tommy Marshall lost interest and his son was too busy with his travel business. The grounds and traps in Yorklyn stood silent but the tournament that grew from obscure beginnings into the nation's second largest lived on. It was adopted by the South End Gun Club in Reading, Pennsylvania, still carrying the original Marshall Trapshooting Tournament name.

The Marshall Marathon in Yorklyn was the biggest trapshooting tournament on the East Coast for thirty years - in prestige, attendance and number of targets. The Auburn Heights property is now a Delaware state preserve.

National Champions at Wilmington High School

In Delaware Leroy Sparks is the Father of Swimming. Sparks was named physical-education director of the Wilmington YMCA in the early 1920s and he quickly became the foremost advocate of aquatic sports in the state. He founded the indoor state championships, which we would be a fixture on New Year's Day for more than three decades, in 1921. He also started swimming as a varsity sport at Wilmington High School.

In 1926 Sparks guided the Cherry and White mermen to eight wins in nine dual meets against top Philadelphia schools. Convinced his swimmers deserved a larger stage Sparks launched a citywide campaign to send the Wilmington swim team to the national high school championships in Evanston, Illinois. Within two weeks the energetic Sparks raised the $1500 necessary for the trip.

His fervor was well-rewarded as Wilmington High swam to victory in the National Interscholastic Championships. Individually, Jack Spargo won the 100-yard breaststroke and James Fraser upset his teammate Franklin Holt, the Red Devils' top sprinter, in the 100-yard freestyle. The Wilmington schoolboys also shattered a national record in the 200-meter medley relay with William Brown, Franklin Potter, Spargo and Holt.

After the 1926 school year Sparks left Delaware for Battle Creek College in Michigan where he would build up a national power over the next 35 years. He trailed behind him not only a legacy in Delaware swim history but in training as well. Sparks introduced a revolutionary energy-producing diet to his charges emphasizing carbohydrates and shunning steak.

His successor Tom Allen continued the controversial training regimen in 1927 and with Holt and Spago returning for their senior years Wilmington repeated as national champions, winning the title by three points even though the Red Devils were disqualified from one relay for swimming out of the lane.

The team was properly feted around Wilmington upon their return but graduation quickly brought a close to the Red Devil dynasty. Franklin Holt was the team's star, swimming eight races in two days at the 1927 nationals; anchoring relays, winning the 100-yard freestyle and narrowly missing the 40-yard title. He went to Lafayette in 1928 where he broke many pool records as a freshman.

Desiring to return home he transferred to the University of Delaware, again setting pool records in practice, but had to sit out a season and dropped out of school. But that was not the last of Franklin Holt. After being away from school for nearly a decade he resumed his education in Newark and began to once again win swimming races for the Blue Hens.

The Prices Run pool was the most popular recreation spot in the city of Wilmington for much of the first half of the 20th century. This shot is from 1926.

Life in the Minors

Matt Donahue could well be the best hitter of a baseball Delaware ever produced. But he came along at a time, between the World Wars, when there were more than 40 minor leagues in operation across America. With more than 300 teams rifling talent to only 16 major league squads many great baseball players never got a chance to showcase their talent in the big leagues.

Matthew Donohue earned 13 letters in football, basketball, baseball and track at Wilmington High School from 1911-15. After high school he played on many teams around Delaware and competed against major leaguers in the Shipyard Leagues during World War I as a member of Pusey and Jones.

Donohue started his professional career with Rochester of the International League, only a rung below the majors. He would climb no further. It was said of Donohue that "he could slash the apple but his arm was a trifle weak."

In 1921, the 23-year old was a reserve outfielder for the Baltimore Orioles, considered the second best minor league team of all-time by MILB.com. He went 7 for 10 in the Little World Series that year.

For the next ten minor league seasons the hard-hitting Donohue averaged .331, never winning even a big-league trial. His minor league travelogue included Mobile, Des Moines, Kansas City, Seattle, and Elmira.

He sat out a couple of years in the late 1920s but staged a comeback in 1930 as a flyhawk for Wilkes-Barre in the New York-Pennsylvania League and made the all-star team by knocking out 202 hits for a .377 average. Still no calls from the bigs.

Perhaps the biggest headline Donohue received in the 1920s came from *The Evening Independent* in his adopted town of St. Petersburg, Florida in 1925 when he remarried his wife five years after the couple's divorce: MATT DONOHUE WINS THE CAKE FOR HIS BRAVERY.

The First Delaware Sports Movie

The first sporting event in Delaware to be captured on celluloid was, of all things, a motorcycle hill climb. In the summer of 1922 more than 4000 speed fans gathered in a field in northern Delaware about 1/4 mile northeast of Smith's Bridge near Granogue.

The Smith's Bridge Hill Climb attracted motorcycle clubs from around the East, including several national champions. Also in the crowd was a motion picture director who filmed the primitive cycles roaring up the steep grass slopes above the Brandywine River.

His resulting movie began appearing shortly thereafter in area theaters as one of the "weeklies," the short reels screened before the main feature.

1930s

If an historian researching the 1930s read only the sports pages he could easily conclude there was no such thing as a Depression. Never had so many sports entrepreneurs attempted new ventures as they did in this decade. On a typical summer day in 1937 a sports fan could spend the afternoon at Delaware Park with the thoroughbreds and that night enjoy outdoor boxing or auto racing in Elsmere or perhaps drive down to Dover for some minor league baseball.

Hard times did not inhibit hard play. Rock Manor Golf Club issued a record 35,247 golf permits in 1931, at the height of the Depression. And in the 1930s, like the first tiny mammals that scurried under the feet of the dinosaurs, softball began appearing in Delaware. The game was tailor-made for the Depression. At the time only the catcher and first baseman used gloves so with a bat, ball and two gloves you had a game.

In 1933 only 14 teams entered the first state softball tournament but by 1936 there were 15 leagues and 2000 softballers, including Milford and Dover. In 1937 the All-Wilmington baseball league, which had been a fixture in Delaware for a quarter-century, stopped play. By the end of the decade baseball was nearly extinct as an adult recreation. There was not even a decent baseball diamond left in Wilmington. One observer concluded, "People aren't satisfied just to watch sports in this day and age, they want to take part. Golf and softball (the fast-pitch variety) are drawing tremendously in this respect."

And if you couldn't afford to go to a game or play a game you could always listen to a game on the wireless. The University of Delaware began radio broadcasting its football games in 1936, the first regular Delaware sports programming.

The Depression's most direct effect on Delaware athletics was on the sporting laws. Boxing was legalized in 1931 after an 18-year battle and in 1935 ballplaying on Sundays was OKed in Wilmington. Both measures helped provide jobs and stimulate the economy to a small degree.

But the biggest boon to the state coffers was the passing of legislation to allow betting on horse racing. It was no secret why Delawareans were now allowed to go to the track and drop $2 on their favorite nag. Prominently reported along with the race results was how much money was sent to the Delaware treasury. And it wasn't just Delawareans who were encouraged to bet. The state placed signs all along Delaware's borders to instruct visitors of the way to Delaware Park.

The opening of William du Pont's magnificent Delaware Park in 1937 was a watershed in Delaware sports history. The racing plant in Stanton cost a million dollars; $50,000 was spent on shrubbery alone. It was big league sports in little Delaware. And it blazed a trail for other sports. Within three years there would also be professional baseball, football and basketball in Delaware.

Delaware Falls Hard for Tom Thumb Golf

Garnet Carter was a traveling salesman with a promoter's soul. He left the road in 1928 to settle on Lookout Mountain in Chattanooga, Tennessee to build a resort and golf course. He also added a small miniature golf course on the property he called Tom Thumb Golf.

Carter's Tom Thumb Golf was so popular that the grass greens wilted under the foot traffic. A new product made of ground cotton hulls called GrassIt was the ideal remedy. He added a patent for a miniature golf course design with hollow logs as hazards to the grass carpet patent and sold "Tom Thumb Golf" kits for $2,000, including shipping. America was about to be swept up in miniature golf mania.

By 1930 there were an estimated 25,000 miniature golf courses across the United States, set up in office buildings and vacant lots and college campuses. Miniature golf made its appearance in Delaware in 1930 when John Metz opened a course at 32nd and Broom Streets in Wilmington. In quick order there was the Rodney Square Miniature Golf Course at 12th and Market, the Robyn Hude Course at 10th and West streets and The Premier on 3106 Market Street. In Newark a Tom Thumb course was laid out on the University Green.

The Delaware state championships, with both the men's and women's winner going to the national Open in Chatannoga, were organized with qualifying targets set - 52 for the men and 62 for the ladies. Hundreds of Wilmingtonians, including the mayor, tried their luck at this new putting game. The eventual men's champion was David Killinger, a 28-year old wire operator for the telephone company, who shot a 123, three under par for three tours of The Premier course.

Mrs. Louis Haywood survived the woman's final, 150-154, when her opponent suffered through an 11 on the 27th hole - no mandatory 6 here. At the nationals Killinger finished five rounds of play at 264, 40 over par and 41 behind the winner. Mrs. Haywood shot a 302 to stumble home 25 strokes back of the leader.

The miniature golf mania spawned what was said to be the largest indoor layout in the United States in the former basketball court and skating rink at 11th and Madison streets. The Auditorium Country Club encompassed 9000 square feet. Spacious felt fairways stretched four feet across with plenty of sporty obstacles including traps, rough and water hazards. The highlight of the loop was a 50-foot putt across a long wooden bridge. The ceilings were painted an azure blue to enhance the illusion of real golf. A mini-clubhouse on the stage overlooked the course.

But like roller skating before it the putting craze in Delaware subsided almost before it began. Tom Thumb Golf was but a brief diversion from the dreary days of the Great Depression.

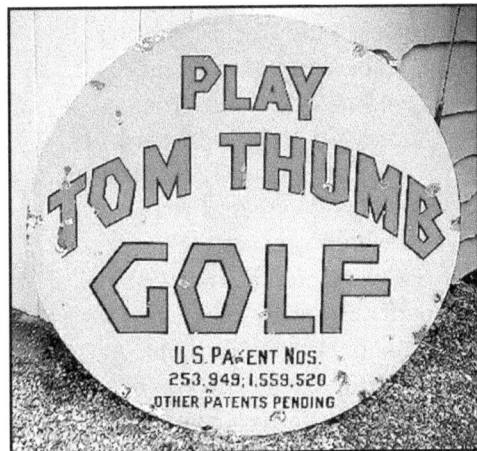

A familiar sign in 1930,
not so much in 1931.

FIRST STATE SPORTS HERO OF THE DECADE:
JIMMY CARAS

Like another fellow who would one day become famous, Jimmy Caras was born in Scranton, Pennsylvania but grew up in Wilmington. After his Greek immigrant father moved to Delaware to run a pool hall Jimmy earned money as a teenage hustler. His prowess earned him an exhibition match in 1926 against Ralph Greenleaf who the *New York Times* would remember as doing for pocket billiards "what Babe Ruth did for baseball, Dempsey did for fighting, Tilden did for tennis."

Greenleaf himself had honed his game in Wilmington after his father had moved from Monmouth, Illinois to manage the Royal Billiard Parlor at 8th & Market in 1915. By the time he won his first world pocket billiards title in 1919 at the age of 20 - the youngest champion ever - Greenleaf was already acclaimed as the "greatest white ball player in the history of his game" for his knack at positioning the cue ball. Greenleaf would hold the world title for nine years in the 1920s. In a decade of dominant sports champions none was more impregnable in his game then Greenleaf.

Greenleaf dismissed young Caras as too inexperienced for his exhibition. Still, when no one else of compatible skill showed up to challenge the champion Caras was called into the 100-ball match. Up first in front of a crowd of over 300, Caras ran off a string of 87 balls before missing. Greenleaf took the table and appeared to be a winner when he pocketed his first 97 balls. But a miss on the 98th ball proved fatal as Caras dropped his final 13 balls to stun the world champion.

Caras was hailed as the "Boy Wonder of the World" and later remembered that Greenleaf's wife, a vaudeville actress named Princess Nai Tai Tai admonished the stunned stickman, "What? A world champion? And you let a high school kid beat you?"

Six years later the two men would meet again - this time in the national championships. At the nationals ten men would gather, playing each competitor once in a game to 125; the player with the best nine-match record winning the title. In 1932, Caras, playing in his first nationals, was

Jimmy Caras won the first of five pocket billiards world championships in 1935. He would become a charter member of the Delaware Sports Hall of Fame.

matching Greenleaf win for win. When it came down to the two men with Wilmington ties, Greenleaf, now living in New York City, captured his 12th title.

Caras would again be runner-up in 1933 before breaking through for the championship in 1935, winning 7 of 9 matches with Greenleaf and defending title holder Andrew Ponzi absent. In 1937 Greenleaf, Ponzi and Caras were part of an historic four-way tie for top honors and after a second round-robin elimination only the three ex-champions were left to shoot-out for the title, a celestial triumvirate from which Greenleaf would emerge the winner.

The 1938 championship again played out into a three-way tie. This time Caras downed Ponzi and newcomer Willie Mosconi to bring his second title back to Delaware and his Tenth Street Billiard Parlor. In the ensuing years Caras would carry the name of Wilmington, Delaware across the country in over 1500 exhibitions.

After World War II Caras moved to Upper Darby, Pennsylvania where he would win more titles in the late 1940s, the product of Wilmington billiard halls still dominating the pocket billiard world. He spent much of his time traveling the world as an ambassador for Brunswick, a leadign maker of pool cues.

In 1967, at the age of 57, he got a hankering to see if he could still compete at the highest level of the game and beat a field of 47 of the world's best players in St. Louis and capture another championship, this time called the U.S. Open.

In 1976 Caras was voted as a charter member of the Delaware Sports Hall of Fame. The next year the Billiard Congress of America Hall of Fame came calling. *Billiards Digest* would come to rank Jimmy Caras as the 10th best player of the 20th century.

Caras was still showing up at his local billiards hall in his 90s in Jacksonville, Florida each day to shoot a few racks. Yet he never tired of telling stories from his days in Wilmington when he would come into the pool hall after school and his father would have set up $100 matches for him. His favorite tale was about the time he glanced in the cash register and saw only $35. When he asked his father what would happen if he lost his father just told him he wouldn't lose. "Talk about pressure," Caras liked to say.

The Dogs

In 1930 the Delaware Whippet Club ran dogs at the Elsmere track on the old State Fairgrounds. Most Delawareans had no idea what a whippet was and the venture met with considerable curiosity. The track featured a 200-yard straightaway with six lanes and was considered one of the swiftest in the country. High speed photography was used to call the break-neck finishes.

The 7-race cards went off under floodlights at 9:00 p.m. Included in the races were popular steeplechase events for the lightning quick canines. Most of the finishes were cavalry charges in just under 12 seconds but the novelty of the whippets wore off without betting allowed. Crowds for the Wednesday and Thursday races began over 1000, with more than half women, but dwindled to fatal levels before the summer was through.

The Fates

In 1937 the fates deprived Delawareans of seeing two of the top sports performers of the decade at the peak of their game.

Triple Crown winner War Admiral was nominated for the $10,000 Kent Handicap on the first racing card of the new Delaware Park but the son of the fabled Man O' War hurt his leg in winning the Belmont Stakes and was scratched.

In the fall, the new Wilmington Clippers were poised to make their professional football debut against the NFL Washington Redskins. The Redskins came to town with their prized rookie making his professional debut - Sammy Baugh, football's first ever pure passing star. Fresh from a storybook career at TCU Baugh's big league bow was eagerly anticipated by sports fans across the country.

But rain washed out the Clippers-Redskins game on a Monday night and didn't let up in time for the game to be played the next night. The Redskins and Baugh left town to embark on their NFL schedule, never to return.

The Wilmington Clippers rewarded their sell-out crowds with wins over the best minor league teams in the East during the 1930s.

1940s

The Golden Age of Delaware sports was the 1940s.

Baseball your sport? There were some years during the decade when as many as five Delaware towns had minor league teams.

How about football? Wilmington's minor league football team, which operated throughout the 1940s, was good enough to beat the Philadelphia Eagles. Down at the University of Delaware there were some students who matriculated on the Newark campus and never saw their team lose before they graduated.

Basketball? The Wilmington Blue Bombers were competing at the major league level - and winning championships.

Golf? Snowball Oliver, who graduated from the Wilmington caddy yards, was tearing up the PGA tour.

Boxing? Delaware sent forth a steady parade of title challengers and enjoyed the skills of Louis, Graziano, and Robinson in local arenas.

Wilmington Park was at the center of a golden age in Delaware sports in the 1940s.

Horse Racing? A Delaware horse went to the post in the Kentucky Derby four years in a row.

Bowling? In one year Delaware sent more bowlers to the American Bowling Congress national tournament than all but nine other states.

Tennis? Wimbledon and U.S. Open trophies graced Delaware mantels.

And Delaware sports virtually ground to a halt for several years during World War II...

In 1937 there was not even an athletic field in Wilmington and there was no clamoring for teams. By 1941 Wilmington had minor league champions in baseball, basketball and football. Papers around the country acclaimed Wilmington as one of the leading sporting towns of its size in America. There were rumors of Wilmington hosting major league franchises in all those sports.

The sporting renaissance was fueled by du Pont family money. Lammot "Brud" du Pont, Jr. was a pioneer of this rebirth of pro sports with his Wilmington Clippers football team which operated through the decade. William du Pont's showcase at Delaware Park was first class all the way, widely praised as a model operation in racing. Bob Carpenter Jr. kick-started the University of Delaware sports program, brought the minor league baseball Blue Rocks to Wilmington and even promoted boxing and auto racing.

World War II halted all this momentum. The University of Delaware stopped playing football, pro basketball and football sputtered, and Delaware Park closed. Transportation problems curtailed scholastic sports and many schools dropped varsity sports to concentrate on intramurals. Rock Manor Golf Club, which had typically done 35,000 rounds a year during the Depression, did less than 9000 during the war.

The sports that fared best in Delaware during the war were baseball and boxing. The Blue Rocks continued to operate and thanks to gas rationing and travel restrictions Delaware became a spring training site for the major leagues. The Philadelphia Athletics did their preseason preparation in Wilmington and the Toronto Maple Leafs of the International League set up camp in Milford. The sensation of the Maple Leafs in 1943 was one-armed outfield wonder Pete Gray who was cut by Toronto but later made the major leagues with the St. Louis Browns.

In boxing heavyweight champion Joe Louis sold war bonds in a 3-round exhibition at the Armory. The champ used

Boxing fans could see Sugar Ray Robinson, whose record was once 128-1-2, in Deleaware during the 1940s.

big gloves but was not coasting, saying, "I don't want to take chances with those big guys." Still, he sent his opponent to the canvas three times before the ref stopped the bout. Sugar Ray Robinson fought several times at the New Castle County Army Air Base and, in fact, was in New Castle with Louis when the Japanese asked for surrender in August of 1945.

After the war Delaware was ready to play. The first Delaware State Horseshoe Tournament was played in North Brandywine Park. The first Delaware Amateur golf tournament teed off at DuPont Country Club in 1945 with Pennsylvania invader Bob Davis of Harrisburg winning. Pari-mutuel betting was allowed on harness racing for the first time in 1946 and attendance at Harrington Raceway exceeded all expectations. Also in 1946 more than 200,000 swimmers used the five Wilmington city pools and the first Delaware State Swimming and Diving Championships drew 2000 to Canby Pool for 30 events. In 1948 came the first annual Delaware State Track & Field Championships at Wilmington's Baynard Stadium.

There was plenty to see in Delaware sports as well in the post-war years. There was stock car racing at four tracks downstate and minor league baseball in Wilmington, Milford, Dover, Seaford and Rehoboth. In golf the Delaware Open brought PGA stars Gene Sarazen, Lew Worsham, Dutch Harrison and others to Rock Manor during its four-year run. Frank Stranahan, the famous weightlifting millionaire amateur won the event in 1948 with a two-day total of 138. And if that wasn't enough sports fans could take special trains to race tracks at Bel Air, Havre de Grace, Laurel and Atlantic City and to see the Phillies or Athletics at Shibe Park.

FIRST STATE SPORTS HERO OF THE DECADE:
ED "PORKY" OLIVER

For want of a kinder fate Ed "Porky" Oliver might be remembered today as one of America's all-time golfers instead of only Delaware's best player ever. In the 1952 Masters Oliver equalled the tournament record but finished second to Ben Hogan who scorched the Augusta National course to a new mark by five strokes.
Earlier, in the 1946 PGA Championship final, then contested at 36 holes of match play, Oliver led Hogan 3-up after 18 holes. At the break between rounds Oliver headed for the lunchroom while Hogan went to the practice tee. In the afternoon Hogan shot 33 on the front nine and routed Oliver 6 and 4.

But it was the U.S. Open where Oliver suffered most. In the 1940 Open, at Canterbury Country Club in Cleveland, Oliver was among the leaders after three rounds of play. As a storm brewed from Lake Erie Oliver and his playing partners dashed to the first tee to start their round early. The official starter was still at lunch and there was confusion about whether the players could tee off before their assigned times. The players forged on.

Oliver finished with a 287 total, tied with two others for the lead, but he was disqualified for playing out of turn. The other players objected, insisting Porky be included in the playoff for the championship. It was no avail, the disqualification stood. Oliver was heartbroken. "It's not just the honor of having a chance to win the Open," he said in the locker room, choking back an occasional tear. "I need the money, and I need it badly."

Oliver finished second so often that he earned the tag "America's runner-up." In two decades on the PGA tour Porky piled up 14 second place finishes and tied behind the leader another 9 times. He won 11 championships.

Born in Wilmington in 1915, Oliver got his start in golf as a caddie at the DuPont Country Club, earning $.50 to $1.00 per loop. He shortly went on to tote bags at the Wilmington Country Club where he anchored the Kennett Pike club caddy team in the Philadelphia District matches. Known as "Snowball" because of his propensity for hurling ice balls as a youngster, Oliver won two straight Philadelphia caddy titles, dominating more than 250 area boys. Before deciding on a career in golf he was a standout athlete at Alexis I. du Pont School, excelling in football, baseball and track.

Oliver turned pro in 1933 as the second assistant at Wilmington Country Club and quickly established himself as one of the longest hitters around. He played in money matches around the Delaware Valley with area pros and in 1936 captured his first professional tournament, the Central Pennsylvania Open. That year Oliver met tour pros for the first time at the Hershey Open and finished 14th out of 160 to take home $90.

Buoyed by his success three Wilmington Country Club members, Bill Denham, Simpson Dean and Sonny Baker, pooled $1000 to send young Snowball out on the winter PGA tour. Once on tour Oliver teamed with another rookie, Sam Snead, in profitable 4-ball matches. Oliver's best finish was a third at the Miami Open where he won $300 but putting problems dogged him throughout his southern swing.

He bought nine different putters and discarded five. It was an incurable affliction. In his later years Oliver would call putting the bane of his career, lamenting that "it has killed me for over 15 years. I've usually had to play 63 golf to shoot 68."

Back in Wilmington Oliver added victories to his resume in the Wood Memorial at Jeffersonville, Pennsylvania in 1937 and the South Jersey Open and a second Central Pennsylvania Open in 1938. It was at theSouth Jersey Open that Snowball Oliver served notice to his fellow professionals. Playing in a brisk Atlantic wind Oliver shot a final round 64, seven strokes better than any pro in the field. Veteran touring pro Leo Diegel called it "the greatest round I've ever seen in over 20 years of golf." And Oliver did it with borrowed clubs.

After a stint as club professional at Hornell Country Club in New York state Oliver became a regular member of the PGA tour in 1940. His first tour victory came at the Bing Crosby Pro-Am in the fourth year of the popular Clambake with a 68-67 at Rancho Santa Fe Country Club. Among his amateur partners were Crosby himself and Johnny Weismuller, a.k.a. Tarzan, who remained lifelong friends. Oliver won the next week, too, at the Phoenix Open with a final round 64.

By the time the tour had reached Texas Oliver was a gallery favorite, renowned for his good humor and happy-go-lucky attitude. A San Antonio paper noted, "This Oliver is a comical fellow to watch on the course. With a battered felt hat mashed in some outlandish fashion around his cranium, he just tramps along, apparently without a care in the world, laughing and clowning. But, boy, oh boy! How he can crash that ball. He doesn't seem any more worried about his missed putts than he does his ample waistline. Which is none at all judging by the way he can tuck away the groceries." Indeed, his friends on tour tagged him "Porky" for his celebrated feats at the dinner table, melting the "Snowball" forever.

Then came the tragic lost U.S. Open at Canterbury, near Cleveland. Although devastated by his disqualification Oliver emerged from the incident a national celebrity. He was in great demand for exhibitions, given to approaching the first tee with a twinkling grin and asking innocently, "Is it all right if I start now?" He even won the next week

Ed Oliver was one of the most popular golfers to ever play the PGA Tour - and but for better fortune almost one of the most successful.

at St. Paul, a victory he cited as his biggest thrill because it came against the same field he had just met in the U.S. Open.

Oliver won the 1941 Western Open, then considered one of golf's most prestigious tournaments before being drafted in March. After a four-year stint in the Army he enjoyed his finest year in 1946, placing fourth on the money list with $17,941. The next year the 32-year old Oliver left the tour for a club job in Seattle at Inglewood Country Club. "I was the fourth leading money winner last year, yet when I got through paying my taxes and expenses I didn't recognize my income. I'm a family man with three kids and long overdue to settle down."

Oliver played some of his best golf in the Northwest. He won five straight minor professional events, the PGA Tacoma Open and brought home $5000, one of his biggest paychecks, by capturing the Phillipine World Open. By 1951, however, Oliver was a full-fledged member of golf's "Gypsies" once again. His fine play on tour earned him berths on the Ryder Cup team in 1951 and 1953. In 1952 Oliver again finished runner-up in the U.S. Open, four strokes back. Of little consolation was a fifty-foot putt Porky holed on the last green to nose nemesis Hogan for second place.

Oliver's career came to an abrupt end in 1960 when a lung was diagnosed as cancerous. When he left the tour he was the 13th all-time money winner in golf history. As his condition deteriorated "Porky Oliver Days" were held across the country, in many sports besides golf. Early in 1961 his old friend Sam Snead came to Wilmington for an exhibition summing up the feelings of many of the tour professionals when he stated that, "Porky's the only person in the country I'd do this for - play for nothing." The event was rained out and re-scheduled for September 30 but Oliver passed away ten days before his final reunion with Snead.

Porky Oliver was eulogized as "the greatest athlete to represent Delaware in national and international competition." Perhaps his most fitting epitaph came from Snead who said, "On a given day Porky could beat any golfer who ever lived. But golf to Porky was just a means to have fun." Years later the Green Hill Municipal Golf Course in Wilmington was renamed in honor of Ed "Porky" Oliver, the golfing star who had narrowly missed capturing each of America's three greatest golfing prizes.

Lost Dreams

World War II wreaked havoc with many athletic careers, big and small. In Delaware, Casimir Klosiewicz was an Olympic caliber weightlifter in 1940, a 165-pounder able to hoist 720 pounds in the three Olympic lifts. Klosiewicz, a one-time Wilmington High School grid star, had been lifting since 1936 as a member of the Delaware Bar Bell Club.

The Olympics were not held during the war years of 1940 and 1944, years when Casimir was out-lifting everyone. Klosiewicz joined the Signal Corps of the Third Army and landed in Europe in the Normandy invasion. In 1948 Klosiewicz, now 27, could manage only a third place in the 148- pound class and failed to make the United States team. That was the last try for Klosiewicz who retired to the Wilmington post office.

"...of Wilmington, Delaware"

Whenever an athlete performs well in a national or international competition the reporting of his/her hometown brings desired notoriety around the country and invariably boosts civic pride. As a desirable place to live Delaware has always attracted transplants of all sorts, including athletes. Recent examples include boxing champion Michael Spinks and golf's U.S. Open winner Laurie Merten, both of Greenville, Delaware.

The first of these champion transplants to settle here was *Marion Zinderstein*, a Massachusetts tennis star. Miss Zinderstein won the national doubles title as an unranked team in 1918. Only seeded fourth the next year she won again. A third national doubles crown came in 1920 and Zinderstein finished runner-up in singles play as well.

Also in 1920 Miss Zinderstein came to Delaware and won the state woman's title - and a husband as well. Marion married a Wilmington banker named John Jessup. Mrs. Jessup won the Delaware tournament in 1921 and 1922, retiring the trophy and becoming the first Delaware resident to win the state title. A baseliner who seldom came to the net, she also won her fourth national doubles championship, teaming with 16-year old sensation Helen Wills.

After a brief retirement Mrs. Jessup was back representing Wilmington in competition in 1924. Always a standout indoor player she won both the national singles and doubles and became Delaware's first female Olympian, winning the silver medal in Paris in the only mixed doubles competition ever held. Mrs. Jessup began fading from the national scene in the mid-1920s as she devoted more time to her family but she continued to win Delaware titles into the late 1930s.

Never did Delaware receive more national press from its immigrants than the 1940s. In 1945 *Bill Talbert*, America's #2 tennis player, moved to Brandywine Hills in Wilmington. Although a Delawarean for only a little over a year Talbert was splashed across the sports page in the middle of a run that would see him collect 17 wins in 21 tournaments.

Announced as "...of Wilmington, Delaware" Talbert, a diabetic, reached the finals in 97 of 103 events in singles, doubles and mixed doubles. He went on to win 8 national doubles tournaments, was ranked in the Top 10 thirteen times and was elected to the Tennis Hall of Fame in 1967.

In golf *Betty Bush*, wife of Brandywine Country Club pro Eddie, represented Delaware in the United States Open and reached the match-play finals of the Canadian Open in 1948. But unquestionably the greatest Delaware import to move to the Diamond State in the prime of her career was *Margaret Osborne*, a native Oregonian. She came to Delaware as a 24-year old in 1942 at the invitation of William du Pont, Jr., who offered his private courts at Bellevue to practice for upcoming big events in the East. Du Pont thought that the Osborne and another guest, Louise Brough, both hard-hitting aggressive net players, would make an excellent doubles team. His acuity was well-placed - the two would win a phenomenal nine consecutive national doubles titles, twelve in all. They tasted defeat in only a handful of more than 300 matches.

Miss Osborne found more than a doubles partner at Bellevue. She married Mr. du Pont in 1947. For the rest of her career one of the world's greatest woman's tennis players picked up her mail in Delaware. She won three consecutive U.S. Open championships in 1948, 49 and 50. A master of lobs and spins, she was ranked number one in the world for those three years.

Mrs. du Pont also won Wimbledon in 1947 and the French Open in 1947 and 49. Her international Wightman Cup record was a phenomenal 18-0, with ten wins in singles and eight in doubles. Fourteen times she was ranked in the Top 10 among tennis players, at age 40 she was still #5. She retired with 37 major titles; only Margaret Court, Martina Navritilova and Billie Jean King ever won more. In 1967 Mrs. du Pont was elected to the National Tennis Hall of Fame along with her longtime doubles partner Louise Brough.

A Truly Old Master

When the Wilmington Country Club formed in 1901 Joshua Ernest Smith was already 51 years old. No matter, he still had four decades of golf left in him. In 1944, at the age of 94, Smith holed his last putt, saying he reckoned it was time to leave the game to the younger fellas. Thus ended one of the most spectacular careers in early American golf.

A lawyer by trade, Smith also stopped practicing law in 1944 after 67 years at the bar. In 1880 he drafted Delaware's famous corporation law. Smith served as judge advocate general under five governors and was a member of the Delaware National Guard for 24 years. He was appointed a Brigadier General by Governor Denney. He began playing golf in his forties at the Delaware Field Club, quickly becoming the best of the three dozen or so golfers who played tournaments regularly at the Elsmere grounds. He was the first player to break 100 and was assigned a club handicap of -13. Smith captained the club's first golf team which represented Delaware in interstate matches. Against a club from Philadelphia Smith defeated Hugh Wilson, who would later design the world-famous Merion golf course.

General Smith was one of the first three subscribers to the Wilmington Country Club when it formed in 1901. He continued to play fine golf at the new Kennett Pike course until his career really hit its stride - at age 70. The General won all five national senior tournaments he played in for golfers 70-75 years of age. It was just a tune-up.

Upon reaching 75 General Smith played in seven more national championships for golfers 75 and over. He won six. At the age of 83 he posted an 88 in tournament play.

He retired as America's best "experienced " golfer.

Well into his 90s Smith hosted an annual dinner for the Wilmington Country Club caddies each Christmas. The General maintained no recipe for his great longevity, advising inquisitors just to "stay healthy." He smoked 20 cigars a day but boasted that he "never knew what whiskey tasted like."

A widower late in life, Smith donated the trademark Japanese cherry trees in Brandywine Park as a monument to his wife, Josephine Tatnall Smith. He also gave money for the Italian-inspired fountain in the park in 1931 which became known as Josephine Gardens.

Smith was a fixture in Wilmington Park, seated in Box A-11 opposite first base. In his later years the General often boasted he could count the number of Blue Rocks' baseball games he had missed "on one hand." Among his last words before slipping into a coma shortly before he died at age 98 was a request for the Blue Rocks score.

In the early 1930s Joshua Ernest Smith took time out from being America's finest senior golfer to donate Josephine Gardens to Brandywine Park in memory of his wife.

Sports Boom at the Beach

The 1940s witnessed the emergence of Rehoboth as a sports center in Delaware. In 1941 promoters started an ocean swim from Dewey Beach to the Hotel Henlopen which became known as the Delaware Mile. World War II interrupted the Labor Day event and when it started again organizers were surprised at the strength of the field, headed by 400-meter former Olympic champion Alberto Zorilla of Argentina.

Zorilla traded championships in the Delaware Mile in 1947 and 1948 with 1941 winner Willard McConnell of Wilmington. With such stars on hand top collegiate swimmers began spending Labor Day at Rehoboth and the ocean swim grew into nine events over two days, including women's divisions. By the mid-1950s the Delaware Mile had been re-named the International Swim Races. There was such an influx of aquatic talent, especially from the Washington DC area, that a separate division had to be established for the overwhelmed Delaware swimmers.

Along with the growth of the ocean swim minor league baseball came to Rehoboth in 1947. A brand new Rehoboth Beach Baseball Park was built which hosted outdoor boxing and auto racing as well as baseball. With the passing of the Rehoboth Beach Sea Hawk baseball team after 1949 the ball park was converted into a 1/4 mile banked track. It was the fastest clay track in the East and the races, with 20-lap features, attracted capacity crowds. In the winter the Rehoboth Lions hosted the 8-team Atlantic Coast Basketball Championships.

These sporting ventures were successful enough that the Delaware Greyhound

Argentine swimming star Alberto Zorilla, who won a golf medal and set an Olympic record in the 400 meter freestyle in 1928, was a regular winner of the Delaware Mile offshore swim.

Racing Association formed with the intent of building one of the East's premier dog racing tracks at the beach. The plant was planned for the E. Thornton Hobson farm less than three miles from the boardwalk. For three years promoters of dog racing tried to get approval from the Delaware legislature. But when it failed the project was abandoned and the sports boomlet at the beach began to subside. Rehoboth returned to being "America's Family Playground" and promoters of spectator sports drifted elsewhere.

The Sportsman: William du Pont, Jr.

No one ever built a greater sporting resume in Delaware than William du Pont, Jr. Horse racing, tennis, golf - he brought national recognition to the state for his efforts in all three sports.

The great grandson of the founder of the chemical conglomerate, William was born in the bucolic horse country of Surrey, England in 1896. Schooled in America, he was active in tennis, soccer and marksmanship. In horse racing he became an internationally recognized authority on the design and construction of steeplechase courses. He was architect of more than two dozen courses around the world, including the National Cup Course on his 11,000-acre estate at Fair Hill, Maryland.

At his primary residence at Bellevue in north Wilmington du Pont maintained a 1 1/8-mile oval and six training tracks. His quarter-mile indoor track was the most modern in the nation. His Foxcatcher Farms horses raced under sapphire blue silks with a gold fox on front. Five Foxcatcher horses started in the Kentucky Derby; Dauber and Hampden were the most successful Delaware entries ever with a second and a third.

He favored fillies, especially those that could whip the boys. His best was Fair Star, a Pimlico futurity winner and Fairy Chant who won the Beldame twice. Du Pont would typically rise at 4 a.m. to train his horses personally before heading downtown to take the reins of the Delaware Trust Company.

William du Pont was the leader of the horsemen who brought pari-mutuel racing to Delaware. He designed Delaware Park and oversaw construction of the plant that brought major league sports to Delaware. Ironically, after sheperding Delaware Park into existence du Pont missed the grand

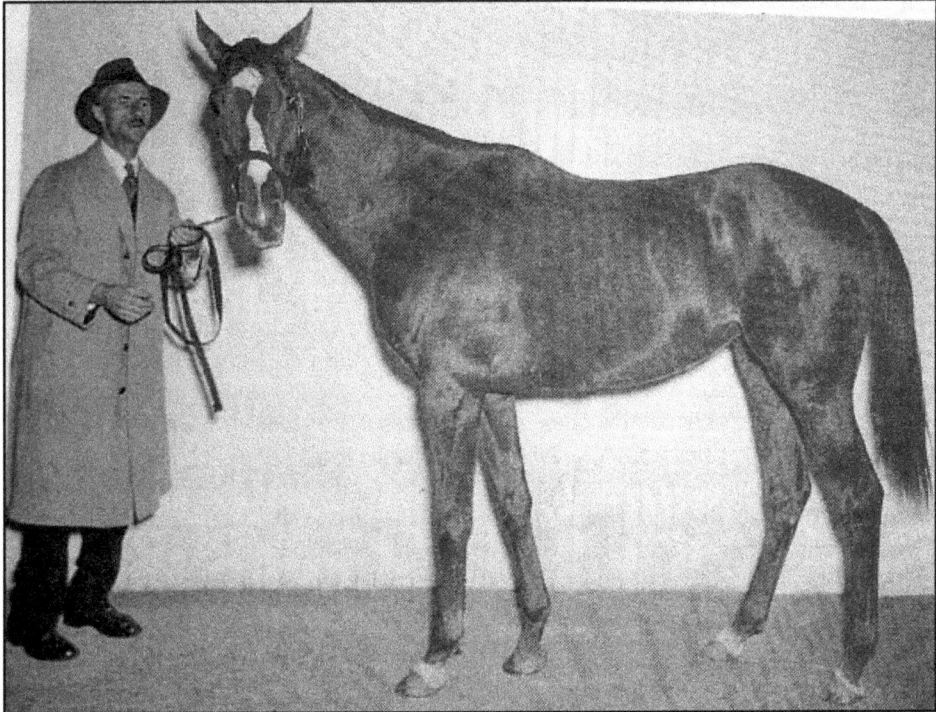

If there was a sports movement going on in Delaware in the 1940s chances are William du Pont, Jr. was likely part of it.

opening. He decided to go to Aqueduct to see his star Rosemont run, nursing a broken collarbone while schooling a jumper at Bellevue the day before.

Only his tremendous contributions to horse racing could dwarf what du Pont did for tennis in Delaware. The courts at Bellevue evolved into one of the greatest private tennis complexes ever. Du Pont employed three resident tennis pros and hosted international tennis stars at his famous "tennis Sundays." He married one, Margaret Osborne, in 1947.

If you played tennis in Delaware after World War II chances are you played on a court William du Pont had a hand in. He was president of the Delaware Lawn Tennis Association for eight years, building a nationally recognized junior tennis program. He contributed half the cost of more than 60 all-weather tennis courts in Delaware. He also gave money to the Wilmington Park Department for construction of public courts.

Du Pont served as president of the Wilmington Country Club and in 1958 donated 108 acres, including 15 golf holes, to the city of Wilmington. The following year he gave another 15 acres to assure the city an 18-hole golf course, now known as Porky Oliver Golf Club.

William du Pont Jr. was committed to advancing the thoroughbred breed and perhaps his greatest recognition in the racing industry came after his death which accompanied the dawn of 1966. Six weeks later his stable of 51 thoroughbreds was put up for auction. Bidders spent a record $2,401,300 for Mr. du Pont's string of Foxcatcher broodmares and stallions, some of the finest ever bred.

So, it's time to add up what Delaware sports enthusiasts owe to William du Pont Jr. Ever place a bet at beautiful Delaware Park? Played a round of golf at the only public golf course within Wilmington city limits? Hit tennis balls at a Delaware state public court? Picnicked or ridden the horses at Bellevue State Park? Thank you William du Pont, Jr.

Delaware's Frank Merriwell

One of the most versatile athletes in Delaware history was Willard McConnell, a banker by trade and sportsman by avocation. McConnell was reared in Delaware City and first made his mark in Delaware sporting circles on the softball field when he won a state record 21 straight games. When he took up duckpin bowling he ruled the lanes for nearly 20 years. McConnell's high game of 278 is one of the highest on record.

At the age of 23 he jumped into the Chesapeake & Delaware Canal on a lark and swam 15 miles in six hours and 18 minutes without any preparation. He then got it in his head to swim from Cape May to Rehoboth and was in the water 8 hours and 26 minutes when exhaustion hit and he was forced to abandon his quest only 1.5 miles from shore. In 1941, at the age of 37, McConnell won the first Delaware Mile Swim in the Atlantic Ocean at Rehoboth Beach.

His marathon swimming career was interrupted when he took up golf, which chewed into his training time. McConnell became perennial club champion at Kennett Country Club but still got enough water time to set a record in the Delaware Mile with a clocking of 21:57. When he approached his 50th birthday he began working on a lifelong goal to swim from Delaware to Florida.

Golf, however, became McConnell's primary sport in his later years. He won five Delaware senior titles and qualified for the United States senior championship. At the age of 58 he shot a 62 at Kennett to tie the course record, although the March round was played with winter rules and temporary tees. The "Old Gray Fox" won the club championship at Kennett 18 of 23 years before succumbing to a heart attack on the Rock Manor Golf Course in 1969 at the age of 65.

1950s

"Major league crazy." That best describes Delaware sports in the 1950s. Bob Carpenter, Jr. was slow to appreciate the power of television but by 1950 he was declaring that he intended to broadcast as many Phillie games as he could fit on the air. There was no need to continue going to low-class boxing matches when there were better ones every night on the tube.

And so spectator sports died in Delaware. The Blue Rocks disbanded in 1952. Wilmington Park, the envy of every minor league town in America a decade earlier, no longer could support itself with the odd rodeo, wrassling show, or polo match and it was razed in 1955 after only 15 years of use.

The highlight of the 1950s was the new Brandywine Raceway in northern Wilmington in 1953. The $2,500,000 harness track was a success from the first post time. Head Pin flashed under the wire to win the first race in 2:10, returning $7.90 to win and by closing night The Big B handled $6,000,000 in its 20-night meet. Delaware Park was hardly hurt by its new neighbor. The Stanton plant averaged 15,017 fans in 1953, including a one-day record attendance of 35,473. Horse racing was the major sport in Delaware.

Another success story was the annual high school all-star football game, founded by Bob Carpenter and Jim Williams, begun in 1956. The first Blue-Gold charity game matching the best players from upstate against the downstate stars pulled 6594 to Newark to raise $17,000

for the Delaware Foundation for Retarded Children. It has gone on to raise over two million dollars. Few states are blessed with such a worthwhile sporting institution as the annual Blue-Gold football game.

The Delaware State Golf Association formally organized in 1952 with eight clubs and a series of tournaments for men, women and seniors. Al Dollins, president of the DSGA, won the first "official" Delaware Amateur, then contested at match play, 2 and 1 in the 36-hole final over Ronnie Watson.

Little League baseball was already in 37 states when it came to Delaware in 1951. The Wilmington Optimists was the first league organized with games at the park on New Castle Avenue and New York Avenue. Bus Zebley was instrumental in keeping the fledgling Little League going, umpiring all the games and calling time to do a little coaching if needed. If kids weren't playing baseball they could be found at the swimming pool. A string of suburban pools dotted the outskirts of the region and peaceful summer evenings in many neighborhoods were routinely pierced by the shouts from swim meets.

There was a suburban exodus in New Castle County in the 1950s but the new suburbanites found few recreation areas waiting for them. There was only one public golf course in the state and developers outpaced the builders of parks. What organized recreation existed was managed by local sporting stores. That was soon to change.

First State Sports Hero of the Decade: Dave Nelson

Dave Nelson came to Delaware in 1951 from the University of Maine at the age of 30. In four years with the Black Bears he had clawed out a 21-6-4 record while tinkering with a new offensive scheme. His first three years in Orono Nelson used the single wing and his final year he employed the T-Formation, both offenses gleaned from his days as a University of Michigan backfielder. He brought an entire new offense to Newark, one he said, "must have on every play the look of a run and the threat of a pass." Nelson had built a reputation for stressing tackling and defense but his first spring practice at the University of Delaware was devoted totally to offense: goal-line blocking and timing with his Winged-T offense.

Although he inherited precious little talent, a special Korean War provision enabling freshmen to play gave Nelson a field general he would rely on for his first four years - Don Miller. With Miller at the controls Nelson's new-fangled offense began driving Delaware to national prominence once again. After a 19-7 win over Kent State in the 1954 Refrigerator Bowl win in Evansville, Indiana - "the refrigerator capital of the world" - Nelson seemed ready to leave Newark for the "big time."

His first offer came from Indiana University to become Athletic Director, a post he also manned in Newark. But Nelson, respectfully called "The Admiral," wasn't ready to leave the sidelines just yet. Over the years Nelson would be mentioned in connection with jobs at Harvard, Baylor, Pittsburgh, Colorado, Florida and the Los Angeles Rams. "It isn't important to me," explained Nelson on why he shunned the big schools. "The game's the thing. I get as much satisfaction out of beating Connecticut or Rutgers as I would out of beating Illinois or Minnesota if I were coach of Michigan." And so he stayed in Newark and built a legendary career at Delaware.

In 1957 Nelson published *Scoring Power With The Winged-T Offense*, co-written with ex-Michigan teammate and Iowa coach Forrest Evashevski. The book contained over 300 detailed diagrams and action photos based on the offense Nelson devised at Maine in 1950. When Evashevski went to two Rose Bowls with the Winged-T in the late 1950s Nelson was acclaimed as one of football's great offensive minds. Marv Levy, who would go on to Super Bowl infamy as coach of the Buffalo Bills, was named coach of California in 1959 and cited Coach Nelson as his greatest influence.

Nelson began to reach his greatest coaching success during the same era. His teams won the Lambert Cup, symbolic of Eastern small college supremacy in 1959, 1962 and 1963. The 1963 Blue Hens, Nelson's greatest eleven, went 8-0 and were voted the national small college champion by United Press International. Back in 1957 Nelson was chosen as a member of the NCAA Rules Committee, at age 36 the youngest on the board and also from the smallest school. In 1961 Nelson, became head of the Rules Committee. And by 1967 Nelson was ready to sacrifice his life on the sidelines for his administrative duties with the NCAA and as Athletic Director at the University of Delaware.

Nelson left coaching after 19 years with an overall record of 105-48-6. At Delaware in 15 seasons he won 84 games, lost only 42 and tied two. Nelson was 45 when he retreated from the coaching wars, only five years older than his hand-picked successor, Tubby Raymond. For the rest of his career he resisted the occasional overture to return to coaching andover-saw the burgeoning Delaware athletic program, both at the varsity and intramural levels. In 1991 came the richly deserved election to the National Football Foundation College Football Hall of Fame for Dave Nelson.

Passing Through

In the post-war years sharp-eyed Delawareans had many a chance to see embryonic legends and say, "I knew him when..."...

The Rifleman. He didn't make much of an impression on Delaware fans as a low-scoring forward for the Wilmington Blue Bombers but the wisecracking Kevin Connors was always a favorite with the local sports scribes. Connors also played a little professional baseball and when he manned first base for Los Angeles one summer he began picking up bit parts in movies, usually as an imposing bad guy. The next time Connors, now known as Chuck, came to Wilmington it was in Pat and Mike at the Loew's Theatre in 1952. Connors would go on to even greater fame as the fast-drawing, slow-burning Lucas McCain in television's *The Rifleman.*

Chuck Connors played major league baseball and minor league basketball for the Wilmington Blue Bombers before becoming **The Rifleman** *on television.*

Say Hey. In the disintegrating days of the Wilmington Blue Rocks in 1950 the few loyal fans received one final treat before the team dissolved two years later. Willie Mays, the first black player in the Interstate League, played before 1663 fans in Wilmington Park as a Trenton centerfielder. Willie went 5-9 in a doubleheader with two doubles.

Followers of the Negro Leagues also had a chance to see Jackie Robinson cover shortstop for the Kansas City Monarchs as a youngster out of UCLA in 1945 and a skinny 17-year old infielder play several games in Wilmington Park in 1951 with the Indianapolis Clowns. His name was Henry Aaron.

The Softball Player. Bill Bruton was born and raised in Panola, Alabama but came to Wilmington during the war in 1943. For recreation he played catcher on a local softball team. Although he played no baseball in Delaware, Judy Johnson recommended him to a Boston Braves scout, who signed him for the National League club. Bruton could not even make his high school track team home in Alabama but soon he was breaking minor league base stealing records. When he reached the majors he led the league in steals his first three years. Bruton relocated to Milwaukee with the Braves but before he left he took a bit of Delaware with him - he married Judy Johnson's daughter.

The Doctor. In 1952 Dr. Jack Ramsey, then 27, was named basketball coach for the Mt. Pleasant Green Knights. It was Ramsey's second coaching job in a pilgrimage that would stretch all the way to the Portland Trailblazers and the Hall of Fame. At Mt. Pleasant High School Ramsey, who taught English and Social Studies as well, inherited only one player from a 6-14 team. He nonetheless forged three winning seasons with the Green Knights, going 40-18, before returning to his alma mater, St. Josephs, to build a program of national reputation. Ramsey was 234-72 at the collegiate level and won 834 NBA games, the second most ever.

The Stilt. Almost from the time he graduated elementary school Wilt Chamberlain was the most famous basketball player in America. In 1954 he came down from Philadelphia to play in a schoolboy game at the Walnut Street YMCA in Wilmington. Four years later, after leaving Kansas University early, Wilt played here again as a member of the Harlem Globetrotters. Performing in the Salesianum gym before 1900 Chamberlain led all scorers with 19 points, mostly on stuffs. It was not a history-making night - the Trotters won again.

Wilt Chamberlain played on Delaware basketball courts in the 1950s both as a schoolboy phenomenon and a member of the Harlem Globetrotters.

The Speedster, human-powered. Charley Jenkins, Olympic gold medal winner in the 400 meters at the 1956 Olympics cooled his heels for a year in Delaware when he spent 8th grade at Howard High School, living with his aunt when his mother was ill.

The Speedster, motor-powered. Mario Andretti is considered the most versatile driver of all time, having won championships with all types of racers from Indy cars to Formula One machines. Andretti cut his teeth racing "big cars" on dusty tracks up and down the East coast, one of which was Harrington Race Track.

The Rookie. Jake Wood came and went to Delaware State almost before the registrar could record his name. Wood left the Hornet baseball team after his freshman year and the speedy second baseman was next seen as a rookie in 1961 igniting one of the strongest offensive teams in history at the top of the Detroit Tiger line-up. Wood played in every game, scored 96 runs, stole 30 bases and led the American League in triples with 14. But just like at Delaware State the mercurial Wood would soon pass from the scene, never enjoying anything like the success of his rookie year.

The Recruit. In his long career at the University of Delaware who was Tubby Raymond's most famous recruit? That would be Carl Yastrzemski, who was anxious to come to Newark and play for Raymond's baseball team in the 1950s. Yaz went so far as to come down from Long Island and travel with the Blue Hens to a game at Ursinus College, where he watched the game from the bench. Alas, an academic problem kept Yastrzemski from enrolling at the University of Delaware and he took his future Hall-of-Fame bat to Notre Dame.

The Brandywine Canoe Slalom

Here's one that is certain to win a few bar bets. What Olympic sport started in America in Delaware? Kayaking.

Bob McNair, the founding force behind the Buck Ridge Ski Club in 1945, literally wrote the book on *Basic River Canoeing*. In 1954 McNair and Buck Ridge started the Brandywine Canoe Slalom, the first event of its kind in the country. About 150 canoeists and kayakers from as far away as Toronto came to test the boulder-strewn waters on the historic river. There were divisions for men and women and one and two-person canoes and kayaks.

The Brandywine Canoe Slalom, held each April, quickly developed into one of Wilmington's most popular springtime events. Up to a thousand spectators would line the banks of the river in Brandywine Park along the course that ran for 200 yards south from the Washington Street bridge.

A canoe slalom is like a ski slalom down a mountain, only trickier. Contestants had to not only pass through gates hung from wires stretched across the Brandywine but they had to pass in the proper direction - which sometimes meant having to battle upstream. Contestants could also be required to navigate gates in reverse. The craft entered the river one at a time and the race was against the clock.

In 1972 white water kayaking achieved Olympic status and the rest of America caught on to the excitement Delawareans had enjoyed for nearly twenty years. The Brandywine Canoe Slalom was, at that time, a qualifying event for national and international competitions. For several years the course was designed by Mark Fawcett, a Wilmington area canoeist who raced three times in the world championships between 1965 and 1969. He managed the United States Olympic team in 1972.

The Brandywine Canoe Slalom passed from the Delaware sporting scene in the late 1970s. But for a quarter of a century it provided Wilmingtonians with world-class competition of the sort the Tour DuPont would bring to Delaware a decade later.

The first inter-club canoe slalom races started on the Brandywine River in the 1950s.

Salesianum Football

High school football in Delaware will never be confused with Ohio or Texas or even Oregon for that matter. Wilmington High School, known simply as "High" in the state, drew the biggest football crowds in Delaware for the first half of the century. The rivalry between the Cherry and White and Chester High School was one of the oldest in America, dating back to 1891 when few secondary schools were playing ball and neither had any in-county gridiron foes. The two played for 53 years, often with as much action in the stands as there was on the field. Enemy fans were typically chased out of town and often wound up chatting with the local gendarmes. Chester won the first meeting 6-0 and the last battle 6-0 in 1944, when the series ended so Chester could schedule Delaware County schools. Chester was on the long end of the rivalry 31 wins to 23.

For many decades high school football in Delaware meant Salesianum. The school's legacy in the sport began modestly in 1921 with the stated objective of building "a team capable of coping with any school in the country." Lofty aspirations for a school founded only 18 years earlier with a student body of 12.

That first year Salesianum went 3-3-1. The first win came in the second game, a 7-0 whitewashing of New Castle High. Later that year Sallies held state football power Wilmington - bigger and more experienced - to a 0-0 tie before 8000 fans squeezed into 18th and Van Buren streets. But success did not come quickly. There were but 11 wins in the first 38 games.

Salesianum became a charter member of the Philadelphia Catholic League in 1923 - a school of 180 squaring off regularly with institutions of 1800 and more. The Wilmington school held its own in this competition and even claimed a share of the championship in 1934 before dropping football in 1938. Football resumed after World War II and Salesianum once again took up chase of its dream.

National status came in the 1950s with the arrival of coach Dominic "Dim" Montero, a former Sallies' All-State lineman. In ten years Montero lost only ten games, piling up 70 wins and three ties. While in-state schools became focused on the new conferences that were finally allowed to form Salesianum played an increasingly tougher out-of-state schedule. Never would a Delaware scholastic eleven enjoy a period like this. Sallies games were carried exclusively on local radio and games were played conspicuously on Friday nights - a rarity in Delaware. In 1957-58-59 Salesianum went undefeated and molded a then-state record 29 consecutive wins. College recruiters routinely harvested Sallies players; five played on the 1960 University of Minnesota Rose Bowl team.

By the mid-1960s enrollment had grown to more than a thousand. In 1964, in his penultimate year, Montero was named National Catholic Coach of the Year. But its monopoly of Catholic schoolboy talent in Delaware was ending. St. Mark's High School opened south of Wilmington and siphoned enough warriors from the old school on 18th & Broom to win state championships of its own in the 1970s.

1960s

With an increase in leisure time in the 1960s Delawareans took to the playing fields. Slow pitch softball, which had been unheard of in Delaware in 1960, had five leagues and 700 players in Wilmington alone by 1963. By the end of the decade there were 3000. Between 1958 and 1961 twenty-eight swimming pools were built in New Castle County, nearly doubling the state number and swimming was suddenly Delaware's second most popular participant sport. Foreshadowing the coming running boom the first Caesar Rodney half-marathon in 1964 attracted 48 racers, twelve from Delaware. Two-time Olympian Browning Ross won in 1:07.24. In 1968 Delaware staged its first state-wide bowling tournament – previously competitions had been divided between lower Delaware and Wilmington - and 1550 kegelers entered.

There was more to do and less to watch in Delaware in the 1960s than ever before. It was the first decade in nearly 100 years with no minor league baseball. Only basketball's Blue Bombers and an occasional football game offered a pro ticket in Delaware in the 1960s.

Fans could watch the first Delaware state high school tournament games. There had been high school playoffs in Delaware before, in the loosely regulated Delaware Interscholastic Athletic Association in the 1920s for instance, but it wasn't until the formation of the Delaware Secondary School Athletic Association, 68 members strong, in 1966 that Delaware got true statewide competition. The first state tournament in any sport was boys basketball, in 1967. Before a sellout crowd in the University of Delaware Fieldhouse Mt. Pleasant High School bumped cold-shooting Brandywine 49-38 to become the first Delaware high school state champion.

The 1960s were still glory days for horse racing in Delaware, albeit their last. Delaware Park and Brandywine Raceway gave the state a thoroughbred-standardbred daily double unsurpassed in America. Delaware pioneered Sunday racing in the country and in 1969 the tiny state was supporting four harness tracks. There was racing 11 months a year.

The 1960s could rightly be called the Decade of Women in Delaware sports. Margaret Varner, an El Paso native teaching in Delaware, won an unprecedented four consecutive national squash singles championships in 1960-63. She was also a member of the United States Wightman Cup tennis team and a two-time national champion in badminton. Gretchen Vosters Spruance was winning the first of 20 consecutive women's Delaware state tennis championships. Rosemary Miller won trap-shooting's greatest prize in the Grand American in 1968. Rita Justice was on the women's pro bowling tour; Patsy Hahn on the LPGA tour. All these women were the best ever in their sports in Delaware.

But the most significant happening for women's sports occurred quietly on October 8, 1969. Behind the infirmary on the University of Delaware campus in Newark a group of women played the first intercollegiate women's game in

Delaware - almost 80 years to the day after the college's first football game. The "Blue Chicks" or "Delaware Co-Eds" as the women's field hockey team was clumsily called, beat Salisbury State 4-1 in that historic contest. There was enough money - $1500 - to fund only three sports and 768 university women selected basketball, swimming and field hockey as the first triumvirate. That hockey field, barren, unlined and sandwiched in the corner of the campus at Academy Street and Park Place was the Madison Square Garden of the women's three venues. In Hartshorn Gym the pool was too shallow for diving so the first swim meets had to be held away. And for basketball the court ended abruptly in a brick wall under the baskets. The windows were welded shut so the players would roast during practices and games. It was of no concern to the fans however - there weren't any bleachers for anyone to sit in anyway. The coaches, of course, worked for free.

From this deprived beginning the University of Delaware developed a strong women's athletic program featuring 11 sports - with winning lifetime records in all. Their success filtered down through the high schools in Delaware and encouraged women to continue competing after graduation. Women were now commonplace in Delaware sports.

The Streak

Bill Billings came to Middletown High School in 1962, taking over a football program that had struggled to a 14-54-3 record in its first nine years. Billings arrived from Edenton High School in North Carolina where he put together 77 wins and three ties in 95 games. On September 14 Billings' Cavaliers, molded from a school of fewer than 500 students, got by Caesar Rodney in his first game, 19-6. Turn the calendar forward to 1967. Bill Billings was still dodging his first defeat at Middletown.

The unbeaten streak stretched through 53 games, although one game, a 52-6 thrashing of Smyrna, was disputed over an ineligible player. It was the longest such streak in Delaware history, the longest in America at the time. Only four of the games were decided by less than a touchdown. The average margin of victory was more than five touchdowns.

In 1966, with the streak at 44 games, Middletown tackled powerful Salesianum, previous holder of the record for consecutive wins with 29. The team from Wilmington outweighed the Cavaliers by 30 pounds a man and observers who knew about these things favored the Sallies by three touchdowns. Seating capacity at Middletown Stadium was 3,500; police estimated the crowd at 8,000. The Cavaliers scored a late fourth quarter touchdown to whip Salesianum 14-13. They were still streaking.

Middletown continued to try to upgrade its Diamond State Conference schedule by lining up larger schools. In 1967 proud Newark, themselves on a 24-game run under Bob Hoffman, ended the Middletown streak. Newark was the state's winningest program at the time, having won 137 and lost only 32 in the previous 20 years. Middletown's success would, however, continue under Billings. In 1971 the Cavaliers, then 91-4 under Coach Billings, reached the finals of the first Delaware state football tournament, losing a close 13-6 battle with big school Wilmington.

FIRST STATE SPORTS HERO OF THE DECADE: KELSO

"Once upon a time," wrote Joe Hirsch of the *Daily Racing Form*, "there was a horse named Kelso. But only once." Delaware may never have had any ties to a Kentucky Derby winner but it can claim kinship with Kelso, the only horse who could ride in a posse with Man O'War and Secretariat.

Kelso was bred by Allaire du Pont, originally of Pennsylvania's Main Line and former resident of Granogue. Although Mrs. du Pont, widow of Richard du Pont, moved to her Woodstock Farm in Chesapeake City, Maryland, where Kelso was stabled, she always considered herself a Wilmingtonian. Kelso was a grandson of Triple Crown winner Count Fleet and the son of Mrs. du Pont's mare, Maid of Flight. He was named for Mrs. du Pont's friend Kelso Alsop of Adams Dam Road in northern Delaware when he was foaled in 1957. Cosmically, in the racing sense, Kelso Alsop was co-owner of a party organizing firm known as Secretariat Limited.

Before he reached the racetrack Kelso was gelded, a genetic tragedy that inspired the Red Smith line, "the unkindest cut since Kelso." His juvenile campaign produced one minor win and a pair of seconds. He was not a contender for the traditional Triple Crown events and was put in training with Carl Hanford, who it was written, "made a good horse great." Kelso came on to win eight of nine starts as a 3-year old and was named Horse of the Year. The magnificent gelding went on to win that most coveted of all racing awards every year from 1960 through 1964.

Before being forced from the track at age nine by a hairline fracture of the right ankle Kelso won at everything from six furlongs to two miles, on grass, in slop six inches thick and often burdened with top weights up to 136 pounds. In almost half of his victories - he had 39 in 63 starts - Kelso set or equalled track records.

At distances greater than a mile and a half he was probably the greatest race horse who ever lived. No horse ever beat him at two miles; he won the Jockey Club Gold Cup a that distance an unthinkable five straight times. Nearing eight, in his last big race at the 1964 International, Kelso romped home in 2:23.4 on grass - the fastest any horse had ever run on this continent.

Kelso banked only a small fraction of his record lifetime earnings of $1,977,896 in Delaware. He raced at Delaware Park only once, as an eight-year old in the 1965 Diamond Handicap. Kelso thundered home 3 1/4 lengths ahead that day. He had his own mail box for fan letters and received the social calls of respectful grooms and jockeys. Episcopal bishop of Delaware, Arthur McKinstry, was his private chaplain.

In retirement Kelso was lovingly cared for and ridden regularly on fox hunts by Mrs. du Pont. The old champion died in 1983 at the age of 26, one week after a rare public appearance at Belmont Park to lead the field onto the track for the 65th running of the Gold Cup, his former private showcase.

Hanford retired in 1968 and became a steward at Delaware Park where his daughter was a trainer. When he was inducted into the National Museum of Racing and Hall of Fame he said, "I'm here because of one horse and one horse only. I had a few stakes horses before, but they didn't compare with Kelso."

Delaware Tourists

While male Delawareans on the professional golf and bowling tours have been as rare as a double eagle or a 7-10 conversion women pros have been virtually nonexistent. The Sixties featured Delaware's best distaff offerings in both sports.

Patsy Hahn first came to the attention of Delaware's golfing community in 1952 when she won the first Delaware state junior girl's championship with a 111 as a 12-year old. The next year the DuPont Country Club prodigy made the quarter-finals of the state women's amateur. She won the state championship for the first time at the age of 16.

By 1963 Hahn was an eight-time medalist and five-time winner of the Delaware state championship, a quarter-finalist in the National Amateur and 12th place finisher in the professional Kelly Girl Open tournament. She turned pro and finished second in her first tournament, the Sunshine Open with scores of 81-81-84. She won $760 with a third place finish in Los Angeles and tied for 7th in the US Open shooting 74-73-78-78-303 to wind up 14 strokes back. She won $312.

Hahn ended the 1963 season 31st on the money list with $2,035.50 in 25 tournaments. Tendonitis in her wrist forced a premature retirement from tournament golf a year later and Hahn returned to a club job in Delaware. She eventually became head pro at DuPont-Louviers Country Club, one of the first women in America to run her own club.

In 1958 Rita Justice was a 23-year old part-time model bowling one night a week. She carried a 148 average. Four years later the Majestic, Kentucky native who came to Delaware as a 4-year old became the first state resident to turn pro. The next year two more Delaware women, Marge Renai and Jean Lapinski, both turned pro.

Pickings on the women's bowling circuit were even slimmer than on the fairways. Over the next decade Justice accumulated numerous honors. In 1966 she was a finalist for the prestigious All-Star Bowl Tournament and finished 13th. Three times she earned a spot on the Bowler of the Year ballot, reserved for the top ten bowlers in the country. In 1972 Justice won the Pearl Cup and World Challenge Cup in Japan; the next year she was third on the tour in earnings with $6,775 and third in Bowler of the Year balloting. When Rita Justice left the women's tour she also took over her own operation, buying the First State Lanes in Wilmington.

Hard Courts: Terry Hassall

Before there was a Jimmy Connors or a John McEnroe there was Terry Hassall. A typical Hassall tennis match in the 1960s would be punctuated by a flying racket or pierced by a self-chastising scream. Fans never knew what to expect from the flamboyant Hassall. But one thing could always be counted on - Terry Hassall would leave the court a winner.

For the better part of a decade the P.S. du Pont High School product never lost a match in Delaware. After winning the state high school championship from 1964-66 Hassall compiled the finest men's tennis record in the history of Delaware, including winning the Middle States singles title 10 times. An attacking serve-and-volleyer, he traveled the pro circuit a few times, playing the European tour, before settling in Pennsylvania as a teaching pro at the prestigious Merion Cricket Club in Philadelphia.

Each grew up and starred in sports elsewhere but found in Delaware an ideal petri dish for their young athletes. One took local boys and girls and drilled and trained them into Olympians; the other attracted future Olympians from across the land. Between them they have brought as much international attention to the state as any transplant since E.I. du Pont.

Bob Mattson came to Wilmington in 1955 as a chemist for the Joseph Bancroft Co. At North Carolina State University he had been a four-time All-American swimmer, one-time holder of American and world records in both the breaststroke and individual medley. With the 1956 Olympics on the horizon he delayed his plunge into the everyday work world but failed in his quest. Had he had the training facilities he would one day give Delawareans Mattson may have been an Olympian himself.

In his spare time away from Bancroft Mattson started a swim team. Soon his young charges numbered 400 and Mattson found himself spending as much time seeking out water for his burgeoning army as he did teaching. By 1963 he had reached a decision point in his life - maintain a comfortable life as a chemist or make swimming a full-time vocation. In Delaware it has always been easier to earn a living as a chemist than as a swimming coach but Mattson set out to build his own swimming facility.

Four years and many tens of thousands of dollars later the state-of-the-art Wilmington Aquatic School in New Castle was a reality. In 1968 Mattson developed his first Olympic swimmer, Dave Johnson. The most successful of his early pupils was Jenny Bartz who dominated Delaware and regional competitions until she departed for California in 1969 and then

the 1972 Olympics. At Montreal in 1976 Wilmington Aquatic School member Steve Gregg brought home a silver medal.

Perhaps the best swimmer Mattson ever coached never made it to the Olympics. Jenni Franks was a 16-year old Mt. Pleasant High School All-American when she shattered the American record in the 400- meter individual medley. She tore through the Pan-American Games but failed at the 1976 Olympic Trials. Seeded first, she finished 11th. Shirley Babashoff won the event in a time four seconds - a swimming eternity - slower than Franks' record.

Mattson once estimated that 10,000 people had gone under his tutelage at the Wilmington Aquatic School, aged three on up. He also helped several national teams prepare for major competitions. Despite his heavy teaching schedule Mattson found time to train himself, dominating Masters competitions for years. In 1994, besieged by economic reversals, Mattson was forced to move his Wilmington Aquatic Club to Alloway, New Jersey after 27 years. All in all Delaware has been well-served for having one less chemist.

Like Mattson, Ron Ludington was having trouble finding adequate facilitates for his students. The 1960 Olympic pairs medalist was seeking more ice time for his skaters while working in Indianapolis. The Wilmington Skating Club offered the additional hours, albeit after 10:30 p.m., and Ludington moved his small stable of pairs skaters and ice dancers to Delaware.

His first champions, ice dancers Judy Schwomeyer and Jim Sladky, came with him in the mid-1960s. In the next three decades Ludington-trained skaters would pile up more than three dozen national championships. Ron Ludington made Delaware a mecca for aspiring pairs skaters.

In 1973 six of the 13-member United States Skating team were coached by Ludington. In 1976, with ice dancing now a part of Olympic competition, Susie Kelly and Andy Stroukoff of the Wilmington Skating Club represented the United States. They finished 17th of 17 couples. In pairs at the Innsbruck Olympics that year Alice Cook and William Fauver placed 11th.

At Sarajevo in 1984 Ludington's most famous stars, Kitty and Peter Carruthers, won a silver medal in pairs skating - the first U.S. medal in the event since Ludington's own 24 years earlier. Since then a Ludington team, while never duplicating the Carruthers' success, has been at every Olympics. In 1988 at Calgary dancers Suzy Semanick and Scott Gregory finished sixth; in pairs Kim and Wayne Seybold skated to 10th.

In 1992 Ludington, now training his skaters at the University of Delaware, produced champions from the combustible "blue collar" team of Calla Urbanski and Rockie Marval. The story of Urbanski, a 31-year old Wilmington waitress who had skated 23 years, and Marval, a New Jersey trucker, captivated America but there was no storybook ending for the oft-feuding pair. They wound up 10th. At Lillihammer in 1994 the Delaware skating Olympians were Karen Courtland and Todd Reynolds.

It has been quite a legacy in exchange for a little ice time.

Howard Sets The Pace

The 1962 Howard High School track team sported only six members but four - Lee Williams, Courtland Camper, Randy Brittingham and Spencer Henry - welded together into the fastest schoolboy 440-yard relay quartet in America that year. Flashing flawless baton passing the foursome won the Championship of America at the Penn Relays track and field carnival, the first conquering Delaware team ever at the meet, begun in 1894. The time for the Howard team was 43.0 seconds, equalling the fifth-fastest winning time at the Relays up to then.

George Johnson had seeded the 1962 team before retiring after 14 years at the helm of Howard track. The Bobcats seldom lost a meet in his tenure and during his last seven years there were seven state championships. Johnson's Howard teams won six events at the Penn Relays, the nation's oldest and largest track and field competition. Johnson, a track star at Howard and Indiana University, started the school's cross country program and won 33 straight inter-school meets. There were state titles from 1956 thorugh 1959. When the state started a Track and Filed Hall of Fame in 1994 Johnson was a charter member.

1970s

In 1971 the Wilmington Country Club hosted the United States Amateur golf championship, the first national tournament staged in Delaware since the 1913 U.S. Women's Amateur. Gary Cowan, a Canadian, holed a memorable eagle 2 from the rough on the 72nd hole to win the championship. Trailing Cowan that day were a number of unknown young amateurs who would go on to greater fame, golfers such as Gil Morgan, Bruce Lietzke, Howard Twitty and four who would one day win a major championship - Bill Rogers, Andy North, Ben Crenshaw and Tom Kite.

The 1970s in Delaware sports were like that. A time to look ahead. Professional baseball in the state was buried deep in the obituary files, minor league football had rasped its last breath and basketball was gasping through one final embarrassing death throe. But there was plenty of sporting potential on display.

The greatest crop of Delaware professional football players - Randy White, Steve Watson, Joe Campbell, Anthony Anderson - were all playing high school football in the Seventies. And it was a good decade for scholastic athletes. Chris Moore of Lake Forest broke the state high school scoring record in basketball and Purnell Ayers of Cape Henlopen eclipsed Moore's mark. Jenni Franks, a Mt. Pleasant junior, broke world swimming records. A college student, Blaise Giroso a Brandywine High graduate, won the first of a record ten Delaware Amateur golf championships in 1979. In Newark the University of Delaware won three Division II national football championships, in the polls in 1971 and 1972 and in the playoffs in 1979.

Another organization looking ahead was the Delaware Special Olympics, the state chapter of international competitions for the mentally handicapped, which began training and competing in 1971. The program would eventually expand to provide tournaments in 13 sports.

By the mid-seventies eleven Delaware high school baseball players had graduated to the minor leagues but none was in the majors. Delaware did, however, sport a professional softball player. Audie Kujala, one of the University of Delaware's all-time athletes who batted .530 in her Blue Hen career, starred in the outfield for the Connecticut Falcons in the short-lived women's professional league. She was the AIAW softball player of the year in 1977.

Horse racing was less popular than it had ever been and there was even talk of bringing jai alai to Wilmington. It was a manifestation of a trend away from spectating and towards participation. State recreation facilities were expanding like never before. Multi-use facilities like the showcase Delcastle Recreation Complex in northern Delaware became magnets for softball players, tennis players, soccer players and volleyball players. More and more, if Delawareans wanted to watch sports they only had to follow their neighbors and friends to the games.

First State Sports Hero of the Decade:
Randy White

The most honored athlete ever to come out of Delaware never made All-State during his high school career. No matter. Such an award would be lost in Randy White's brimming trophy case. By the time White ended his 14-year Dallas Cowboy career in 1989 he had been an All-Pro defensive tackle eight times, a Super Bowl co-MVP and a certain Hall-of-Famer.

Randy White was born in Pittsburgh before his father, a butcher, brought the family to Dunlinden Acres in Delaware. At McKean High School White was a bruising fullback and standout on defense but was unable to lift his team to a winning record. Consequently he was never singled out for anything better than 2nd-team All-State honors, but he was invited to the annual Blue-Gold All-Star game.

Although Delaware All-State voters were singularly unimpressed White stirred the passion of college recruiters. Still, he had pretty well been wrapped up by ace University of Maryland scout Dim Montero since the 10th grade. At College Park White rapidly matured, sculpting 248 pounds onto his 6'4" frame. A fanatic for work - even among those who considered themselves fanatics for work - he improved his bench press to 450 pounds without losing a step from his 4.6 speed in the 40-yard dash. After his junior year in 1973 White was named to the Associated Press All-America first team as a defensive end.

As White's fortunes climbed, so did Maryland's. The Terrapins made their first postseason appearance since 1955 in the Peach Bowl in 1973. The next year it was off to the Liberty Bowl and White won the coveted Outland Trophy, emblematic of the nation's top lineman. He was the second player chosen in the 1975 NFL draft, going to the Dallas Cowboys with a pick obtained from the New York Giants.

At Dallas, White seemed almost too talented for his own good. Where do you play someone that quick, yet that strong; that big, yet that agile? For two seasons White languished as a special teams player and reserve middle linebacker, picking up pass receivers coming out of the backfield. In 1977 Coach Tom Landry switched White to the defensive line and he immediately became one of the NFL's premier defensive performers. He was voted Co-MVP with teammate Harvey Martin in Super Bowl XII following the 1977 season for helping the Cowboys lasso the Denver Broncos 27-10.

The next year White was NFC Defensive Player of the Year after making 123 tackles, 16 of them quarterback sacks. He would be selected to every Pro Bowl from 1977 to 1985. White's legendary intensity earned him the monicker "The Manster," part man, part monster. Landry once remarked, "I don't think I've ever coached a player who brought everything to the field on every play like Randy White."

After 14 years White retired to the farm. Growing up White had never lived on a farm but shortly after visiting teammates' ranches in Texas he purchased a 21-acre spread of his own in the rolling Chester County hills. His record of 1100 tackles and 114 sacks guaranteed his installment as Delaware's first member of the Pro Football Hall of Fame in Canton, Ohio. But still no Delaware All-State football player has been a Hall-of-Famer.

First State of Mascots

Dave Raymond, son of Delaware football coach Tubby Raymond, created sports mascot history as the personality inside the impish Phillie Phanatic for 16 years. But before there was a Phillie Phanatic there was a Lawrence Hunn.

Hunn, from Dover, was a senior at Georgia State College working part-time for the Explorer Scouts in 1966 when the newly imported Atlanta Braves contacted the Scouts looking for someone to do an Indian dance at Braves games. Hunn took the assignment and in the dark ages before political correctness set out to create the most authentic woodland Indian he could.

He dressed in leggings, a beaded apron and vest, black moccasins and feather decorations - all topped by a gaudy horsehair headpiece. In an attempt to appear fearsome, and hide an un-Indian-like mustache, Hunn smeared his face with blue war paint. Chief Noc-A-Homa, as the Braves' mascot came to be affectionately known, perched inside a teepee on a platform beyond the leftfield fence during games, emerging amidst a plume of smoke to greet every Brave home run with a celebratory war dance. For most of the game Hunn, a marketing major, would hide in the teepee reading the *Wall Street Journal*.

Raymond, a kicker for the Delaware Blue Hens, was a student working as a clerk in the Phillies promotion offices when Bill Giles asked if he would climb inside a new costume and appear at Veterans Stadium during Phillies games. The character had no name and the Phillies did no special promotion prior to Raymond's first appearance on April 25, 1978.

Raymond was given no instructions. Phillie experience with mascots heretofore had been limited to those staid patriots Philadelphia Phil and Phyllis. Raymond was paid $25 a game to bound on the field and through the stands and see how fans reacted. He slipped into the 35-pound costume and made the green furry creature with the megaphone mouth and bulging eyes a Philadelphia institution.

Raymond continued in the role of the Phanatic for 16 years before bowing out after the Phillies' National League Championship year of 1993. In that time he missed only eight home games. Away from Veterans Stadium he made more than 250 appearances annually and reaped an income estimated at over $100,000. In his wake Raymond, along with the Chicken, spawned a legion of less-talented imitators in sport's Era of the Mascot. To wit, the Phanatic was voted 'best mascot ever' by *Sports Illustrated for Kids* and *Sports Illustrated*.

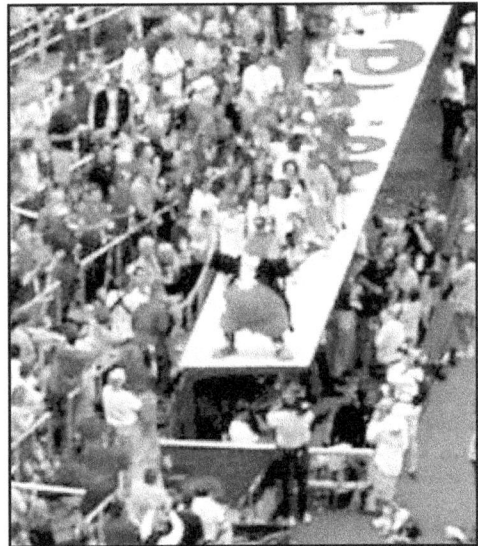

If there was something going on in the stands at Veterans Stadium in the 1970s it was likely the Phillie Phanatic was in the middle of it.

A Swing at Soccer

For anyone who has ever driven around residential Delaware on a summer evening and seen the thousands of kids playing soccer on area fields the state would appear to be a natural for professional soccer. The first to try it were the Delaware Wings in the American Soccer League in 1972.

The Wings were founded with the philosophy of giving Delaware players a chance to play soccer after college and developing local talent. While most teams in the ASL relied on foreign talent the Wings started nine or ten Americans. Playing under this experience handicap the Wings enjoyed a successful 5-4-1 first season and coach Ron Gilbert was named ASL Coach of the Year.

In 1973, now playing in Baynard Stadium, the Wings completed a respectable 5-7-2 season, narrowly missing the playoffs. Attendance averaged between 500 and 700 but after an 0-2 start in 1974 only 160 were on hand for the home opener. The talent discrepancy began to overwhelm the Wings and coach Al Barrish. The Wings finished with the worst record in league history, 1-14-2, and that lonely win was by forfeit. The only bright spot was forward Charlie Ducelli, a second-team All-League forward, who was fourth in the ASL in scoring with 9 goals and 3 assists.

The Wings averaged only 407 fans in 1974 while its big league opponents were drawing ten times that number. The franchise expired in 1975 but a foundation had been laid for big-time soccer in Delaware. When Baynard Stadium was the site for a United States-Mexico Olympic Regional Soccer Elimination later that year a near-capacity 4700 fans packed the stands, even though the United States was already eliminated from the competition. Mexico beat the inexperienced Americans 4-2 in Wilmington, but had to come from behind twice to do so.

The evolution of pro soccer was stalled for almost two decades until the formation of the Delaware Wizards in 1993, playing as one of 43 teams in the more localized U.S. International Soccer League. The Wizards, like the Wings, bore a heavy Delaware flavor. On their opening roster the Wizards had 21 players, more than half of whom played either high school or college soccer in the state.

The Wizards finished 11-8 in the Atlantic Division, making the playoffs in their first year where Delaware lost to Greensboro, the eventual league champion. The Wizards pulled 3000 fans to each game at Glasgow Stadium and the team earned recognition as a model franchise in the USISL.

Rolling Through Obscurity

What is it about ice? Strap on skates with a blade and swirl and swoop with your partner and people line up and television lights blaze. But perform the same routines on wheels and the world will try and stifle a collective yawn. Over the years Delaware roller skaters have built as enviable a record as their ice skating cousins but there have been no parades, no streets renamed and little recognition.

Warren Danner was Delaware roller skating's Ron Ludington. He coached Jane Panky and Richard Horne to the 1972 World Dance Championship. Panky and Horne defected to the ice themselves after 1972 and Danner orchestrated the fortunes of Concord High graduate James Stephens and Jane Perucchio of Cleveland Heights, Ohio. For several months the pair could train only on weekends as the 16 year-old Perucchio commuted from Ohio. But with a summer of regular work the young pair captured the 1973 International Roller Dance title.

The next world champions from Delaware were Anna Marie Danks and Scott Myers who trained at the Christiana Skating Center in the late 1980s. Roller skating is now on the verge of being an Olympic sport. When that happens don't be surprised if Delaware's roller skaters bring the state as much recognition as its ice skaters.

1980s

Andre Agassi, Greg LeMond, Betsy King, Bill Elliott, Patty Sheehan, Brad Gilbert, Donna Adameck, Darrel Waltrip, Michael Chang, Nancy Lopez, Tim Mayotte, Bobby Allison. These were the stars that came to be Delaware sports in the 1980s. For the first time since the coming of professional sports to the state a century earlier there were no play-for-pay team sports to be found in Delaware. No minor league baseball, no football, no basketball. In their place Delawareans discovered individual sports.

The standard bearer for these national events was the bi-annual NASCAR races at Dover Downs. For two weeks each year the capital city is transformed under a sea of trailers and thousands of stock car fans. The NASCAR races grew ever more popular until attendance topped 60,000, doubling the population of the town. Dover was a favorite of fans and drivers alike and many people around America know of Delaware only as the home of Dover Downs.

The next sports beacon flashing from Delaware across the country was the LPGA McDonalds Classic, the richest event on the women's golf tour. The meticulously organized tournament drew daily crowds in excess of 30,000 from its first day at DuPont Country Club and soon its action was picked up on national television. That TV signal from Delaware went around the world when DuPont picked up sponsorship of the Tour de Trump bicycle stage race and made Wilmington its focal point for the East Coast event.

With its reputation for hosting first class big time sporting events professional tennis came to the state in 1987 with the Wilmington Tennis Classic at the Paladin Club. In the 8-man singles draw were Andre Agassi, Brad Gilbert, Tim Mayotte, Emilio Sanchez and Miroslav Mecir, five of the top players in the world. Mayotte upended the top-seeded Mecir in the finals 4-6, 6-2, 6-3. In 1988, the final year of the event, Michael Chang and Andres Chesnokov joined the impressive draw.

In 1989 professional bowling returned to Delaware. The ladies' tour had stopped briefly in New Castle in 1970 but now a more extended stay began with the Columbia 300 Delaware Open at Holiday Lanes in Claymont. The tourney packed bleachers on loan from the University of Delaware as Donna Adameck won the first title in 1989. By 1993 the pro-am portion of the tournament was attracting more than 1300 bowlers - an LPBT record. The event grew into the third richest on the women's tour for the ten years it lasted.

In 1988 Delaware staged its inaugural First State Games. The fruition of eight years of work by founder Erik Conrad, the Games were an Olympic-style sports festival with 15 medal sports and seven demonstration sports. Nearly 1,400 amateur athletes from across Delaware competed in events ranging from judo to fencing to cycling. By 1990 the festival attracted more than 2,200 Delaware athletes but the First State Games never caught the fancy of fans and the sports carnival would not survive into the 1990s.

First State Sports Hero of the Decade:
Frank Masley

In 1976 Masley was a pole vaulter at Christiana High School who had never heard of luge until he saw it on television during the Olympics. Three years later, at the age of 18, Masley was the United States singles champion and in 1980 he was an Olympian in luge doubles with partner Ray Bateman. Masley and Bateman, the national doubles champions, finished 18th in Lake Placid, New York.

At Sarajevo Masley was named captain of the luge team and selected to lead the American team into Olympic Stadium as the carrier of the American flag. The computer draftsman placed 14th in singles and 13th in doubles through snowy and windy conditions.

After the 1984 Olympics and six years as America's top slider Masley's career appeared in decline. The Newark resident won no national championships in either 1985 or 1986, the first time that had happened since his first title in 1979. But in 1987 Masley once again won the national singles championship and was a silver medalist in the World Cup with his fastest time ever. At the Calgary Olympics Masley became Delaware's only three-time Olympian and had his best-ever showing with a 12th place finish, the highest ever for an American in the Olympics. After Calgary, America's "Mr. Luge" retired, a nine-time national sliding champion, six in singles and three in doubles.

After three Olympiads in the 1980s there was no going pro in luge. Even though Frank Masley had helped make luge a permanent part of the American Winter Olympic vocabulary there are still only two full-size luge tracks in the United States, one in Salt Lake City, Utah and the other in Lake Placid where he had traveled back in 1976 and enrolled in a beginner's program. Masley designed a starter luge track at Muskegon, Michigan and continued to support the development of luge when he could.

Masley took his degree in mechanical engineering to W.L. Gore and Associates where he woked as a textile engineer. He eventually developed a military glove that shields against fire and germs while remaining supple enough to be allow soldiers to handle weapons in extreme conditions. He was able to plug his company, Masley Associates, by delighting David Letterman during an appearance of "Audience Show and Tell" on the *Late Show* in 2006.

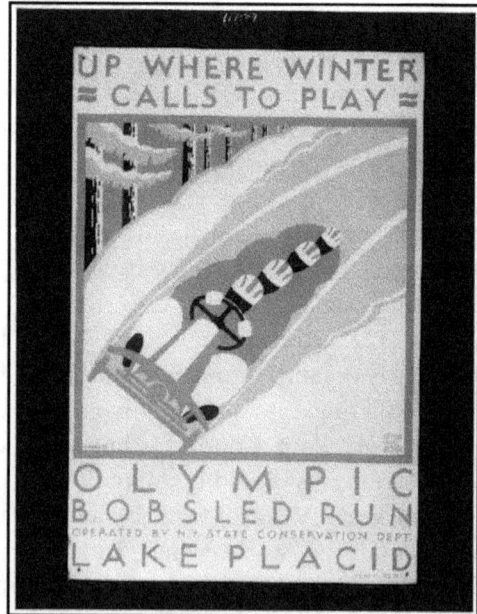

UP WHERE WINTER ≈ CALLS TO PLAY ≈

OLYMPIC BOBSLED RUN
OPERATED BY N.Y. STATE CONSERVATION DEPT.
LAKE PLACID

Delaware State Emerges

There's an old saw about publicity that it doesn't matter whether it's good or bad, just so the name is spelled right. For decades Delaware State College played football like several hundred other small schools - in total anonymity. There were some good years in the under coach Eddie Jackson, the 1934 team went 8-0 and allowed only two points, but few beyond the 200 or so students knew of the Hornets' exploits. And so it went, good or bad, until November 8, 1980.

On that Saturday afternoon Delaware State made all the televised scoreboard shows for the first time. The next morning the name "Delaware State" was plastered in headlines across the country. The Hornets happened to be on the short end of a 105-0 humiliation by Portland State.

An injury-depleted 1-7 team flew across the country to play the powerful Vikings and their NFL-bound quarterback Neil Lomax. The game was over before many fans had settled in their seats. Portland State had four touchdowns less than five minutes into the first quarter. On offense the decimated Hornets fumbled 16 times. As the score mounted even ambulance attendants were jumping around the sidelines cheering for the Vikings to reach 100 points.

The next week Delaware State rebounded to shock Central State 20-14 at Alumni Stadium. But America didn't hear about this victory. The Hornets were buried back in the small type on the sports page.

The Portland State game had long-term ramifications in Dover. It cost coach Charles Henderson his job. Plans for a long-anticipated meeting with the University of Delaware, made viable by a Hornets' trip to the 1977 Orange Blossom Classic, were scuttled. And in a response most controversial, officials at Delaware State brought in Joe Purzycki, the college's first white coach, to resurrect the football program.

Purzycki was an All-American defensive back at the University of Delaware in the late 1960s before beginning his coaching career at Woodbridge High in 1972. He guided the state's third smallest school to its first winning season ever, barely missing the state tournament. In 1975 he moved to Caesar Rodney and won a state championship. Purzycki's college coaching career began with three years under his college mentor, Tubby Raymond. He would then re-tool the Hornets with the potent Winged-T offense imported from Newark. Within three years Purzycki had the moribund Delaware State football team nationally ranked.

More importantly he was bringing talent to Dover that would build a lasting program. He found an ex-Army tank driver playing a touch football game in town and made him a fullback. Gene Lake went on to rush for 1,722 yards in his junior year, the most for any running back in college football in 1984. Purzycki's most important player was never recruited. John Taylor arrived on the Dover campus after a year of baseball at tiny Johnson C. Smith Collge in North Carolina. He had played football as a 130-pound defensive back and when he transferred to Delaware State to be closer to his New Jersey home, Taylor, now 6'1" and 185 pounds, decided to walk on as a non-scholarship wide receiver.

Delaware State didn't feature much of a passing game at the time and the coaching staff was so oblivious to Taylor they called him "Jake" for three weeks. When he caught a game-winning touchdown as a freshman Taylor wasn't even listed on the Hornets' roster. But Taylor's skills forced Purzycki to find a way to get him the ball. He scored 13 touchdowns as a sophomore, two on electrifying punt returns. By graduation Taylor had 100 catches and 42 touchdowns. He was drafted in the 3rd round by the San Francisco 49ers and would become the first player from a Delaware college to make All-Pro.

Purzycki left Delaware State after only four years. He was 15-5-1 in his final two years before moving to James Madison University. Assistant coach Bill Collick took over and the Hornets' ascendancy continued, reaching the 1-AA Top-10 for the first time in 1987. Delaware now boasted two quality college football programs.

The First Family of Delaware Tennis

Of all the sports Delaware has made less national impact in tennis than any other - with one glaring exception, the Vosters family. In 1964 and in 1988 the Vosters were named the United States Tennis Association Family of the Year. The national recognition is bestowed annually to the family that has done the most to promote amateur tennis in the country, especially on a volunteer basis. But the Vosters play a bit too.

Madge "Bunny" Vosters, the matriarch of Delaware's most distinguished tennis clan, began playing with her family as a teenager in the 1930s when she became a nationally ranked junior player in Pennsylvania. At Ursinus College she won two Eastern States Clay Court Singles championships and was an All-American reserve in field hockey. Vosters also played basketball.

In 1942 Vosters, known for "a nearly unretrievable drop shot," reached her highest United States Tennis Association national ranking - No. 9 - at the age of 23. She moved to Delaware in 1952 and the next year she was state champion. Her eldest daughter, Nina, won 16 letters at Friends School and was nationally ranked in Girls 18 singles in 1963. Bunny and Nina won two national mother/daughter titles.

Meanwhile, younger daughter Gretchen was polishing her game. Gretchen Vosters won her first Delaware State Women's Tennis Championship in 1967. Lyndon Johnson was President. She retired, unbeaten in state play, 20 years and five presidents later. In winning 20 consecutive Delaware titles she lost only one set in the finals, in 1972 to Connie Von Housen. In that time she dropped only 54 games in 41 sets of championship play. She dispatched 13 different aspirants to the throne during

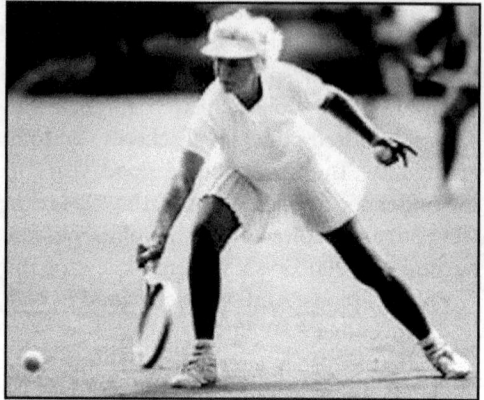

Bunny Vosters won 48 national tennis titles and 12 more on the squash court.

her reign.

Unlike many champions Gretchen Vosters Spruance was hardly obsessed - or impressed - by her accomplishments. She had two children during "The Streak." She virtually stopped playing all competitive singles and often had to be goaded into defending the state title by her husband and mother. Her favorite tennis was with her mother. Bunny and Gretchen won 24 national mother/daughter titles. In the winter months Spruance played squash, well enough to win five national singles and five national doubles championships. Bunny and Nina also won national doubles squash titles.

In 1981 Bunny Vosters won her first national singles crown. Playing on the home turf of Wilmington Country Club the unseeded Vosters defused top-ranked Betty Pratt's drop shot to prevail 6-7, 7-6, 6-4 to capture the USTA Womens 55 and Over Grass Court Championship. There would be more age division titles for Vosters. The Delaware Sports Hall of Fame, for one, couldn't wait for her to retire. They waived the normal five years of retirement rule for qualification and inducted Bunny Vosters in 1980.

A Delaware Sporting Dynasty

Prior to the 1940s if the average Delawarean knew the name "Carpenter" it was in some vague connection to the du Ponts. But in 1943 R.R.M. Carpenter, vice-president of E.I. du Pont de Nemours and Company, rescued the foundering Philadelphia Phillies franchise - a team that had lost 100 games five years in a row - from stewardship by the National League by purchasing the club for $400,000. Carpenter turned the team over to his 28-year old son, Bob Jr., a prominent Wilmington sportsman.

The young Carpenter, a graduate of Tower Hill, spent three years as a reserve end for Duke University before returning to Delaware. He became president of the Wilmington Sportsmen Club and tried his hand at boxing promotion in Wilmington Park. In 1940 he was elected President of the Wilmington Blue Rocks, a team the family had purchased 50% of from Connie Mack. Also in 1940 Carpenter began a lifetime of benefaction to the University of Delaware by helping entice new football coach Bill Murray from North Carolina to Newark.

Out of the office Carpenter was just as active in athletics. He started the Dilwyne Badminton Club at his home and it became one of the focal points for the game in the East. In the Army, as a leftfielder he led his softball team to the championship of Camp Union. Tending to business as the youngest club president in baseball he reversed the Phillies fortunes and was named Executive of the Year in 1949. The next year the Phillies were National League champions for only the second time.

At the end of the 1972 season the 57-year old Carpenter turned the Phillies over to his son, R.R.M. Carpenter III, familiarly known as Ruly, then 33. Ruly Carpenter had naturally grown up wanting a baseball career - but on the field, not in the executive suite. He threw three no-hitters for Tower Hill in 1958, captained the baseball team at Yale and starred in the Delaware Semi-Pro League before settling into his Phillies career in 1965.

Although the Phillies had once again slipped to the bottom of the National League following an infamous 1964 collapse his father hardly left a barren line-up. Larry Bowa, Greg Luzinski, Bob Boone and Mike Schmidt had all recently graduated from the farm system and Steve Carlton just arrived in trade.

Ruly Carpenter knew what he wanted to do with the flagging franchise. He replaced three-quarters of the scouting staff although most baseball decisions were left to Dallas Green, recently installed in charge of the farm system, and Paul Owens, the new general manager. The Phillies were off on their most successful decade in their history, culminating with the team's first World Championship in 1980.

The world championship was the highlight of the Carpenters' ownership of the Phillies. Within a year the Carpenter family had sold the team, reportedly from Ruly's frustration with fellow owners paying outrageous salaries for average players in the free agency era. "I'm going to write a book one day," Carpenter once cracked. "It's going to be called *How To Make A Small Fortune in Baseball - Start With A Big Fortune.*"

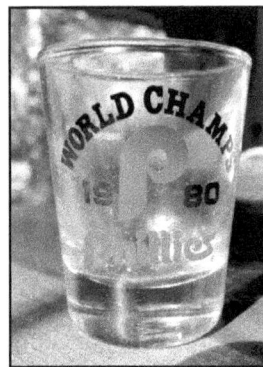

Carpenter family ownership of the Philadelphia Phillies culminated in a World Championship in 1980.

Delware's Own World Series Champions

Little League baseball came to Delaware in 1951. Over the years several state teams advanced to various youth baseball World Series - Stahl Post played in several American Legion World Series and a Delaware all-star team made the 14-15 Babe Ruth World Series in 1975. In 1976 three Delaware teams reached the World Series: Newark in the 13-15 Babe Ruth World Series, Suburban-New Castle in the 13-15 Little League World Series and Delaware in the 16-18 Babe Ruth World Series. But all these teams fell short of the grand prize.

In 1981 a 13-15 year-old Senior Little League All-Star team from Georgetown snuck out of the Delaware tournament with a comeback win against Suburban Little League and then caught fire. In the double-elimination format Georgetown lost only once in the Mid-Atlantic Division and were unbeaten in the regionals to advance to the 1981 Senior League World Series in Gary, Indiana.

Georgetown bludgeoned its first two opponents in Gary, crushing Belgium 15-1 and Taylor, Michigan 12-2. Pitching ace Guy Wilkins shut down Danville, California in the third game 2-1 before Georgetown lost its first World Series game, 7-4, forcing a deciding final game. With Wilkins back on the mound hard-hitting Georgetown crushed San Ramon Valley, California 15-4 to capture the Senior Little League championship.

The world championship was the first ever for a Delaware youth baseball team. The Georgetown all-stars, culled from a tiny community of 2000, were the first to unseat the powerful Taiwanese in the World Series in nine years. Georgetown finished tournament play with 18 wins and only three losses. Wilkins won ten of those game and shortstop Bill Savage slugged 14 home runs and hit .446 during Georgetown's championship run.

Delaware was a force in youth baseball throughout the Eighties. Two years later the Delaware 16-18 Babe Ruth League all-star team went on to win the Babe Ruth World Series in Newark, Ohio. Five players of the 1983 champions would eventually be drafted by major league baseball: Mark Brockell, Scott Mackie, Bobby Britt, Jeff Vickers, and Bill Dorsey. And Seaford, riding the arm of future National League star Delino DeShields, became a regular visitor to national tournaments.

An Executive Battery

When Ruly Carpenter was an All-State end at Tower Hill it was Pat Williams tossing him passes. And when Carpenter was baffling opposing hitters on the mound for the Hillers, Williams was his catcher. After Tower Hill Williams and Carpenter parted ways, Williams going to Wake Forest and Carpenter to Yale.

After Wake Forest Williams had a brief minor league baseball career. An injury ended his playing days in Miami in 1963 and he was offered a front office job. He showed an immediate flair for the work. As general manager for Spartanburg he pioneered usherettes in the box seats and handicapped entrances. In 1967 Williams, 26, won the Larry McPhail Promotion Trophy as the minor league's top executive.

After four years at Spartanburg, he switched sports and became business manager of the Philadelphia 76ers. The Chicago Bulls made Williams a general manager and after turning around a moribund franchise he came back to the 76ers in the same capacity. Under Williams - and Julius Erving - the Sixers became one of the NBA's showcase franchises. The best days of the Phillies and Sixers were guided by the old Tower Hill battery.

America's Greatest Multi-Stage Bike Race

World class bicycle racing had been dormant in Delaware for a century when Wilmington became involved in America's premier bicycle stage race, the Tour de Trump in 1989. In 1991 E.I. du Pont de Nemours and Company took over sponsorship of the newly named Tour DuPont. The 11-day race that meandered down the East Coast now started in Wilmington and included a lengthy race to Dover. That year the final stage was a time trial through Winterthur and Hagley Museum. Opinion among the riders was nearly unanimous - it was the most beautiful course they'd ever raced across. Organizers of the race estimated that 200 million people in 100 countries watch the Tour DuPont each year.

The highlight of the Tour for Delawareans was the Prologue, a three-mile-plus time trial on the eve of the race proper. More than 20,000 people would gather along the race route through Wilmington with most eyes - and television cameras - riveted on Monkey Hill to see the world's best cyclists hurl down treacherous cobblestones at over 30 mph. Over the years such international stars as Emil Breukink of the Netherlands, Raul Alcala of Mexico and United States superstar Greg LeMond all won the Prologue. Racing for French team Z, the Minnesoate-bred LeMond became the first American winner of the Tour DuPont in 1992.

In 1993 an unheralded 21-year old Texas rider named Lance Armstrong finished a strong second. He repeated the feat the next year and then won the race in both 1995 and 1996, competing for the Motorola team. That year Armstrong was diagnosed with life-threatening metastatic testicular cancer. He would come back and win the Tour de France seven consecutive times beginning in 1999. Back in the States, meanwhile, DuPont dropped its sponsorship of the race after the 1996 Tour. It would not stage a comeback.

Greg LeMond battled the cobblestones of Monkey Hill and cold, stiff winds to take the Prologue of the 1992 Tour DuPont. He also won the 11-day race that year.

When There Was No Semi About It

Pro baseball is not what it used to be. Once the undisputed "national pastime" the sport has been steamrolled by football in popularity. So imagine how vital "semi-pro" baseball must be. Games for the eight teams in the Delaware Semi-Pro Baseball League attract about as many spectators as a Sunday afternoon softball kegger.

But such was not always the case. The league formed in 1941 and developed teams and legends every bit as colorful as those toiling in the bigs. Any recounting of the Delaware Semi-Pro league must begin with John Hickman, whose Parkway team made the playoffs for 38 consecutive years. His lowest finish during that time was 4th place, of 11 teams, in 1956.

Under Hickman Parkway won 16 league pennants and 13 playoff titles. There were eight straight pennants from 1965-1972. The heyday of Parkway was the heyday of the semi-pro baseball in Delaware as other teams chased Hickman's champions. In the 1960s playoff games at Rockford Park, Canby Park and especially 18th & Van Buren Streets would routinely attract crowds over 2000 (there were many seasons in the 1960s when the Phillies would not draw 10,000 fans a game to Connie Mack Stadium).

Teams featured many of the top college players from around the East. Many semi-pro players were on either side of major league careers: Chris Short, Jack Crimian, John Wockenfuss, Dave May. Parkway's greatest player was Bob Immediato, who played into his 50s. The 6'2", 190-pound first baseman joined Hickman in 1962, after three years in the Cleveland Indian farm system. With Parkway he established career league marks in hits and RBI.

But despite Parkway's success many longtime league observers consier the team assembled by Brooks Armored Car, Parkway's great rival, in 1963 to be the finest semi-pro team to ever take a Delaware diamond.

That year Brooks' third baseman-manager Lou Romanoli mounted his greatest challenge to Parkway's dominance. He rounded up three former major league pitchers for his rotation - Crimian, Bob Davis and Ray Narleski, who at 34 years of age was only five years removed from winning 13 games with the Cleveland Indians.

To bolster his line-up Romanoli recruited Ruly Carpenter, the Yalie future Phillies owner who had led the Ivy League in batting, and ex-big leaguer Harry "The Horse" Anderson. Anderson was only 32 years old and had finished 18th in MVP voting in 1958 when he belted 23 home runs to abet a .301 batting average.

The two nines clashed in the championship finals and with fans overflowing the bleachers and hanging from tree branches Brooks swept Parkway four games to none.

By 1988 Parkway was suddenly not only out of the playoffs entirely but struggling to win a game - and field a team. The misfortunes piled up, growing so bad that Hickman, then in his seventies, played right field in one game to prevent a forfeit. Six games into the 1990 season the franchise disbanded.

It was only a precursor to the fate of the league as a whole. By the 1980s major league games were on television every night and fresh air and good semi-pro baseball on Wilmington fields was no longer the attraction it once was. And shortly there would be other professional baseball in town as well.

Hiding Out In Delaware

Until the 21st century there was no more public persona in sports than the heavyweight champion of the world. Bigger than life figures to hold the title stretch back through Muhammad Ali past Joe Louis all the way to John L. Sullivan. Where can a champ go to avoid the constant glare of the media spotlight? For one unassuming champion that place was Delaware.

In 1985 light-heavyweight champion Michael Spinks moved to Greenville, Delaware, following the earlier path blazed by his manager/ promoter Butch Lewis. Shortly after arriving in Delaware Spinks became the first light-heavyweight champion to take the belt from a heavyweight champion when he stopped undefeated Larry Holmes.

But unlike Holmes, who constantly plugged his hometown of Easton, Pennsylvania, Spinks' new adopted residence wasn't even listed in his fight programs. The champ came to northern Delaware to disappear in the wooded hills and conducted his boxing life elsewhere. Philadelphia was for workouts, New York for business meetings and television interviews, glitzy resorts for training. Delaware? It was for privacy.

Another champion joined Spinks in secluded Greenville several years later. Golfer Laurie Merten was not in danger of being mobbed by adoring fans when she moved to Delaware. Early promise on the LPGA tour had been washed away by eight winless years when the popular Greenville resident emerged to win the 1993 U.S. Women's Open. Her golf had been so spotty she had not even bothered to enter the tournament from 1987 to 1991. Merten went on to finish the 1993 LPGA season as the sixth leading money winner on tour with $394,744.

1990s

In the first decade of the 20th century the three big sports in Delaware were baseball, trapshooting and horse racing. At the start of the last decade of the 20th century there was no professional baseball in the state, no trapshooting and horse racing was rapidly disappearing. That was soon to change. With a bang.

On April 9, 1990 the best everyday player Delaware had produced since Judy Johnson - Delino DeShields - made his major league debut by banging out three singles and a double against the St. Louis Cardinals. At that time only ten players had collected four hits in their first game, one being Delawarean Spook Jacobs. DeShields would go on to finish second in Rookie of Year balloting to David Justice.

On April 16, 1993 minor league baseball came back to Delaware after its longest absence since the game was introduced to the state some 110 years earlier. More than forty years had buried past failures and disappointments before new optimistic owners. The Blue Rocks were back on the field. The new Wilmington nine played to near-capacity crowds in its inaugural season and won five division and four league titles before the decade was out.

Horse racing came back in the First State as well, but not on its own. It was called in Legislative Hall the Horseracing Redevelopment Act but the people of Delaware knew it as legalized gambling. The state's three remaining horse racing tracks - Delaware Park, Dover Downs and Harrington Raceway - were permitted to install video lottery slot machines and the profits would be sliced up among

the casino, the state, the vendors and horsemen. The one-armed bandits made their debut on December 29, 1995. More prize money and better horses materialized as promised. Crowds as big as decades before? Not so much.

Professional soccer was also reintroduced with the formation of the Delaware Wizards in 1993, playing as one of 43 teams in the more localized U.S. International Soccer League. The Wizards, like the Wings of the 1970s, bore a heavy Delaware flavor. On their opening roster the Wizards had 21 players, more than half of whom played either high school or college soccer in the state.

The Wizards finished 11-8 in the Atlantic Division, making the playoffs in their first year where Delaware lost to Greensboro, the eventual league champion. The Wizards pulled 3000 fans to each game at Glasgow Stadium and the team earned recognition as a model franchise in the USISL in the first two years as a farm team for the New York/New Jersey MetroStars. By 1997, however, attendance was diminishing and the franchise slipped across the border into southern Chester County. The Wizards would not see the new century.

There was also news in the 1990s from another keystone Delaware sport that had not been in the headlines for many a year: bowling. James "JJ" Johnson had been drawing kegeling notoriety at Bowlerama and Holiday Lanes and First State Lanes and Blue Hen Lanes since his junior bowling days, accumulating a record 67 perfect games certified by the United

States Bowling Congress.

Johnson was the finest bowling talent Delaware had seen since commercial artist and semi-pro baseball player Robbie Robinson busted his knee in a play at the plate and took up the sport in the 1960s. Robinson rolled on the PBA Tour and won the prestigious Hoinke Singles Amateur Tournament in Cincinnati, Ohio.

In 1988 Johnson joined the Professional Bowling Association and in Portland at the Hollywood Bowl in 1997 he became the first Delaware-born PBA winner when he downed Hall-of-Famer Pete Webber 232-197. Before leaving the tour in 2001, Johnson earned over $176,000 in 142 tour events.

But alas, there was still no world-class trapshooting competition in Delaware.

The Wizards brought professional soccer back to Delaware after a two-decade absence in the 1990s - but only for the 1990s.

Delaware Special Olympics

The first International Special Olympics Summer Games were held in Chicago in 1968 with swimming and track and field events. The Delaware Special Olympics organized its first track & field competition in June 1971 with 100 athletes gathered at Wilmington High School. In its early years the chapter grew to include basketball and bowling and soccer and participation ballooned to over 400 athletes.

In 1989 the Delaware Summer Games found a new permanent home at the University of Delaware. There would eventually be some 4,000 athletes competing in 20 sports and training in Special Olympics programs statewide. At competition time more than 3000 volunteers assisted in the seasonal sports festivals with winners advancing to national and international meets.

In 1997 Renee Baldwin Kalokitus became the first Special Olympics athlete to be inducted into the Delaware Sports Hall of Fame. In 15 years of competition Renee had participated in swimming, long-distance running, softball, cross-country skiing, basketball, volleyball, track and sailing. She competed in two World Games in the 1990s and excelled at aquatics. Her performances in the 100-metre individual medley and 200-metre freestyle earned her recognition as the United States Olympic Committee's 1991 Outstanding Female Athlete of the Year and the National Swim Coaches Association Female Aquatics Athlete of the Year -- both firsts for a Special Olympics athlete from any state.

First State Sports Hero of the Decade:
Delino DeShields

When Montreal Expos general manager Murray Cook announced the selection of Seaford's Delino DeShields as the 12th overall pick in the 1987 Major League Baseball draft he called the second baseman "the best athlete in the country." He certainly had the resume, beginning with two state championships with the Nanticoke Little League in 1981 and 1982. At Seaford High School he was an All-State defensive back as the Blue Jays won a Division II state championship. He was an All-State infielder and won a state championship in baseball in 1986. And basketball was DeShields' best sport and he set a school record with 1,751 points.

DeShields was such a dynamic basketball player that Rollie Massamino, still basking in his 1985 NCAA championship, offered the Seaford star his one available scholarship to play for Villanova University. DeShields committed to the Wildcats and planned to pursue both sports but after a first taste of minor league baseball he concluded that there absolutely was a future in the major leagues. He rescinded the basketball scholarship to concentrate on groundballs and curveballs.

DeShields, known as "Bop," was in the Expos starting line-up in 1990 at the age of 21. He was part of one the finest core of rookies ever assembled, along with Marquis Grissom and Larry Walker. DeShields batted .289 and finished second in the Rookie of the Year race. Two years later he was 16th in MVP voting. The young Expo core would produce 94 wins in 1993 and a baseball-best 74-40 in 1994 before the season was cancelled. For good or ill, Deshields was not in Montreal for that disappointment.

After the 1993 season DeShields was dealt to Los Angeles for a rookie pitcher named Pedro Martinez. The move would work out poorly for the Delaware star on both ends. While he struggled through the three worst years of his career with the Dodgers Martinez became of the all-time great pitchers. Once out of Los Angeles, DeShields finished out the decade batting .295, .290, .264 and .296. Always possessing a good eye at the plate he was among the league leaders in on-base percentage among middle infielders.

Delino DeShields wrapped up his playing career in 2002. He had come to the plate in a major league game 6,652 times - far more than any Delawarean. He was ranked in the top 50 of all-time for career steals with 463. Fewer than 50 players ever played more major league games at second base.

In retirement DeShields started the Urban Baseball League which barnstormed with ex-big leaguers in urban communities to promote the game and in 2009 he got back into the professional game as a batting instructor for the Billings Mustangs in the Pioneer League. He became a manager for the Dayton Dragons in the Cincinnati Reds organization in 2011 and has worked his way up to be manager of the Triple A Louisville Bats. He also coached his son Delino DeShields Jr. who broke into the majors as an outfielder with the Texas Rangers in 2015. And also his daughter Diamond who was a two-time Miss Georgia Basketball in 2011 and 2013 and stars in the University of Tennessee backcourt.

Delaware Sports Words

When *Al Cartwright*, then 29 years old, walked into the newsroom of the *Journal Every Evening* in 1947 to take over the job as sports editor he looked around and saw only one other full-time member of the sports department. Cartwright was born and raised in Reading, Pennsylvania, a sports town much like Wilmington that harbored major league ambitions while orbiting in the sphere of Philadelphia, and he knew how important first-rate reporting was to readers. Cartwright himself was most recently of the *Philadelphia Record* and his immediate goal for Wilmington was to provide professional coverage of local sports.

To create a big league sports page required talent and Al Cartwright had that in spades. His sports column was called "A La Carte" and he wrote about anything and everything, usually flecked with equal parts insight and humor. He injected his columns with fictional characters such as "Blewynn Gold," a purported University of Delaware graduate Class of 1890, who "had seen them all" and "Kenton Sussex" who picked horses. In 1950 the National Headliners Club recognized Cartwright as America's "Most Consistently Outstanding" sports columnist.

With Cartwright, small-town Wilmington had a reserved seat at the nation's top sporting events. He would cover World Series games and attended the Olympics in Tokyo in 1964 and Mexico City in 1968. But his greatest impact on Delaware sports came at home. Many of the state sporting institutions that are taken for granted came about because Cartwright championed them in the newspaper: high school athletic conferences, Little League sports, the Delaware State Golf Association and organized swimming leagues among the suburban pools that sprang up in the 1950s.

All-state teams? Cartwright's idea. The Delaware Sports Hall of Fame? Cartwright

again. He started the Wilmington Sportswriters and Broadcasters Association and in 1950 the organization began giving out its coveted award to the outstanding sports performer of the previous year. The award was named for *John J. Brady*, who had segued from a semi-professional football and baseball manager into the sports editor's chair at the *Morning News* in 1924 and was the print voice of Delaware sports for over twenty years.

Cartwright set about giving Wilmington a sports department the envy of cities many times the size of Wilmington. In 1950 he recruited *Izzy Katzman* from the *Harrisburg Patriot*. Katzman was nimble enough to write on any sport but he found his sweet spot when the Brandywine Raceway opened on Naamans Road in 1953. When the United States Harness Writers Association began giving out its John Hervey Awards for excellence in standardbred jornalism in 1962 Katzman picked up one of those. In 1994 he was inducted into the Harness Racing Hall of Fame, in the "Writers Corner." Katzman stayed at the *News-Journal* for 36 years.

When Cartwright brought *Matt Zabitka* down from Delaware County in 1962 his mandate was "to increase local coverage and maintain rapport with news sources." Zabitka was a Chester, Pennsylvania native who had already done enough work as a sports talker on WDRF and a writer with the *Delaware County Daily Times* to earn him enshrinement in the Delaware County Sports Hall of Fame in 1978. His ubiquitous coverage of local sports for 40 years would land Zabitka in the Delaware Sports Hall of Fame as well.

Since Cartwright created the modern sports section in Delaware papers such devotion to the state athletic scene is not uncommon. *Chuck Durante*, who started writing about Delaware sports as a stringer for the *Philadelphia Inquirer* while at Villanova Law School in the 1970s, has covered First State athletes for over four decades. He served as president of the Delaware Sportswriters and Broadcasters Association for 15 years. Since leaving the University of Delaware in 1980, *Kevin Tresolini's* byline has appeared in the *News Journal's* sports section for over 35 years.

But the Al Cartwright sportswriting tree branches far beyond Delaware borders. The writing talent he brought to Delaware took root in markets across the country and quite a few of those who read him took up writing because of his columns. *Gary Smith* was born in Lewes in 1953, one of nine children in residence in a rambling five-bedroom house. At the age of 16 he was working as a clerk at the *News-Journal* and the paper was a launching pad that landed Smith at *Sports Illustrated* in 1982. His stories were included in the *Best American Sportswriting* anthologies, more than any other scribe, and he won four National Magazine Awards. Before retiring in 2015 Smith was hailed as America's finest magazine writer, who just happened to be working in sports.

Harley Ryan Bodley, a native of Smyrna, took his fresh University of Delaware sheepskin to the *Delaware State News* in 1958 to cover baseball. He came to the *News-Journal* in 1960 and worked his way through the sports department to become sports editor in 1969 when Cartwright took a sabbatical to work for his beloved Philadelphia Phillies who were making a transition from Connie Mack Stadium to Veterans Stadium. Hal Bodley would remain as sports editor until 1982 when he assumed the position of baseball editor for *USA Today*. Including his 22 years at the *News-Journal*, Bodley would cover 43 World Series and 41 All-Star Games and watch an estimated 36,000 innings of major league baseball in the guise of a reporter. Bodley won 30 regional and national writing awards, including a dozen times named "Delaware Sportswriter of the Year," as the most honored sportswriter in Delaware history.

Delaware Sports Voices

The first radio programs in Delaware crackled across the airwaves on July 22, 1922 from the WDEL studios. That year listeners could tune in a nightly sports show presented by *Herman "Hoim" Reitzes*, who was working his way through the University of Delaware. In the coming decades Reitzes would provide listeners their first coverage of live Delaware sports with play-by-play of University of Delaware football and the Wilmington Clippers. In the 1940s Reitzes would travel down to Rock Hill, South Carolina and file reports from the Blue Rocks' spring training camp.

In March of 1949 a sister outlet of WDEL went on the air - WDEL-TV, Channel 7. The low-power transmission from the broadcast center on Shipley Road in northern Delaware was so weak it caused no interference with Philadelphia stations only 30 miles away. Even so, Delaware's first television channel would be shuffled off to Channel 12 by 1951. The station's first sports director, signing on after stints with the United States Navy and Temple University, was *George Frick*. In 1951 he launched a nightly 15-minute sports show called "The Sporting Scene" that featured interviews and footage from local sports statewide. The *TV Guide* named it the "Best New TV Sports Show in the Delaware Valley."

After Channel 12 ceased commercial operations Frick continued to be active in Delaware sports, including a three-day-a-week column for the *Delaware State News* - "Frick's Picks." But he was not finished with silver-tongued oratory. There were live broadcasts from the Brandywine Raceway, Dover sports coverage for WDOV, and eleven years as the starter and announcer for the McDonalds LPGA golf tournament. In 2005 when Wesley College refurbished the press box at Scott D. Miller Stadium it was dedicated to George L. Frick.

In Newark, the pressbox of Tubby Raymond Field at Delaware Stadium is a memorial to **Bob Kelley**, the "Voice of University of Delaware Football." Kelley was behind the microphone for 378 consecutive Blue Hen football games from 1950 until his death from leukemia at the age of 64 in 1988. Kelley was also the radio broadcaster for Blue Hen basketball from 1962 until 1979. Kelley had migrated to Delaware in 1950 as a sportswriter when his New York City newspaper, *The Sun*, shuttered after 117 years of operation. Kelley wrote for the *Wilmington Morning News* and handled publicity for Delaware Park for almost two decades. Nineteen times Bob Kelley was honored as Delaware's "Sportscaster of the Year."

During the 1960s and 1980s Kelley teamed with **Bill Pheiffer** who got started in radio and television in 1949. As sports director for WDEL for over 30 years Pheiffer was a familiar voice on Wilmington Blue Bombers basketball, Salesianum football and Big 5 basketball games from the Palestra in Philadelphia. Pheiffer called horse races at Brandywine, Delaware Park and Fair Hill. He also manned the sports editor desk at *Delaware Today* magazine. He once estimated that he had broadcast more than 1000 professional, collegiate and high school games at over 200 venues in 32 states. After retiring from WDEL in 1989 Pheiffer continued working Blue Hen football and basketball until 1999.

For a spell in the 1970s, Bob Kelley's partner in the booth was *Tom Mees*, a Springfield, Pennsylvania native who got his start doing football play-by-play on the the University of Delaware student-run station. After graduating in 1972, he became sports director at WILM for six years, joining Kelley for football and basketball broadcasts. In 1979 Mees broke nationally as one of the original sports anchors at ESPN, where he worked until drowning in a swimming pool accident in 1996.

Few voices are more familiar in Delaware than *Marv Bachrad's*. Bachrad was already in the Communicators' Corner of the Harness Racing Hall of Fame before he went to work with Dover Downs in 1997. Bachrad graduated from Norristown High School in Pennsylvania in 1953 and began working at local radio stations, including a two-year hitch running an Armed Forces radio station. As a local television reporter in Philadelphia he was a fixture on 76ers and Big Five games. Bachrad was a charter member of the United States Harness Writer's Association 1n 1963 and took over public relations duty at Garden State Park in New Jersey in 1975 and pioneered the use of the fax machine for disseminating race results. Bachrad took over the same duties at Brandywine Raceway in 1979 until the track's closing in 1989 before taking his Hall of Fame credentials to Dover.

The Bob Kelley Pressbox at the University of Delaware.

2000s

On every front the new century brought with it a dimming of spectator sports in Delaware. The Internet had arrived in full force and it became awfully hard to sit through three whole hours of live game action. In 2001 Dover Downs increased its grandstand capacity to 135,000 - capable of seating one in every six Delawareans. By the end of the decade track officials were scaling back to 95,000. Even the gold standard of Delaware sport fandom, Blue Hen football, was suffering. Attendance at Delaware Stadium declined every year from 2005 until 2015 with no end to the trend in sight. Students were hardly showing up on Saturdays at all and it was a popular meme that when they did they never lifted their heads from a smartphone. But season ticket sales to the faithful were down from a high of 11,000 to scarcely 6,000.

There was less to watch as well. The McDonalds LPGA Championship pulled out of Delaware in 2004 and left the state without women's professional golf for the first time since 1987, hoping to raise more money for charity (it didn't happen and McDonalds withdrew its sponsorship in 2009). The Delaware Smash also departed after a 13 years of World Team Tennis play in 2009. The Smash won the championship in 2003 by thumping the New York Buzz 24-12 for coach Brad Dancer behind fan favorites Paul Goldstein, Samantha Reeves and Liezel Huber. Goldstein and Reeves were voted Male and Female Most Valuable Players that year as the Smash rolled to a 13-1 record and won their only title.

The face of Delaware sports was changing as well. Since the 1984 Olympics six of Delaware's eight Olympians were women. The best basketball player was a woman, Elena Delle Donne, who became a national figure in the WNBA without abandoning her Delaware roots. The best tennis player was a woman, Madison Brengle who won over a million dollars on the professional tour. Delaware State boasted a nationally ranked bowling team - the women. In 2009 the Hornets made it to NCAA kegeling Final Four before bowing out to eventual champion Nebraska 4-2 in the national semi-finals. Along the way the women unfurled nine consecutive strikes for a school record in the Baker scoring format where each team member rolls two frames.

There were highlights for the Delaware men as well. In 2001 Tubby Raymond won his 300th football game as the Blue Hens ground out a win at home against Richmond, 10-6. Only 11 other college football coaches at any level reached that milestone. After 36 years Raymond stepped down and was replaced by K.C. Keeler, a one-time Blue Hen linebacker, who leaned heavily on transfers from bigger schools to build his program. His bait was that by coming to Delaware those players could take the field immediately rather than sitting out one year. The strategy worked. In only his second year in 2003 Keeler won the university's sixth national title by whitewashing Colgate University 40-0 in the playoff finals. Only four players on the 61-man roster hailed from the First State.

One team where every member was a Delawarean was the Naamans Little League All-Stars who became the first Delaware team to play in the Little League World Series in 2002. The Brandywine Hundred youngsters bowed out in pool play. They would be followed to Williamsport by Newark National in blank who suffered the same fate. A few levels higher up, Bob Hannah stopped coaching at the University of Delaware after 35 seasons in 2000. His teams had won 1,053 games, almost 70%, and he had mentored 23 All-Americans and 32 major league draft picks.

What Is It about the Number 96?

For many years the holder of the Delaware all-time major league home run crown was cut and dried. Dave May, born and raised in New Castle County, thumped 96 round-trippers in his career. But since the left-handed slugger left the game in 1978 things have not been so simple.

Enter Robert Randall Bush, born in Dover in 1958. But he was soon in Florida where he became an all-state outfielder for Carol City High in suburban Miami. After patrolling the outfield for the University of New Orleans Privateers Bush was a second round selection of the Minnesota Twins in the 1979 draft. He played an impressive 12 years with the Twins, got into World Series in 1987 and 1991 and once tied an American League record with seven consecutive pinch hits. Bush retired with a career .251 batting average and - 96 home runs.

Then came John Steven Mabry, born in Wilmington in 1970. But Mabry played his high school ball down the Delmarva Peninsula at Bohemia Manor in Chesapeake City. College was at West Chester University for three years before the St. Louis Cardinals came calling with the sixth pick in the 1991 draft. Mabry also enjoyed a long major league career but it was no Randy Bush ride - he played for eight teams in 14 years after finishing 4th in Rookie of the Year voting in 1995. Mabry retired with a career .263 batting average - and 96 home runs.

So who is the real Delaware all-time home run king? Mabry had topped out at 96 home runs in fewer at bats (3409) than Bush (3481) and May (3670). But wait. Before parsing through all kinds of statistics Paul Goldschmidt, born in Wilmington and raised in Texas, belted his 97th home run for the Arizona Diamondbacks in 2015. An unheralded eight round draft pick who has twice finished runner-up in the National League MVP voting, Goldschmidt had 116 career homers through his age 28 season.

So the player born in Delaware with the most career major league home runs is Paul Goldschmidt. Dave May hit the most major league home runs by a Delaware high school graduate. Does that clear anything up?

First State Sports Hero of the Decade: Elena Delle Donne

Elena Delle Donne first came to national attention for her proficiency at the most mundane of basketball tasks - shooting free throws. While at Ursuline Academy in 2005-2006 she set the girls' national high school record for consecutive free throws made with 80. By the time she the wrapped up her secondary school career with her third straight state championship the nation was also aware what Delaware hoops fans already knew - the 6'5" Delle Donne could play basketball when all the players on the court were moving as well.

Delle Donne was the 2008 Naismith High School Player of the Year and the top-rated recruit in America and she chose the top-rated basketball program at the University of Connecticut. She made headlines again when she left Storrs after only two days of summer practice to come back to Delaware to be closer to her family, particularly her older sister Lizzie who was born deaf and blind with cerebral palsy. The Huskies were able to trundle on without their prized recruit. Geno Auriemma's bunch won their first game of that 2008-2009 season and the next 89 after that to establish a collegiate record for consecutive wins. There were three consecutive national championships as well.

For her part, Delle Donne gave up basketball completely. Burned out and tired of the attention, she attempted a normal college experience by enrolling at the University of Delaware and walking on to the women's volleyball team. She played middle hitter on a 19-15 squad that made the NCAA tournament. But you can't keep Secretariat in the barn forever. She came back to basketball as a red-shirt freshman and pumped in 26.7 points per game to finish third in the nation in scoring. She struggled through a sophomore season while battling the effects of Lyme disease but came back for her junior year to be the nation's top score with 28.1 points per game. She shot .520 from the floor and pulled down over ten rebounds per game. After the season Delle Donne got her first taste of nternational ball by helping the Americans to a gold medal in the World University Games in Shenzhen, China with averages of 15.7 points and 14 rebounds per game.

In her senior year Delle Donne repeated as a United States Basketball Writers Association first team All-American and as an Academic All-American. She led the Blue Hens to a 27-3 regular season record and an unprecedented #6 seed in the Women's Division I Basketball Tournament. Delaware made the Sweet Sixteen with an opening round win over West Virginia and a 78-69 dispatching of #3 seed North Carolina. Both games were played in the Bob Carpenter Center on the Newark campus as the NCAA made the site selection decision a year earlier when Delle Donne announced she would not leave school early for the professional ranks of the WNBA.

The Blue Hens' 2013 championship run ended the next week in Trenton's Sun National Bank Arena when Delaware was dumped by #2 seeded Kentucky, 69-62. Delle Donne finished with 33 points, including 13 in a row to keep Delaware within striking distance in the first half. She finished her career as the fifth all-time leading scorer in NCAA history with 3,039 points and could easily have been the all-time top score had she not missed 22 games during her four years in college.

The Chicago Sky selected Elena Della Donne with the second pick in the 2013 WNBA Draft. She capped off a memorable rookie campaign by leading the Sky to a winning record for the first time in its eight-year existence and Chicago's first-ever playoff appearance. In an eerie mirror of her collegiate career, Delle Donne was slowed by Lyme disease symptoms in her second season and Chicago once again slipped to a losing record. But the Sky qualified for the playoffs and Delle Donne returned to help Chicago reach the WNBA Finals where they lost three games to none to the Phoenix Mercury. Like in college, a healthy Delle Donne led the league in scoring in her third season with 23.4 points per game and was third in rebounding. When the media sat down to cast votes for league MVP, Delle Donne received 38 first place votes out of 39 ballots cast.

Elena Delle Donne had reached the pinnacle of her sport. But what about those free throws that had brought her so much fame in her early school years? Yes, she could still shoot those. In her first 77 games in the WNBA she went to the line 477 times and converted 448 for a career average of 93.9%. Long-time Phoenix Sun guard Steve Nash holds the all-time career free-throw percentage in that other professional basketball league - a measly 90.43%.

Pete Oakley Did What?

"Biggest upset in the history of the British Senior Open." "Unknown wins Senior British." "Little-known pro provides big-time shock." Those were the headlines on the sports pages in July of 2004.

Florida-born Pete Oakley had accomplished quite a bit in his golfing years in the Mid-Atlantic region. Six Delaware Open titles between 1980 and 2000. A four-time Player of the Year for the Philadelphia Section of the PGA. A couple of Philadelphia Open championships. But his fame did not push much beyond Delaware Valley golf circles.

Oakley had considered trying the PGA Tour in his early twenties but realized quickly he was good, but not PGA Tour good. He attempted to qualify for the Senior Tour after he turned 50 years old. He tried four times and missed four times. He won the PGA Senior Club Professional Championship for club pros that year but otherwise directed most of his attention to funding, designing and building a golf course in Milton with partner Chris Adkins.

Oakley would tend to the golf matters and Adkins would handle the maintenance.

In 2004 his brother David talked Pete, then 55, into trying the European Senior Tour, mostly to keep him company. David Oakley had won four times in Europe. To join him Oakley had to survive a nervous qualifying tournament, aided by a skulled 8-iron on the ninth green that crashed into the pin and fell into the cup. By the time July rolled around there had been some success but not much. When he entered the qualifying tournament to get into the Senior British Open at Royal Portrush in Ireland Oakley figured that the 70-pound fee to hire a caddy for one round was a bit steep so he pulled his own golf trolley around the course.

On the 10th hole a man named Mervyn Steed stepped out of the crowd and offered to pull Oakley's cart for him. A 50-foot putt for birdie fell on that hole and Steed became Oakley's caddie for the week when he secured one of the 20 available qualifying sports for the tournament. Oakley, whose natural ball flight is a low, boring shot, found the chilly and brisk conditions of Northern Ireland fit his game. He shot a one-over par 73 in the first round but a splendid 68 in the second round thrust him into contention. Another 73 in the third round gave Oakley the 54-hole lead.

On Championship Sunday Oakley seemed impervious to the pressure. Slight of build, Peter Alliss on ABC television remarked that he looked much like a butler on the course. Oakley made six birdies in the round and the last, a 25-footer on the 14th hole, gave him a three stroke cushion with four holes to play. But up ahead of him Tom Kite was shooting a final round 68 and Eduardo Romero, an eight-time winner on the European Tour who had just turned 50 that week to get into senior event, had fashioned a 67. Oakley would need to make par on the final hole to win the tournament and avoid a three-way playoff.

He drove well but his approach shot to the green came up shot and disappeared into a deep bunker. Without being able to see the flagstick from his position Oakley blasted out 12 feet past the hole. The putt was perfect and Pete Oakley, club pro from Delaware, had won the Senior British Open with a four-under par total of 284. "It was divine the way I putted this week," Oakley, a spiritual man, said after the round.

His best previous finish on the American senior tour had been 35th, at the U.S. Senior Open in 2003. His best finish in Europe had been ninth. The $295,000 winner's check was 12 times more than his best previous payday. No qualifier had ever won the Senior British Open before, let alone one who had been pulling his own clubs aroudn the course.

Besides the money there were perks, including a one-year exemption to play the Senior Tour in the United States. When Oakley arrived back in the United States - minus his golf clubs which the airline had lost - Arnold Palmer came up to him in the locker room at the U.S. Senior Open and congratulated him, telling "the unknown pro from Delaware" how proud he was of him. There were mobs of fans waiting to get his autograph.

Oakley took advantage of his year's exemption on the Senior Tour to take off from the Rookery. He played 26 events, had a couple of Top Ten finishes and won $192,293. It was not enough to earn him additional time on Tour but he proved to himself that he could play at golf's highest level.

His British Open championship won Oakley the right to return and defend his title in 2005. At Royal Aberdeen in Scotland he shot 82-80 to miss the cut. "I'm the luckiest guy I know," he said afterwards. "I'm playing golf. The heck with the score. Life is good." Tom Watson won that tournament, just like he had in 2003 so the names on the gold cup of the Senior British Open winners read: Tom Watson-Pete Oakley-Tom Watson.

Beware of What You Wish For

One small state. Two universities, playing at the same level of ball. One would think natural rivalry. In the case of Delaware and Delaware State one would be thinking wrongly. Throughout the 20th century the two teams, one white and richer and the other historically black and poorer, never met on the gridiron.

For most of its history since being founded in 1891 Delaware State was a small school with no program of consequence. But that began to change in the last decades of the 1900s as Delaware State moved into the Mid-Eastern Athletic Conference and began competing at the same level as the University of Delaware. And eventually First State football fans, especially in Dover, wondered why the two schools never scheduled a football game.

The burden to play was on Delaware, which trotted out the same excuses for years - no flexibility in the scheduling, no one is that interested in playing Delaware State, the games would not be competitive, we play them in other sports. The rumblings grew louder in the mid-2000s until fate settled the matter for the schools. In 2007 coach Al Lavan led the Hornets to its sixth MEAC title with a school-record 10 wins. Delaware State was ranked as high as No, 10 in some regular season polls and earned their first berth in the NCAA playoffs. The first round opponents for the Hornets: the University of Delaware Blue Hens.

The historic game in Newark drew 19,765 fans - the largest in playoff history at Delaware Stadium and one of the biggest crowds ever for a 1-AA playoff game. ESPN showed up to televise the game nationally. Delaware State was the #10 seed in the tournament and Delaware the #13 but the game did not play out that way. Blue Hen running back Omar Cuff ripped off a school-record 288 yards - exactly twice as many as the entire Hornet offense could muster - and Delaware built a 44-0 lead after three quarters to coast to a 44-7 win. The Blue Hens advanced all the way to the finals before losing to Appalachian State in Chattanooga.

Two years later Furman University dropped off the University of Delaware schedule just before the 2009 season and a gaggle of state politicians and school officials announced that not only would Delaware State fill the date but there was a contract signed for an upcoming three-game series. A rivalry was hatched. Or at least one was tried to be manufactured. The Delaware-Delaware State game was given a name - the Route 1 Rivalry although the highway runs nowhere near the Newark campus.

News-Journal readers came up with a name for the trophy to be awarded the winner - The First State Cup and Derek Alexander of the Delaware Industries for the Blind designed the forty-inch high hardware with a walnut base that has room for each year's winner to be engraved. All the trappings were in place for an in-state rivalry. But early returns on the field have not lived up to the hype.

The University of Delaware has won the first six games in the series by an average of 28.5 points. The Hornets have never been ahead at any point in any of the games. More dispiriting the crowds at Delaware Stadium - all the games have been played in Newark with its 22,000-seat capacity - have been some of the sparsest in years. There was uncertainty after the first contracted series ended whether the games would be continued but another four-game contract was signed for games from 2016 until 2020, with a break in 2018 for another evaluation. Football fans are hoping the two schools rediscover the passions that flared when they were not playing other have rekindled by then.

Little League World Series

In 2003, Naamans Little League was in its 46th year and Joe Mascelli had been in the dugout coaching for 36 of them. Heck, he had played in the league in its second year in 1958, when there just 4 teams and 60 boys and games were played at old Cohens Field at Naamans and Ebright roads not far from the highest point in the state.

Mascelli was once again in charge of the Naamans 12-year old All-Stars for the 2003 tournament season and was preparing for the Mid-Atlantic Region championship game at the A. Bartlett Giamanti Little League Leadership Training Center in Bristol, Connecticut where the winner would advance to the Little League World Series. Through the years Delaware teams had made it to this point many times: Newark National Little League in 1980, Brandywine Little League in 1988, 1989 and 1995, Newark American Little League in 1990 and Georgetown Little League in 1995. None made it to the Little League World Series.

Now it was Naamans' turn. In the opposing dugout was the Pennsylvania champion from Lower Perkiomenville who had dealt Naamans its only loss in the round-robin tournament by plating a run in the bottom of the sixth to win 4-3. For the rematch Mascelli sent his best pitcher, Scott Daugherty to the hill. Daughtery had struck out 67 in 36 innings in the tournament but had been nicked by the Pennsylvania champs in his sole loss. In the second inning Ryan Dietrich solved Daugherty for a two-run homer to stake Lower Perkiomen to an early lead. But first baseman and lead-off hitter Dave Mastro clubbed a home run in the third inning to tie the game and third baseman Danny Frate connected in the fourth inning to put Naamans ahead. Kip Skibick stroke a home run in the fifth and Mastro cracked another round-tripper in the sixth inning as Dougherty finished off the 7-3 win. Delaware would be making the drive up Route 15 to Williamsport for the first time.

Daugherty was back on the hill to throw the first Delaware pitches in a Little League World Series. Skibicki knocked in Vince Russomagno in the top of the first against Chandler National of Arizona but the West Champions exploded for four runs in the fifth inning to break open a tight contest, 5-1. The next time out Naamans overcame four errors and a 7-3 deficit to score Delaware's first-ever World Series win against Iowa. A wild fourth inning produced five hits and five runs and Mastro struck out seven of the final ten batters to seal the 8-7 triumph.

In front of a partisan Delaware in the win-or-go-home next game against Richmond, Texas Skibicki plowed through the Lone Star champions' line-up the first time. But the Texans caught up to him in the fourth inning, sending eleven batters to plate, rapping out seven hits and scoring seven runs. Texas advanced and Naamans was out of the tournament with a 1-2 record.

In 2013 Newark National, under the direction of coach John Ludman became the second Delaware Little League to represent the First State at the Little League World Series. It was the third straight state championship for Newark National, a feat accomplished only once before by Middletown-Odessa from 2007-2009. This time the Delaware champs stormed through the Mid-Atlantic Region Tournament with 52 runs in five games. In front of a crowd of 16,600 the big bats of Newark National roared immediately. In the top of the first Delaware used a run-scoring double by first baseman Eric Ludman, a two-run single by Jack Hardcastle and a booming triple by Ryan Miller to build a 5-0 lead which stood up for a 6-3 win over Urbandale, Iowa.

The tables were turned in the next game against the East Lake Little League of Chula Vista, California. Delaware was buried under the assault by the big bats of the West Region champions who used a Grant Holman walk-off grand slam over the trees in centerfield to seal a 15-3 decision ended by the 10-run rule. Newark National now faced the same must-win third game to continue in the World Series. Once again, however, the Newark bats fell silent and Delaware bowed out of the tournament with a 10-0 loss, surrendering another grand slam and enduring another game stopped by the 10-run rule.

Going the Distance

When Doug White ran his first Caesar Rodney marathon in 1971 few had ever heard the word "jogging." No one ran for fun - if you were out running it was "roadwork." Even White never ran at Dickinson High School or the University of Delaware. His passion back then was drag racing, a more common sight on Delaware streets than running shorts. When that hobby became too expensive he traded the burning rubber for running shoes.

A few years later White entered his first Boston Marathon. In 2015, at 72 years of age he completed his 42nd consecutive 26.2-mile Boston Marathon in 4:54:17. In his prime, when he logged over 4,000 miles a year on Delaware roads and tracks, that time was more than two hours faster. White had planned to stop his streak at 40 in the 2013 edition of the race but the bombings that year made it an unsatisfying conclusion to a storied career. So the streak continues. Another runner, Ben Beach, has a current streak six races longer.

White worked for New Castle County but devoted nearly as much time to organizing road races in Delaware. For over thirty years he put together a caravan for Delaware runners to get to the Boston Marathon. In 1978 White was in on the planning for Delaware's first certified marathon, part of a training exercise for the military reservists called the Delaware National Guard Minuteman Marathon. White painstakingly measured the course along Route 9 around Delaware City which included a trip across the Reedy Point Bridge. To avoid conflicts with more established road races the "first marathon in the first state" was scheduled for March 5, 1978. Six inches of snow fell on March 3 and race day remained frosty as the runners maneuvered between recently plowed snowdrifts. Running across the exposed 135-foot high bridge in 26-degree temperatures with whipping winds caused considerable gnashing of teeth.

The Minuteman Marathon attracted 178 runners and 114 completed the course. Twenty-five year old Dover Air Force Base High School graduate Dan Rincon won the race in a time of 2:30:02 and 14-year old Debbie Parks paced the women with a time of 3:17:47. Each won a color television. The organizers tried again in 1980, this time in May. Despite being greeted by a spring heat wave 238 runners finished the race but there would be no more Delaware Minuteman marathons.

Downstate, the Lewes Seashore Marathon started in November 1978 with White besting a field of 67 runners and 43 finishers. The low-profile Lewes race continued for 11 years and one of its noted winners was Gary Fanelli who ran races in costume, often as a Blues Brothers character. He represented American Samoa in the 1988 Seoul Olympics. In the 1990s the the Delaware Schweizer's Marathon was staged in Middletown for several years.

Those fits and starts were so 20th century. In the 2000s Delaware runners have typically been able to pick from at least a half-dozen marathons up and down the state. The Delaware Marathon Running Festival began in 2004 and is a qualifying race for the Boston Marathon as it winds from the Wilmington waterfront to Brandywine Park. The Delaware Trail Marathon makes two scenic loops through White Clay Creek State Park near Newark. The Monster Mash Marathon is another Boston qualifier that starts with a lap around the track at the Dover International Speedway before heading off into the historic state capital. The Trap Pond Marathon is another trail run through Delaware's first state park. The Coastal Delaware Running Festival is favorite for PRs (personal records) as the flat course pads through the paved roads of historic Fort Miles in Cape Henlopen State Park before finishing in Dewey Beach. In December the Rehoboth Beach Marathon always fills its 1200 marathon slots and 1700 half-marathon registrations. No wonder Doug White is closing in on 100,000 miles of competition.

No one who ran in Delaware's first-ever marathon is likely to forget the Reedy Point Bridge.

Delaware Sports

Auto Racing

The Green Flag

Auto racing first supplanted horse racing at the Delaware State Fair in Elsmere in 1919. There were many pile-ups on the non-banked dirt horse track and many of the 5000 in attendance agreed with the newspaper accounts that it was "greatest auto show ever witnessed in Delaware." At Harrington, the auto races were the highlight of the Kent-Sussex Fair.

By 1925 the turns at the Elsmere track were banked and the dirt was rolled hard. Manager Dave Coxe staged regular programs that included time trials, 5-mile races and 10-mile features. There were 70 deaths in auto racing in 1924 but none at the Delaware tracks.

Through the 1930s the only night racing in the East was at Elsmere. For a time midget racing was the biggest speed show in Delaware but it gradually gave way to the excitement of the big stock cars. The old speedway at Elsmere would not see the age of stock cars, however. In 1939 the track gave way to the Elsmere Gardens housing project.

In Delaware, as elsewhere in America, stock car racing took root in rural areas. In the 1940s there were four state tracks; all downstate, in Little Creek, Bridgeville, Magnolia and Georgetown. Georgetown was the biggest and Sunday races would attract drivers from as far away as Mississippi for $500 purses. More than 3000 fans would watch the factory cars skid around the half-mile oval at speeds averaging 65 mph. Some could click over 100 mph on the straightaways. Top Drivers included Russ Bennett of Rehoboth, Bob Burkhart of Wilmington and Johnny Martin of Milford.

In the early 1950s stock car racing spread northward. Augustine Beach Speedway opened and enough Wilmingtonians drove the 17 miles south that the Wilmington Speedway was built on the Du Pont Parkway in 1952. That year the new asphalt plant hosted a $3000 NASCAR event on the Grand Circuit. A capacity crowd of 5360 turned out for Delaware's first national stock car event. Twenty-five drivers from seven states roared off the starting line and followed 50-year old Pappy Hough of Paterson, New Jersey to the checkered flag.

The races at Wilmington Speedway were the best attended Delaware sporting events, save for Delaware Park and Brandywine Raceway. Capitol Speedway joined the state roster of stock car tracks when it opened on Route 113 in Cheswold. It was all a warm-up act for the super speedway at Dover Downs.

Most Delaware sports fans had never seen anything as exciting as early auto racing on the state's dirt tracks.

Delaware's Indy Star

One of the racers who emerged from the Elsmere driving wars was Russell Snowberger. Snowberger was born in Denton, Maryland in 1901 but raised in Bridgeville. He started racing at Harrington in 1921 and set the half-mile track record at Elsmere with a lap in 31.3 seconds. In 1927 Snowberger, then a Philadelphia resident, got a car in the Indianapolis 500 as a relief driver and was in the starting line-up for 1928. His Marmon front-drive racer was forced out of the race on only the fourth lap with mechanical problems but as a relief rider for Jimmy Gleason he led the race for thirteen laps.

Snowberger went on to specialize in revamping stock cars into Indy cars. In 1930 he spent $156 to prepare a production car for the Indianapolis 500 and came in 8th against $25,000 cars. The next year he won the pole position for the Memorial Day classic and wound up the race 5th. The next three years he came in 5th, 8th and 8th again. In an era when fewer than half the starters completed the 500 miles Snowberger was the only driver to finish in the money five straight years. He won $17,300 for those five races.

Busy most of the year at his day job as an engine inspector at the Packard Plant in Detroit, the 500 was the only race he entered. Although several times he was running among the leaders deep into the race Snowberger never again finished as high as fifth.

By 1947 Snowberger had made 15 starts in the Indianapolis 500. Only a handful of drivers had made the Memorial Day run more times. That year he covered only 74 laps. It was his final appearance at the Brickyard. His last competitive turn behind the wheel came in the Pikes Peak Hill Climb in Colorado in 1949. After putting down his goggles he signed on as chief mechanic for the Federal Engineering team running out of Detroit before retiring from racing in 1960.

Russell Snowberger was the fourth-ranked American driver in 1931.
For the 1932 Indianapolis 500 he selected this Hupmobile Eight Comet for his ride.

The Midgets

In 1935 the Delaware Sports Center was chartered to promote sports in the state, including wrestling and boxing. But the main activity was to be midget auto racing. This exciting spectacle had started on the west coast and the racing plant on Route 13, one mile south of Hares Corner, was the first track built especially for midget racing east of the Mississippi River.

Former driver and promoter Dave Coxe graduated from his pioneering work at Elsmere to beat the drum for the midgets. The track was 1/5 mile around and most races featured 20 laps of non-stop action. There was seating for 5000 and room for another 5000 at the Thursday evening events under 90,000 watts of light.

Admission was 50 cents and 5000 fans lined up to get in for the debut as drivers swathed in shoulder pads and helmets and heavy boots (to protect from the hot oil and water spraying from broken hoses) squeezed into the little racers. Coxe's ads promised "spills, thrills and chills" and no one left disappointed. The cars crashed into the infield only to reemerge time and again. Wheels locked and cars flipped end over end. The powerful, noisy engines added to the flavor of the evening. The crowd loved it. Most everybody agreed it was the best sport to come to Delaware in a long time.

The first card of nine events was dominated by locally built and piloted cars. Wilmington driver Lee Minnick carried off several prizes but the action quickly attracted the big-timers from New York who started to sweep all the awards. Coxe's promotions kept the track humming; he brought in real midgets under 3'5" to race the little cars and on July 4 he featured Indianapolis 500 drivers.

Midget racing continued at Hares Corner for several more years. Tragedy occurred in 1938 when 38-year old Bob Harper of Chester, the starter, was killed while flagging the field to signal the final lap. Danny Goss coming in front of the grandstand in heavy dust never saw Harper and struck him going 65 mph, sending the body 100 feet down the track in front of 2000 spectators. Ironically Harper's brother was on that final lap on his way to winning the race.

The midgets gave way to the "big cars," the stock cars, before World War II but racing fans did not soon forget their summer evenings with the spills, thrills and chills of the midget racers.

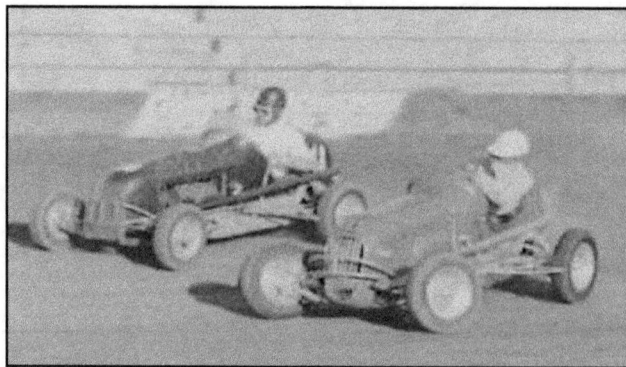

Midget racers in the 1930s were promoted as providing "spills, thrills and chills" and they seldom failed to deliver on the track.

DELAWARE DRIVERS

Johnny Pierson. At the age of 24 in 1941 Pierson created a sensation on the midget racing circuit by winning the Eastern championship crown. Pierson was a student in auto mechanics at Brown Vocational School in Wilmington and working part-time in a city garage when he got an offer to drive in 1938. Working his way through the circuit he drove every night, maybe five races a night, earning $250 a week at the pinnacle of his sport.

Bob Mattson. Mattson was a native Californian who came to Delaware during World War II to work in the shipyards. He settled in Wilmington, building race cars in his garage at 1301 Philadelphia Pike. Mattson was the second leading stock car driver in the East in 1947 and third in 1948 when he won 5 of 38 races.

He attempted to qualify for the Indianapolis 500 in 1949 but failed after he cracked up his car in a race back home in California. Mattson returned to the dirt tracks but died tragically several months later after locking wheels and flying over an embankment in a race in Salem, Indiana.

Lou Johnson. Johnson began racing stock cars on dirt tracks in the 1940s, including Augustine and Georgetown in Delaware. Over the next quarter-century he travelled to tracks up and down the East Coast during the boom time of sprint car racing. The loosely organized circuit developed into the United Racing Club and Johnson won its driving championship three times.

George Alderman. After two years at the University of Delaware and two in the Army, Newark native George Alderman began racing cars in 1956. His specialty was road racing and he soon won the Sports Car Club of America driving championship. In 1960 Alderman was the Formula III driving champion at age 29. An expert mechanic, Alderman continued winning races on the sports car circuits for three decades.

Brett Lunger. Princeton political science student by day, race driver by night. Brett Lunger was home in Wilmington for the summer in the 1960s when he happened on a couple of evening auto races. Hooked by the competition he began asking questions and came under the tutelage of George Alderman. In his first season, while still in school in 1966, Lunger was competing in the Canadian American Challenge Cup Series, the premiere road-racing series in North America.

After a tour of duty in Vietnam in 1969-70 Lunger decided to make a career of auto racing. At first he tried being an owner-driver but soon concluded his best opportunities lay in driving. He went to Europe, apprenticed against some of the top road racers in the world, weathered the oil crisis and emerged in 1975 as a Grand Prix driver. In 1976, as the only American-born driver in Formula One, Lunger finished in the top ten four times.

Home of the Monster Mile

In 1940, Melvin Joseph went to work with a sixth grade education, a dump truck and a shovel. He was 19 years old. 1949 became a big year - he became a partner in a downstate Ford dealership, he scored his first big contract for Melvin L. Joseph Construction Co. and he got involved in racing by building the Georgetown Speedway. Joseph was known to break a few speed limits on the back roads of Sussex County in his souped-up Mercurys.

Joseph was a pioneer in early NASCAR and a fixture on the sands of Daytona Beach in the 1950s. All his cars and, later, horses, carried the number 49 from his "lucky" year. He set his sights on designing and building a dual track for fast horses and fast cars.

That dream was Dover Downs, which opened in 1969 as America's first multi-purpose sports complex, a distinction it retains today. The busy agenda called for thoroughbred and standardbred racing on the interior 5/8 mile oval and world-class auto racing on the outside one-mile track. For auto racing Dover Downs boasted a new design principle - "variable degree," which promoted a smooth transition from straights to high-banked turns that allowed drivers to reach unheard of speeds on the one-mile lap. Hence the Dover track's nickname: "The Monster Mile."

The first event at Dover Downs was the Mid-Atlantic 300, the longest scheduled race in United States Auto Club history. Lining up in the starting grid were A.J. Foyt, Bobby Unser, Al Unser and other Indy stars. Foyt won the race which was halted after only 158 laps due to heavy rains. Later that year Andy Granatelli captured the Dover 200 over Mario Andretti and Gordon Johncock.

Richard Petty christened the new speedway for NASCAR racing with a victory in the Mason-Dixon 300 on July 6, 1969. "The King" averaged 115.772 mph for the 300 laps in his Ford Torino Talladega and the win was the first of seven trips under the checkered flag for Petty at Dover, tying him with Bobby Allison for the most NASCAR wins in Delaware.

Jimmie Johnson pushed the record to eight in 2013. Two years later Johnson became only the fifth driver in NASCAR history with at least ten wins at a single track when he captured the spring event. When 2015 ended Johnson had led 2,999 laps at the Speedway.

Since 1971 the Dover Downs International Speedway has hosted two NASCAR Winston Cup stock car races each year. The two race weekends are by far the largest spectator sporting events in Delaware, with the equivalent of one-half the state's population attending Friday qualifying sessions, the 200-mile NASCAR Busch series races on Saturday and the classic 500-mile tests on race Sunday.

In 1995 Dover became the first supersweedway in NASCAR to be paved with concrete, providing a faster and more competitive racing surface. In 1997, with the Sprint Cup race shortened from 500 miles to 400, Mark Martin established a race record by averaging 132.719 mph and coming within 50 seconds of finishing in less than three hours. In 2014 Brad Keselowski ran the fastest qualifying lap in 164.444 mph - true Monster Mile.

Baseball

The Town Ball Era

Early Delaware baseball matched local teams. Here was a chance to offer prideful tradesmen, for instance, a chance to meet on level ground. When groups of butchers squared off it was the "Cows" and the "Steers." There is an early account in Delaware of "a match game of baseball played between the painters and printers for a keg of beer. The printers beat, but the painters refused to pay." Another popular match-up was teams of single men against nines of marrieds.

These new games of baseball were often arranged for charity. In one novel game a "fat" nine of Wilmingtonians totaling 2300 pounds engaged a "lean" nine of but 1125 pounds. The admission fee of 25 cents was given to the House For Friendless Children. The big men took the first game but the "leans" exacted a 51-22 revenge in the next game after "the heavy men came on the grounds not only fat, but saucy, and pranced around in gay ribbons, smiling broad smiles at the recollection of their former victory." The two games raised $51.25.

Baseball, in all its various forms, swept the country rapidly. In 1866 it was observed that "the game of baseball has now become beyond question the leading feature in the outdoor sports of the United States." Inevitably towns began presenting their best players against those from the village down the road.

The first teams in Delaware were the Lenapis of New Castle and the Atlas Club of Delaware City, the latter being a family affair featuring three Reybolds and two Prices.

Games were arranged by letter, often printed in the local papers. When a challenge was accepted the game would be played according to the regulations adopted in New York in 1865 by the National Association of Baseball Players. Most important was the selection of an umpire through negotiation. The team first up was decided by a coin toss.

The games were heavily bet on and the atmosphere was often less than gentlemanly. A good match could be expected to draw 500 or more fans. The game was rough, both on the field and off. At one game it was reported, "that some man, whose mind was more thoroughly imbued with the love of money-getting than with common sense or decency, had set up a stand for the sale of beer in the judge's stand, and some boys and young men having drunk too much, commenced a fight. This drew all the spectators from the game and stopped the play for a short time."

By the 1870s baseball clubs were organized throughout Delaware, including several black nines: the Flat Foots of Georgetown, the Long Nine of Bridgeville, the Independent Baseball Club and the Hercules team. The best ball was played in Wilmington and it was no trifling matter. From the local Wilmington paper came this report: "The Academic Baseball Club of Milford, so badly beaten by our city clubs while on a visit here recently, make all sorts of excuses for their defeats but the local paper of the town tells the club the best and most truthful excuse is, 'they could not play well enough.' Correct."

While professional baseball was at best a spotty proposition in Delaware throughout the nineteenth century, amateur ball at the town level remained popular, especially in the rural environs. Junior teams were formed for boys and challenges were accepted in the same manner as their adult counterparts. As a result baseball games could be found in every town in the state on any Saturday well into the 1900s.

The Diamond State Baseball Club

In 1865 a group of young businessmen gathered in a broker's office at the corner of Fifth and Market in Wilmington and excitedly discussed the formation of a team to play this new game that was sweeping the country. The Diamond State Baseball Club was born.

Early in May of 1866 the young men, resplendent in their new suits of black and white checkered shirts, black pantaloons and blue skull caps, marched proudly through the streets of town to the baseball grounds at Delaware and Adams for their first game with the powerful Athletics of Philadelphia. It would be charitable with too much credit to term the contest a "battle."

The Athletics were acknowledged as the champion nine of the country and were too much a team for their novice opponents. Home runs over the fence were the rule rather than the exception. One Diamond State fielder so wearied of jumping over the outfield fence after baseballs that he stationed himself out of the field of play. After awhile the home team placed all of their club in the field. Even with 20 or 25 players scattered about the lot the Delawareans had difficulty in holding down their formidable foe.

The crowd for the novel event, however, was hardly dissuaded by the lopsided goings-on and when deliberate Philadelphia errors enabled a Diamond State player to circle the bases with the first Wilmington run the fans went wild with delight. The final score was Athletics 104, Diamond State 5. Undeterred, the vanquished Delaware team feted their visitors in grand style that evening at a local hotel.

Weeks of hard practice followed and the Diamond State club deemed itself ready to challenge the more established Lenapis of New Castle to a series for the state championship. Playing on their home grounds the New Castle ball tossers won the first game handily by 10 runs. The rematch in Wilmington looked much the same until Diamond State exploded for nine runs in the final inning to prevail 35-32. They banqueted their defeated opponents and sent them home with three hearty cheers.

Buoyed by their spectacular come-from-behind first victory the Diamond Staters swept over the Lenapis 30-7 in the deciding tussle. By this time the Wilmingtonians had lured into the fold, "Fergy" Malone, who would later become the greatest pitcher of his day. Although no players were paid at the time, not even expenses, Malone was assisted in setting up a cigar store at Seventh and King Streets for his diamond exploits. Malone was worth the investment; he never lost while in the box for the Diamond State Baseball Club.

The Wilmington team took a boat to Delaware City and beat the Atlas Club resoundingly 32-15 to clinch the state championship before a large turnout of partisan supporters. Diamond State did not have long to enjoy their laurels in peace. Another Wilmington team, the Wawasets, organized and were as strong as any Diamond State had yet met in Delaware.

The two nines met often over the next few seasons. For most of that time Diamond State, especially with Malone handling the pitching chores, was clearly superior. But against other pitchers Wawaset was able to win its share of games as well. The Diamond State Club was able to retain its mythical state championship until it disbanded in the early 1870s.

The Quicksteps

With the dissolving of the Diamond State Baseball Club in the early 1870s there was no acknowledged champion baseball nine in Delaware. After a couple important wins in 1872 the Quicksteps were quick indeed to claim the mantle but they still had much to prove on the field. Late in 1872 the Quicksteps fell to Wilmington's Eckford nine before an overflow crowd at the diamond at Delaware and Adams streets.

In 1873 the Actives of Wilmington were the leading team as the Quicksteps did not reorganize until July. The new Quicksteps within a short time became the strongest baseball club to yet represent Wilmington. With star pitcher Frank B., better known as "Flip," Lafferty in the box, this club never suffered a defeat at the hands of a local club. In the summer the Quicksteps travelled to southern Delaware dispatching nines from Milford and Georgetown and declaring themselves "Champions of the Peninsula."

By 1874 the Quicksteps were firmly established as "Delaware's team." The celebrated nine was by now combatting mostly out-of-state teams and their exploits were assiduously detailed on the front pages of the Wilmington papers. They held their own in games against Philadelphia clubs and crowds of 500 fans were common at their afternoon games at Scheutzen Park.

In 1875 the Quicksteps joined the national Amateur Association, playing games against professional and amateur teams. The resourceful nine displayed an uncanny knack at tallying in the late frames to win games on their field out by the 3rd Street Bridge. On July 15 the Wilmington Maple Leaf engaged the Quicksteps for the state championship. There was considerable wagering on the game with the Quicksteps only slight favorites as the Leaf featured two players from powerful Philadelphia teams. The Quicksteps at first refused to contest against a non-Wilmington team but finally agreed to play and jumped to a 11-1 lead after two innings. The Quicksteps thumped the Maple Leaf 24-4 for the state title.

On August 7 the Quicksteps played their first game against a professional nine, the Chicago Whitestocking. The contest got off to a less than auspicious beginning. According to game accounts, "The first batter knocked the first ball pitched to him to right field and made second. The ball fell on the track and rolled under a horse's feet, and while Stock was getting it the horse lifted his hind foot and made an ugly wound on the player's face, necessitating the stoppage of the game for some time and the substitution of Kelley for Stock." The Quicksteps slipped behind 5-0 after two innings and fell 11-4 but the Chicago manager praised the nine as one of the finest his team had yet met.

The Quicksteps again marched through the south crushing Milford 27-5 and demoralizing Dover 29-0. Before the Smyrna game their arrival was thus heralded in the local paper: "The Quicksteps came to town last night and will beat the club of this place this afternoon." They did, 29-1. In the sixth inning, when Lafferty was "pitching most wickedly," one of the prettiest girls present, after consulting a dozen of her companions, penciled the following note and had it sent to him - "Dear Frank: Please let our boys have one run; just one. Affectionately yours, the ladies of Smyrna."

Upon receipt of the plaintive missive Lafferty bore down even harder and the ladies appealed to other Quickstep players. After the letter was printed in the Wilmington paper rooters took up the refrain against futile visiting teams. The Quicksteps built new grounds and forbade betting. They pummeled the reorganized Diamond State club 26-4 and even beat the fabled Philadelphia Athletic 6-4. The Quicksteps were now playing to great fanfare and 50 fans followed the team to Reading on an excursion train. The Wilmington team lost to the Reading Active before a record crowd of 1800. The Quicksteps complained of shabby treatment by the Reading fans and when they won the rematch 16-7 in Wilmington a bitter rivalry was hatched.

The rubber game was arranged in Philadelphia to accommodate the large followings of each team. Each side put up $100 with the winner taking all. The Quicksteps led 6-2 into the 8th inning but then surrendered 12 runs, playing so poorly there was talk the game had been sold. The jubilant Reading nine returned home to a full parade.

The games had been so entertaining no time was wasted setting up another three-game match. By this time Reading had notched wins against teams from Philadelphia and New York and were boasting that they were the best amateur team in the country. The first game in Reading spilled over to 10 innings before the Active prevailed 9-8. The match was acknowledged as "the finest game yet played in Reading" and was so popular an exhibition was scheduled after the Quicksteps returned from a trip to Harrisburg. Wilmington won the "practice" game 8-6. Back in Wilmington the series resumed with the Active winning 14-8 and then sweeping the series by thrashing the Quicksteps 16-3 in Reading.

The Quickstep players got no money for their exertions and a large benefit was held to defray expenses. Late in October an eighth meeting was arranged between the Active and the Quicksteps in Reading. The contest degenerated into a mob scene forcing the Quickstep team to flee from the field. The Active had set up the game

Meet the most celebrated Delaware nine of the 19th century: the Quicksteps.

only as revenge for what they considered shabby treatment for the last game in Wilmington when the Quicksteps delayed the start of the game causing Reading to miss the last train home and incur extra expenses. In retribution Reading turned over only $25 of a $60 guarantee. The great rivalry ended in festering bad blood.

In the Centennial year of 1876 the Quickstep Association formed a stock company and joined the professional National Professional Association. Al Hindle of the Quicksteps was selected president of the league featuring teams from Philadelphia, Reading, St. Louis, New Haven and Brooklyn. The team was stocked with players brought in from out of town and paid about $10 a week to play ball in Wilmington. The new team donned snappy new white uniforms with blue stockings, red belt, blue trimming and white shoes. "Quickstep" was emblazoned across the breast.

Delaware's first professional team won laurels on the field but only a modest following among Wilmingtonians. Meanwhile the former Quicksteps reorganized to form the Quickstep Amateurs. Evans and Lafferty, spirited away from the professionals, were key pitchers on one of the strongest amateur nines in the country. The team opened with a 24-3 trouncing of the Philadelphia Keystones on the new grounds by Pennsylvania and Delaware avenues before a sellout crowd.

Wilmingtonians were regaled with success stories from both Quickstep teams in the daily papers. Inevitably a 7-game series was arranged between the amateurs and professionals. More than 1200 fans packed the grounds for the opening match. Admirers cheered lustily for play on both sides but animosity ran deep between the players. The game was delayed by lengthy rules debates and cries of "pack up the bats and go home" emanated from both sides. The professional nine eventually prevailed 11-6 but the proceedings of the play sent the remaining fans away with diminishing enthusiasm.

The two teams split the next two games but the series dissolved before the result of the fourth game was announced. The decline of baseball in Wilmington had begun. The professional team could not muster enough support to survive the season and the Quickstep Amateurs returned from a western road trip without the services of Lafferty, Evans, Splaine and Smiley, who were all raided by other clubs. In August the manager Manuel Richenberger, who had been the first to enclose a baseball park in Delaware, was ousted and the team reorganized but the glory days of the Quicksteps were over.

In 1877 the Quickstep amateurs were salaried and by mid-season were acclaimed as one of the strongest teams in the country. White flags flew on street cars on game days and monthly tickets were sold for $1 but, while Wilmingtonians were still greatly interested in baseball, they weren't interested in paying for it. A typical Quickstep game would draw about 500 paying customers but twice that would gather on the hills, rooftops and wagons around the park. Wilmington papers implored the fans to watch "from inside the enclosure" and support the team to keep it but the death knell was sounded.

The Quicksteps disbanded before the 1877 season wound down and in the spring of 1878, while amateur games proliferated around the state, there was no top flight competition. The Quicksteps were not revived until July 28 at Eighth and Broom Streets but the effort failed. Delaware's nationally recognized amateur nine was no more.

Dover Baseball

No town loved its baseball more than Dover. It was universally conceded that the grounds of the Dover club were the finest in the state but the best ball played there was seldom by the Dover nine. In 1874 Dover hosted the Kent County championship but was routed by Smyrna and had to watch Milford and Smyrna battle for the title on their home turf.

Cap Anson was the first Hall-of-Famer to play on Delaware diamonds. Unfortunately for Dover he was wearing a Philadelphia uniform at the time.

It was recorded that the Milford win, "notwithstanding the rays of old Sol which were exceedingly scorching, was witnessed by quite a large number of persons, including a small sprinkling of ladies, who seem to take as much interest in the exercises of bat and ball as the sterner sex."

On June 25, 1875 the first professional game in Delaware was arranged in Dover between the Athletic of Philadelphia and the New Haven of Connecticut. An extra 1500 temporary seats were erected for people "regardless of race, color or previous condition or servitude." Anxious spectators began coming to the town at 10:00 a.m. but it was not until the 2:00 p.m. train arrived that the stands for the 3:20 game filled.

An umpire's mistake in the top of the first inning completely snuffed out a New Haven rally and the team seemed not to recover. Philadelphia, led by the great Cap Anson, scored in each of the first three innings and cruised to a 12-1 win.

1875 was a better year for the local nine who distinguished themselves against downstate foes. A visit by the Quicksteps was much anticipated by the Dover faithful; a victory could bolster a claim as state champion. But the game was a fiasco. After four innings the contest was mercifully stopped with the home team trailing 29-0. The Dover nine would never quite meet the expectations of the devoted townsfolk.

The Amateur Leagues of Delaware

In the 1880s Seaford emerged as the leading baseball town in downstate Delaware. In 1888, having not lost a game in three years, the Seaford nine dumped the Delaware Field Club 9-3 and claimed the mythical state baseball championship.

The boastings from down the peninsula did not escape the attention of Wilmington baseball men who instigated the formation of the Amateur Baseball League of Delaware to decide the best baseball team in the state. The league included Seaford and three Wilmington nines: Americus, Wilmington and the Quicksteps. All players were required to be amateurs and residents of the city represented.

The league got off to a rousing start in attendance; the "bleaching boards" were always full and games elicited much spirited betting. More than 1000 people stormed the grounds for the much awaited home opener at Seaford which prompted the observation that "one commendable feature of baseball attendance in this town (Seaford) is the presence of hundreds of ladies at each game. Their presence serves to eliminate the too-prevalent objectionable features at baseball matches and at the same time stimulates the players to exert themselves."

Seaford was less successful on the field, however, as they struggled to an 0-4 start. Americus was far the strongest team in Delaware, winning their first four matches by a combined 49-10 score. When Americus traveled to Seaford, however, they were dispatched 6-0. Immediately there were protests that Seaford had used a professional pitcher and catcher from Baltimore to dominate the game. Wilmington papers termed the local umpiring "criminal."

With new pitcher "Davis," Seaford reeled off two more wins and during a tumultuous league meeting on August 2 all the clubs conceded to using pros except Americus. Manager Ross of Seaford admitted that he could not compete with the Wilmington club on local talent alone. And no wonder; consider the distribution of population in Delaware in the 1880s - Wilmington, 60,000; Dover, 4,000; New Castle, 4,000; Smyrna, 2,500; Milford, 2,000; Seaford, 2,000; and Newark, 1,000. Seaford resigned from the association and the Amateur Baseball League of Delaware fizzled.

The next year another attempt was made to organize the state teams. Dover, Wilmington, Smyrna, Camden and Milford banded together to form the Delaware State League. This time each team was allowed to hire eight players and there were no residency requirements. But even before the league could get underway there was controversy over Dover's use of second baseman Bill Higgins, a Wilmington player who had played 14 games for the Boston Braves the year before. The Smyrna management claimed they had signed Higgins and Dover threatened to pull out before the matter was resolved in their favor.

There were 600 on hand to see Dover nip Wilmington in the League opener and play was combative from the start. Dover led the list with a 5-2 mark with Wilmington a half-game back at 4-2, with both losses to Dover. Dover travelled to Wilmington to administer a third defeat to the big city but the league was beginning to break up for want of downstate attendance. Smyrna couldn't compete with the other clubs in salaries for players and dropped out and within two weeks there was no more tournament for baseball supremacy of Delaware.

After several years in a Rip Van Winkle state professional baseball re-awakened in Wilmington in 1883 when a city team joined the Interstate Association, banding together with nines from Pottsville, Reading, Brooklyn, Trenton and Harrisburg. Delaware fans could expect a game nearly every day and the Union Street grounds were the best in the Association behind the Brooklyn Park.

The new Wilmingtons adopted the storied name "Quicksteps" and proudly posed for pictures in their new white flannel uniforms with blue stockings and belt and blue and white caps. Early play was uneven but the team consistently drew between 500 and 800 fans to the park. By July, however, the Quicksteps had slipped to 11-19 and stirred the wrath of the local press: "The players still have the consolation left that they can continue with their poor exhibitions of baseball until the end of the season without losing their present standing."

By August wins were so rare the team returned from a win on the road to the headline: THE QUICKSTEP ACTUALLY WINS A GAME. Their first win in over two weeks was witnessed at Union Street by scarcely 200 people. The team management couldn't conquer the problems on the field or off. The season was peppered with managerial and roster changes, all to little effect.

As to the fans, it was reported, "quite as many persons witness the game from neighboring trees and buildings as pay their way to the park. An enterprising individual with an old barn and rickety house back of the yard sells privileges to occupy positions where the game can be seen a square away. These spectators are, in the majority, able to pay admission to the grounds, but would rather get an indifferent view of the field at half price. These patrons do more growling at the Quickstep club than all the paying ones together."

The Quicksteps stumbled to a 29-49 finish in what was left of the Interstate Association. Still the team was considered a strong franchise, plagued mainly by mismanagement. Backers easily sold $2000 worth of stock for a new team in 1884.

Brooklyn wound up being the class of the short-lived Interstate Association - not Wilmington.

Despite the dismal minor league experience of 1883 Wilmington entered the Eastern League, one of the four leading professional organizations along with the National League, American Association and Northwestern League, in 1884. Manager Joseph Simmons recruited an especially powerful team, fortified by strong batters, and the Wilmington nine was favored for the title in preseason opinions around the league.

Matched with Allentown, Newark, Richmond, Harrisburg, Baltimore, Reading and Trenton the Wilmingtons - sporting no nickname - were the scourge of the circuit from Opening Day on May 1. They won ten of their first eleven games by the scores of 21-6, 11-1, 15-8, 13-1, 7-8, 13-4, 10-2, 20-5, 10-3, 7-6 and 21-6. Lefthander Daniel Casey and righty Edward Sylvester "The Only" Nolan were phenomenal pitchers who dominated the league with 10 and 19 wins respectively.

Only Trenton offered much of a challenge but the New Jersey men were beaten 12-10 before 1300 Wilmington fans. It was the high point of the season. The lopsided games held as little appeal to Delaware fans as the previous years' hapless losers. Nineteen straight wins pushed the record through 50 games to 40-10, with the team averaging more than 10 runs a game.

Shortstop Thomas "Oyster" Burns led the Wilmington attack with an astounding 12 home runs. Burns got his nickname from his off-season job of selling shellfish; he was known around the league for "an irritating voice and personality."

The pennant chase was over by August. Wilmington stood 46-12. The owners, battling red ink at the gate all season, closed the team down as soon as they had mathematically eliminated all challengers for the championship. It was hardly a triumph draped in glory.

In the ultimate triumph of hope over experience Wilmington once again joined the Eastern League in 1885. This time, with little money to pay players, they were routed early, although barely 100 fans were turning out to witness the slaughter. After a 1-14 start the team relocated to Atlantic City verifying the conclusion reached during the championship 1884 season - Wilmington would not support a team. The third successive attempt to run a baseball club in the city had come to grief before the season was over.

19-year old Oyster Burns led the champion Wilmington nine at the plate in 1884 before embarking on an 11-year major league career.

Delaware in the Major Leagues

"The papers have all been signed and Wilmington's pet club, which had won recognition as the champion of the Eastern League, is ready to worry the nines of the Union Association all the way from Boston to Kansas City," trumpeted the Every Evening on August 18, 1884. And so began Wilmington's hopeful odyssey into major league baseball.

The Wilmington Quicksteps had laid waste to the Eastern League in 1884 winning 51 of 63 games by the middle of August. They had already clinched the pennant when the owners jumped to the Union Association to replace the failed Philadelphia Keystones. The Union Association was in its first - and only - year as a third major league, formed in opposition to the reserve rule that governed the rival National League and American Association.

Fans in Wilmington were ready for the challenge because, as *Every Evening*

Rookie southpaw Dan Casey won Wilmington's first major league game. After the club disbanded he went on to win 96 major league games.

went on to report, "experience has demonstrated that, though many of the matches with Eastern League clubs were enjoyable and hard fought contests, the almost continuous line of victories for the home club seemed to have impressed the admirers of the game with the foregone conclusion as to the result, and to have lessened the attendance so much that the club's existence, for financial reasons, was beginning to look doubtful."

The Quicksteps traveled to Washington where they won their first Union Association game against the Nationals before 1800 fans at Capitol Park, plating two runs in the 8th inning to prevail 4-3. The Washington manager praised the Quicksteps as "a fine set of ball players who gave a beautiful display of fielding and won favor for their quiet, gentlemanly deportment."

Wilmington fell the next day to the Nationals 4-2 but more importantly lost their shortstop and centerfielder who jumped to the Baltimore club. The hastily reassembled Wilmington nine was drubbed 12-1 in the third game of the series, getting no hits and striking out 13 times. Washington administered decisive 14-0 and 10-4 defeats in the last two games, the four runs coming meaninglessly in the ninth inning.

The roster was still fluid. Outfielder Dennis Casey, hero of the opening day win but ineffective in the four-game losing streak, was released, but not for his play. "Dennis Casey's behavior has been despicable and contemptible," it was reported, "and considering also his unpopularity with the rest of the nine, it is well that he has left."

Wilmington departed Washington for a series in Boston, but arrived late and had to forfeit the first game 9-0. It was supposed that some of the team members had stopped too long in New York City and misunderstood the directions to the Boston park when finally arriving in the Hub. The next day the Quicksteps outhit the Bostons 7-6 but lost the game 7-1 under the burden of 23 errors.

Hope emerged the following day when Wilmington jumped to a 4-0 lead after two innings but the advantage could not be sustained. Blame for the 5-4 loss was laid squarely on catcher Tom Lynch: "Lynch's bad catching lost the game here yesterday, as all other games have been lost by poor playing in this position."

After a respite by rain the Quicksteps were once again shut down 3-0, dropping their record to 1-8. The team finally returned home for their first games at the field at Front & Union dragging an eight-game losing skein. 600 fans turned out for the game with Cincinnati and were rewarded with the second Quickstep Union Association win. The colorfully named The Only Nolan twirled a 3-2 masterpiece, felling 11 Queen City batters with his deceptive curve. Local fans could also revel in the work of native Wilmingtonian George Fisher at shortstop.

The next day the Quicksteps enjoyed a 3-1 lead into the 6th when pitcher John Murphy was struck a "terrible blow" with a pitched ball while at bat. He remained in the game but his effectiveness ebbed and Cincinnati came back for a 7-3 win. After the game Wilmington lost John Cullen, a stalwart in the middle of the order, when he fell down an elevator well. Cullen promptly retired to his native California to edit a local newspaper.

Next in town for the Quicksteps was the powerful St. Louis team that was dominating the league on their way to a 94-19 record. Nolan, the team's highest paid player at $325 a month, held the talented visitors in check but fell 4-2. The succeeding games were perfunctory losses; 9-3, 11-3 and 7-1. A soggy 4-3 loss to Baltimore dropped the Quicksteps to 2-16.

On September 15 Kansas City and Wilmington assembled for a game but gate receipts totalled only $40. The visiting team was guaranteed $75 and the Quickstep stockholders were unwilling to go deeper into their pockets to make up the balance. The game was cancelled and the team folded.

Milwaukee played out the final 12 games of the season and the Union Association was gone too. Although Wilmington's adventure in big league baseball was a brief one their 2-16 final log stands as the worst team mark in major league baseball history.

Ed "The Only" Nolan, a 27-year old Canadian pitcher, was the Quicksteps top-paid player. Seven years earlier while pitching in the minor leagues for Indianapolis Nolan threw 76 complete games, won 64 and pitched 30 shutouts - all records in professional ball.

Mighty Casey First Struck Out In Delaware

For the better part of 50 years a trolley conductor in Binghamton, New York entertained riders with a tall tale - he was the inspiration for Ernest Thayer's celebrated baseball poem "Casey At The Bat."

The story Dan Casey told was this: "I was a left-handed pitcher for the Phillies. We were playing the Giants in the old Philadelphia ballpark on August 21, 1887. Tim Keefe was pitching against me and he had a lot of stuff, but I was no slowpoke myself. It was the last of the ninth and New York was leading 4 to 3. Two men were out, and there were runners on second and third. A week before, I had busted up a game with a lucky homer and folks thought I could repeat. The count went to 3 and 2 and he burned one over the plate. What a miss it was." Casey claimed that after that game Thayer, a Philadelphia sportswriter, showed him a poem he had scribbled about the incident.

The next year Thayer was in San Francisco and "Casey at the Bat" became a popular theatrical recitation. The travails of the Mudville nine soon became ingrained in American lore.

In the 1930s as baseball was organizing the Hall of Fame in bucolic Cooperstown, New York the lords of the game went all in on the Abner Doubleday myth of the game's creation. When they heard of Casey's story down the road in Binghamton archives were checked and most of the baseball part of the story rang true.

Even though Thayer always maintained that Casey was a fictional creation, baseball embraced the real-life Dan Casey version. He was an unlikely "mighty" Casey. Primarily a pitcher, that lucky home run was his only one in 710 career at bats. His lifetime batting average was an unfrightening .162.

Was this Wilmington's Dan Casey?

Nonetheless, *Time* magazine ran an article on the "Mudville Man." At the Hall of Fame grand opening festivities in 1939 Casey was interviewed on a national radio show and presented with a lifetime pass to all the ballparks in the land. Seventy-six years old at the time, he re-created his epic failure on the field of an exhibition game.

If Dan Casey was indeed the original mighty slugger of legend his first failures were with Wilmington in the Eastern League in 1884, when he signed his first professional contract as a 21-year old off the family farm just outside of Binghamton. He died in 1943 at the age of 80, going to grave convinced he was "the mighty Casey."

Minor League Baseball - The Middle States League (1889)

In August of 1889 Wilmington baseball enthusiasts staged two exhibitions to gauge local support for a professional baseball team. Turnout was sufficiently encouraging to convince the investors to enter the crumbling Middle States League with teams mostly from central Pennsylvania.

The new team, adorned smartly in gray suits with maroon trim, actually beat the powerful Cuban Giants (48-17), a collection of professional black players from Newark who were an attractive draw wherever they went. The Giants rebounded to drub the Wilmingtons several times to drop the home team to 4-9.

Once again Wilmington would not last to the end of a minor league campaign, but this time the apathy of Delaware fans could not be blamed. In mid-September the worst storm in 50 years lashed the East Coast, devastating many areas in the region. Rather than re-start the schedule with only a handful of games the backers closed operations for the 1889 season, promising to return in 1890.

Minor League Baseball - The Atlantic Association (1890)

Enthusiasm was never higher in Wilmington for a minor league season than for the upcoming Atlantic Association season in 1890. A new ball park was readied at 29th and Market Streets and Governor Benjamin T. Biggs was on hand to throw the first ball into play. The crowd was estimated at 2500 but paid attendance was only 1484. The rest jumped the fence and easily eluded the six overmatched policeman on duty. Once again Wilmingtonians had demonstrated their desire for baseball and their unwillingness to pay for it.

By the third game the team was 0-3 and attendance had plummeted to 300. Joseph Simmons, who had managed the now revered 1884 Quicksteps, was brought in to lead the squad and guaranteed he was not going to finish as the Atlantic Association tailender.

The record deteriorated to 4-31 but the assemblage was still considered a good one. The Wilmingtons pulled together for four straight wins and actually reached 28-50 when local legend Simmons was released. Only mildly despondent, he put together a pro team to tour the peninsula and give Delaware towns a chance to try their hand against professional talent.

Late in the year Wilmington traveled to Baltimore to meet the league-leading Orioles and could muster only 7 players; two more were recruited from the lot at the ballyard. Soon after they were expelled from the league for non-payment of dues. Once again Wilmington did not last a full season in the minor leagues.

After a lull of several years baseball fever once again gripped Delaware in the mid-1890s. The smaller towns fielded teams featuring pro players and strong Wilmington amateur teams like the YMCA and Rockford began attracting great crowds. Thus inspired, Wilmington once again entered the minor leagues, this time joining Newark, Hartford, Paterson, New Haven and the New York Metropolitans in the Atlantic League.

It seemed a strange geographical choice for Wilmington, the only non-New York area team in the circuit. But the Atlantic League was the strongest league Wilmington had yet engaged. All the teams were competitive on the field and each was well supported among the local enthusiasts.

In Wilmington the Union Streets grounds were fixed up handsomely. Padded seats were installed on the players' benches and the grandstand for the fans was spruced up considerably. Smoking was prohibited in the south stands which were reserved for ladies and their escorts. Outside the park accommodations were provided for 3000 bikes. Save the early Polo Grounds, where the Metropolitans played, the Wilmington grounds were the class of the league.

Three thousand were on hand for the return of professional baseball to Wilmington but the faithful were sent home in a sour mood after Paterson scored all their runs in the 9th inning to steal a 3-2 win. On April 29 in the opening series Honus Wagner played first base for Paterson and led the attack in a 6-5 win with a triple and a home run that went through a hole in the fence. He also made 16 putouts in a performance that was still talked about around Wilmington 30 years later.

In the ultra-competitive Atlantic League the Wilmington nine was never more than two games from .500 for the first 31 games. They then dropped a three-game series to league-leader Paterson to fall to 16-21 and tumble into fifth place. Worse, ominous signs were cropping up off the field.

The final game with Paterson, on a Saturday, drew only 800 fans, a crowd that "should have been twice that size." Across town the bicycle races of the Pullman Club, a minor club made up of Pullman Palace employees, pulled over a thousand spectators. Elsewhere, there were rumors that New Haven and the Mets were headed to Troy and Albany and that Wilmington might move to one of the abandoned cities.

Wilmington, under manager Denny Long, won 16 of 22 and glided into second place but the all-too familiar problem of poor attendance dogged the team. A lengthy front page *Every Evening* editorial implored Wilmington baseball fans to support the efforts of the men behind the team who were delivering good, clean baseball to Delaware. Still, the team appeared on the verge of collapse before New Haven and the Mets were replaced by Philadelphia and Lancaster which stirred a local rivalry.

Games with Lancaster attracted 1500 and 2500 in a homestand crucial to the team's survival. The series kept the franchise in Wilmington but only 300 fans graced the grounds when the team moved into first place with a 46-39 mark. It was exceedingly frustrating to the backers who saw their team play regularly in front of crowds of 2000 or more in visiting towns.

Injuries undermined the team's pennant drive and Wilmington cascaded down the list to fourth place, finishing at 60-73. In the front office Long lost $1000 while other owners were making as much as $8000 on their investments. Although the year was a failure, the Atlantic League in 1896 was the first minor league season a Wilmington team had completed from start to finish. There would not be a second campaign, however. Long moved the team to Reading in 1897.

The AAs and the BBs

Wilmington entered the 20th century with no professional baseball and no prospects. In 1901 the management of the Brownson Athletic Club formulated a plan for semi-pro baseball that centered around keeping operating expenses down. Players would be paid on a per game basis, all games would be contested on the Union Street grounds in Wilmington with no travel costs, and the team would remain independent of any league. Manager Harry McSwiney scheduled three or four games a week and constantly adjusted the roster to keep the play of the highest caliber.

Wilmington responded. The games were well-patronized and by August Brownson incorporated the team as the Wilmington Baseball Club, operated by the Wilmington Baseball and Amusement Company. McSwiney, so instrumental in reviving baseball in the city, retired to private business and Thomas Roach was retained as a full-time manager. The Wilmington Baseball Club finished the season playing 103 games, winning 60, losing 41 and tying 2.

The success of the Wilmington Baseball Club did not go unnoticed in the local business community. As the team reorganized for the 1902 campaign they were greeted by a new, rival organization. The Wilmington Baseball and Athletic Association incorporated and built new grounds south of the Market Street bridge. South Side Park was a short 5-minute walk from the downtown business area and was convenient to all city rail lines. The grandstand was erected to accommodate an astounding 4000 fans.

Manager Roach of the Wilmington Baseball Club and the Athletic Association's manager Jess Frysinger spent lavishly to acquire top players from all over the east to stock the two independent teams. By the time the season opened both teams had developed loyal followings around Wilmington. Ardent backers sported badges to indicate their support for the Athletic Association, known as the AAs, or the Wilmington Baseball Club, the BBs.

The AAs, with their superior facilities, attracted much of the early attention. Seven thousand fans poured into the new park for Opening Day, flooding the field and necessitating the adoption of special ground rules for the game. Crowds continued to average more than 5000 through the season. Meanwhile the BBs, playing away from the center of town at the Union Street grounds, played to near capacity crowds of 3000, often on the same day. Wilmington had never seen baseball fever like this.

And the fans of the respective teams did not reserve their passions solely for each other. Four hundred followers of the AAs accompanied their team to Chester and when the steamer returned to the Wilmington & Northern wharf a melee broke out between Wilmington and Chester fans. Some Wilmingtonians jumped overboard into the river and others never did disembark. The steamer pulled away to shouts of "Three cheers for the Wilmington AA!" as Chester fans replied by throwing chairs from the deck.

After a 26-19 start the BBs replaced Roach with Curtis Weigland, a hard-hitting middle infielder. Under his leadership the BBs became one of the strongest semi-pro nines in the country, winning 27 of the next 29 games. They reeled off 22 wins in a row, denied of equalling the independent record of 26 by a 4-1 loss to Pottsville in the opening game of a doubleheader. The majority of the games were tightly played affairs that sent the happy fans home in less than 90 minutes.

As the reputation of the BBs grew the AAs matched them win for win. The AAs built their record to 65-18 and went on a 20-game winning romp of their own, led by catcher Harry Barton, the most popular player ever to wear a Wilmington uniform. The AAs were stopped only when Chester notched four runs with two out in the 9th inning to wrest away an 8-7 triumph.

One of the AA victims was the Brandywine nine of West Chester. In September the Brandywines reorganized and started boasting. The two teams danced around terms of a meeting for two weeks, generating great interest in the two towns, until the sports editor of the *Philadelphia Inquirer* arranged a match in that city.

The game was played on a winner-take-all basis, with each side putting up $500. In addition, the victor would

The phenomenal success of the indpendent Wilmington Athletic Association baseball team attracted national attention and spawned souvenirs like this pin.

cart home all the gate receipts. Connie Mack made his field at Twenty-Ninth and Columbia available for only $75. Special trains carried large delegations from West Chester and Wilmington to the game. An enormous crowd of 15,712 paid their way into Shibe Park.

Wilmington tallied in each of the first two innings to grab a 2-1 lead and nursed the tenuous advantage for six more tense innings. In the ninth Newton led off with a double for Brandywine but was doubled off when the next batter lined to second. After a single, the AAs got the last out on a tapper to the mound.

Wilmington partisans swarmed the field carrying the players to the locker room on their shoulders. The fans, equipped with every noisemaking device that could be found, then marched en masse to the Reading Station behind the Philharmonic Band as Wilmington papers were releasing extra editions to announce the 2-1 final.

The owners of the AAs realized a bounty of $4606 from the gate receipts, not including the spoils of the bet. The money was split with 50% going to the owners, the Stirlith brothers, and 50% going to the players and manager. In addition, players claimed to have won an additional $2000 in side bets. The money was carried back to Wilmington in satchels.

Chick Hartley, surely one of the greatest hitters ever produced in Wilmington, pitched the victory. He used his $400 bonus to get married and signed a major league contract. He became disenchanted with the pro game before the season began however and quit baseball. Hartley left Delaware for Philadelphia where he was a policeman on the beat for more than 30 years.

Left out of the frenzied hoopla Weigland of the BBs offered $1000 for a winner-take-all game with the AAs but Frysinger was not interested. Such a confrontation would surely be a duel to the death. The loss of prestige that would shroud the loser could spell financial ruin. As it was the two teams would never meet on the diamond and the continual debate as to which was the better team served to keep interest in both nines at a high pitch.

On the field there was little to choose between the AAs and the BBs. Playing much the same schedule of strong semi-pro teams from Pennsylvania and New Jersey the AAs completed the 1902 season with an 83-34 log; the BBs checked in with an 88-38 mark. The popular local twirler Billy Day led the way for the BBs with 30 wins, six by shutout.

Frysinger was feted nationally in the October 25 edition of *Sporting Life* in an article titled: "Worthy of Promotion: An Independent Manager Who Made a Great Record Last Season." The teams' six wins over major league teams were noted and it was suggested that the manager was destined for a career in the majors. He would, however, die tragically in 1906 at the age of 33 from complications following surgery to remove an appendix.

By 1903 the fervor for the AAs and BBs had lessened not a whit. South Side Park overflowed with 10,500 fans for the first game, the largest crowd ever to witness a baseball game in Delaware. Across town 4500 squeezed onto the Union Street grounds to see the BBs begin play. Each team had an almost complete turnover in personnel but fans quickly adopted new favorites. Both the AAs and BBs started slowly but by midseason each was playing at a .650 clip when suddenly the town was startled to learn the AAs had bought the BBs.

The Stirlith brothers swallowed the Wilmington Baseball Club whole; they purchased the players, the Union Street lease, the uniform and even the charter. The BBs were breaking even but were making no money due to the generous salaries needed to keep top players in Wilmington. Former heavyweight champion John L. Sullivan umpired the last game in the history of the BBs, a shutout win. Their record for 1903 was 54-32; for the three years they stood at 202-111-2, a .645 winning percentage.

The newly merged Wilmington Athletic Association team continued to roll over its opponents, snapping off 31 wins in their final 39 games. With the rivalry dissipated the most talked about moment of the final part of the season was the first home run hit out of South Side Park, one of the most spacious yards in the country. Thomas of Lebanon crushed a ball fully 20 feet over the 350-foot left field wall to make headlines in all the papers. Overall the AA's finished the year at 91-39, featuring 26 shutouts. Everson led the pitchers with 31 wins and Faulkner notched 29 wins, tossing 76 consecutive scoreless innings at one point.

But the AAs had not heard the last of the BBs.

After the season the AAs represented Delaware in the Tri-State Championship in Philadelphia, against Camden from New Jersey and Harrisburg, skippered by their old manager Jess Frysinger, handling Pennsylvania. Harrisburg won the coin toss gaining the bye and Camden and Wilmington tangled in the first game. It was a sloppy affair with the AAs losing 6-5. The death blows were two home runs knocked over the right field fence by Billy Gray - the former Wilmington BB outfielder. After obtaining his services in the buyout the AAs had released Gray as not being good enough to make their club.

The Major Leagues Come To Delaware

The AAs and the BBs both brought big league nines to Delaware, entertaining the likes of the Philadelphia Phillies, Boston Braves and John McGraw's New York Giants. Great sluggers like Honus Wagner, Nap Lajoie and Ed Delahanty performed in exhibition games with the locals before wildly enthusiastic crowds.

After the Philadelphia Athletics won the American League pennant in 1902 Connie Mack invited the AA's to play a benefit game in Philadelphia as part of the victory day parade celebration. The Wilmington team fell behind early but rallied for six runs in the 6th inning to take an 8-7 lead.

The champions quickly regained the advantage to the delight of 11,000 Philly rooters waving white elephants, given out for the occasion. With the score 10-8 Mack brought in his ace hurler, George "Rube" Waddell. Waddell was unquestionably the greatest talent to yet appear in major league baseball but he was as celebrated on his way to the Hall of Fame as much for his childish antics as for his blazing fastball.

Waddell, who was an imposing 6'1" figure on the mound, was said to spend days on the banks of a river fishing when he was supposed to be pitching. "There was delicious humor in many of his vagaries, a vagabond impudence and ingenuousness that made them attractive to the public," the *Columbus Dispatch* explained to its readers. In his 1902 seasn Waddell did not pitch his first game for Mack until June 26 but still won 24 games and paced the league with 210 strikeouts.

In his outing against the AAs Waddell closed out the game by striking out Wilmington's last five hitters, finishing off the final batter after sending his fielders to the bench. It would become part of Waddell's legend that he routinely performed such feats of bravado but even though Rube waved his fielders in against Baltimore and Boston the players never left their positions. Only against Wilmington did the Athletic players leave Waddell alone against the hitter.

The AAs claimed a measure of revenge the next day when the A's came to Wilmington for an exhibition game. Waddell was struck by a line drive on his hand and driven from the game as the AAs went on to down the American League champs 4-2.

Rube Waddell was baseball's first great strikeout pitcher - as he proved in exhibition games in Wilmington.

Flushed with the success of its independent professional team owner Stirlith and manager Frysinger entered the AAs into a loose aggregation of clubs known as the Tri-State League. Joining Wilmington in the new venture were nines from Camden, Williamsport, Altoona, Lebanon, York and Harrisburg. For the next decade Wilmington's professional baseball fortunes would be cast with this sometimes maddening, sometimes remarkable and always resourceful organization.

A crowd estimated at over 10,000 turned out for the season opener at South Side Park. The players paraded to the grounds in a special trolley car behind the Philharmonic band. Upon entering the park they were greeted with fully ten minutes of applause. Rising to the occasion, the AAs rallied for two runs in the ninth inning to win a 7-6 thriller.

The town buzzed with the goings-on "across the bridge." The lowest admission prices in the circuit, 20 cents and 10 cents extra for the grandstand, brought Delawareans "league ball at amateur prices." But the ills that would haunt the Tri-State League like a prolonged batting slump were already fomenting. On June 18 Camden, which had won only four of its first two dozen games, disbanded. Wilmington, despite a winning record, was thrust into next-to-last place.

More insidious was the escalation of salaries among the teams. As independent teams with no league regulation players jumped routinelyto the highest bidder. Salaries became so great that some major leaguers jumped into the Tri-State League. With its low admissions and a lack of attractive Saturday home dates Wilmington couldn't compete for the best players.

The AAs were built on speed but pitching woes spawned a rash of one-run losses that condemned Wilmington to last place. They slumped to 27-41 and the owners considered transferring the entire York team to Delaware but they stuck with the original squad. Unable and unwilling to hire replacements for stars spirited away by rival clubs Frysinger found himself with only nine players to field and five of them were pitchers.

For the first time in history a league cancelled Wilmington home games for fear of no attendance. The team limped home with a final record of 41-61. Wilmington had begun the 1904 season as the best-paying city in the Tri-State League. But after a year of raiding and warring against other teams there was little thought of re-joining for 1905.

Baseball rumors of the upcoming season swirled around Wilmington for the entire off-season. Fans were anxious for the new baseball campaign but had no pro league representative. The Tri-State League - now minus its New Jersey and Delaware representatives - kicked off with six Pennsylvania teams in the fold. Wire reports indicated things had not changed in the tumultuous circuit: "So far only three of the umpires of the Tri-State League have been assaulted this season." And it was only May 7.

In early June Wilmington was summoned to replace the faltering Lebanon franchise in the Tri-State. Wilmington was forced to assume Lebanon's 4-28 record but they jumped out with three wins, including one against defending champion York, and crowds of three and four thousand supported the team.

But soon the AAs' play began to approach its predecessor, tumbling to 21-67. They were 14 games out of next-to-last place. The visiting towns weren't enticing enough to pull fans and the amateur games began outdrawing the Tri-State League. In an extremely tight pennant race Wilmington sold its last three home games to York. It was a legal move but the league grumblings increased when Wilmington surrendered two runs in the bottom of the ninth to lose the series opener. Then the AAs shocked the Yorksters 3-2 and 11-6 in a doubleheader to deliver the Tri-State flag to Williamsport.

There was no Tri-State League ball for Wilmington in 1906 but the next year the Association joined the National Baseball Commission in an attempt to protect players and keep salaries down with a cap. Wilmington was regarded as the linchpin in the organization and was awarded a majority of the attractive Saturday home dates. The 25- man team left for spring practice in Portsmouth, Virginia on March 30 while enthusiasm back home in Delaware was higher than any season yet. South Side Park was fitted with new bleachers and the grandstand was improved to feature folding opera chairs. Seating capacity was increased to 6000 and every seat was filled for Opening Day.

Despite the heftiest payroll in the league the Wilmington "Peaches" stumbled to a 1-9 start, swatting the ball at an anemic .182 clip. Tension mounted on and off the field. When outfielder Rube Vinson, a former American League outfielder and Dover native, was tossed out of a South Side Park game in a bellicose argument with an umpire he waved encouragement to several hundred fans who stormed the field. It was the ugliest incident in Wilmington baseball history; eight policeman were required to escort the besieged official from the grounds. Vinson was suspended and soon traded but the tone for the season had been established.

The Peaches cascaded to a lowly 3-16 as the press bemoaned hard luck and bad umpiring calls. Owner Chris Connelly changed managers and attempted to strengthen his roster with former major league talent. Hank Mathewson took the hill for Wilmington but hardly invoked images of his Hall-of-Fame pitching brother Christy when he didn't survive the first inning, yielding four runs and never appearing again.

The dismal performance of the Wilmington Peaches left fans in a surly mood. Dover native native Rube Vinson incited a riot when he called for fan support in an argument with an umpire.

The team continued to struggle and changed managers again. This time popular catcher Mike Grady from Kennett Square took the helm. Grady had enjoyed an eleven-year career in the major leagues, compiling a .294 lifetime batting average and smacking 35 home runs in the dead ball era. But he is best remembered for making four errors on a single play while filling in as a third baseman for the New York Giants in 1899.

His time with the Peaches more resembled his follies as an infielder than his triumphs as a backstop. Grady pushed the Peaches all the way to 5th place but they remained mired there for the rest of the year. Through all the travails the fans continued to support the team, although many were calling for even Grady's scalp.

The season ended in farce as Johnstown and Wilmington played the league finale in 57 minutes to get the season over with, not running the bases and being purposely put out. The crowd of nearly 2000 left totally disgusted with its 43-79 team. But even the rancid exhibitions of 1907 couldn't dissuade Wilmington baseball fanatics from their game.

Eight teams began the 1908 Tri-State campaign and Wilmington actually started 16-16. Then a two-week downturn sent the Peaches plummeting into the familiar environs of last place. They captured only 4 of 26 August games but attendance still averaged nearly 1500. When stadium rent was raised to $25 a game the owners decided to play out the season on the road, ending the longest continuous stretch of professional baseball in Wilmington history.

The "homeless team" stumbled in as the league's tailender, dropping 87 games against only 40 wins. They were 42 games out of first. Another several thousand dollars in the red, the owners decided to abandon the Tri-State League. In four years the Peaches had finished last, last, next-to-last, and last - despite being the highest paid team in the league most of that span. Never at any point in the season had the team reached higher than fifth place. Their four-year mark was 157-318, winning barely more than three of every ten games.

Wilmington could not remain out of league ball for long. With over 110,000 people it was by far the largest unattached city on the east coast. The economy was booming and amateur games were always well-attended. As a baseball town there was no more attractive or eligible temptress to potential owners than Wilmington.

By 1911 plans were ready to re-join the Tri-State. The fans were waiting; 2500 showed up for the season opener on a bitter April afternoon. The Wilmington Chicks, as they were now known, displayed pitching woes from the start. They returned from a bad road trip and committed ten errors. It was reported that some of the misplays looked intentional and the games were called "disgusting articles of baseball."

When a former Wilmington hurler twirled a 5-hitter against the Chicks the team was savaged in the local press: "Pitcher Daly,

who, when with Wilmington was banged all over the field by every old club that came along and who since joining Altoona has also been hit to all corners of the lot, simply played with the locals yesterday." As the team began playing better the hitting stopped and the Chicks settled once again into the basement.

Still, 3000 fans turned out for Saturday home games and even a modest four-game winning streak stirred local passions. But the team seemed jinxed on and off the field. When Weeks, the team's best all-around outfielder, left the team because his mother was ill it was noted that, "It is seldom that a ball player gives up baseball entirely because his mother is ill." Between the white lines the Chicks suffered through an unbearable 49 one-run defeats.

They finished the 1911 campaign in last place, 12.5 games from 7th and 39 games away from first place. The owners Peter Cassiday and Thomas Brown admitted

JACKSON, BALTIMORE

Jim Jackson, a rare college man in the early days of baseball, turned the Wilmington entry in the Tri-State League, into a winning nine.

they got off to a bad start by following poor advice on securing players. It was the worst year ever financially for any Wilmington team in the Tri-State League but the owners proved their mettle as sports- men by not resorting to benefits and "$1 games" - where the owners asked a dollar admission rather than 25 cents - to recoup losses.

The 1912 season held the dual promise of a new beginning: a switch to the revitalized Union Street grounds and the hiring of a new manager who had apprenticed under the greatest manager of his day, John McGraw - Jimmy Jackson. Jackson, a hard-hitting centerfielder, kept the team bobbing around .500 for the entire season, finishing in fifth place at 58-55.

Strangely, as the team improved the fans became apathetic. In the midst of an 8-game winning streak fewer than 500 people dotted the stands. The main attraction at Union Street seemed to be the Bull Durham tobacco advertising sign at the park. The company awarded 72 bags of tobacco for any home run and $50 for any homer striking the bullseye. For the season 2500 round-trippers were hit in professional baseball resulting in 180,000 bags of tobacco. There were only 208 bulls-eyes and none of the 29 balls hit out of the Wilmington park plunked the Bull Durham bull.

The next year Jackson had his troops at the head of the Tri-State list from Opening Day. Combining timely hitting and solid pitching the Chicks raced to a 6-1 record and were out of first place for only 24 hours the entire season. With 30 games left the Chicks had gouged a 7-game lead and the owners dug a five-foot hole in centerfield for the pennant pole. When they clinched the pennant thousands packed the streets of Wilmington to enjoy "Noise Day" as 1000 athletes from every baseball club in the city marched to the baseball park.

The 1914 season looked much the same as the Chicks leaped out to a 26-18 mark and first place but the Chicks, the Tri-State League and all of minor league baseball were suffering. A third major league, the Federal League, had siphoned off the cream of the minor league talent, especially from a Class B league like the Tri-State. The quality of ball suffered and the fans noticed.

The Chicks were forced to go with younger players as Jackson moaned that, "the men sent to me are weaker than some on the town lots." When clean-up hitter Jackson went down with a broken hand the irreversible decline began. The owners fell behind on player salaries and the team limped home fourth at 47-63.

The Federal League did not survive but it succeeded in killing off the Tri-State League. After nearly a decade of frustration Wilmington had finally fielded a winner only to have the league fold.

The team that finally won the Tri-State pennant - just before the league collapsed.

The Reading nine - here pictured from the Tri-State League in 1908 - was a perennial rival of the Wilmington baseballers in many leagues.

Minor League Baseball - The Union League (1908)

The Union League held promise as the strongest minor league ever to play in Wilmington. Its tight geographic boundaries with Brooklyn to the north, Washington to the south and Reading to the west promised economical travel and the inclusion of Philadelphia, Baltimore, Washington and New York gave it the greatest population base outside the major leagues.

The Wilmington ownership leased the Riverview grounds at 29th and Market and spared no expense in outfitting the park. Bleachers to accommodate nearly 3000 extra fans were installed and 1200 seats with backs were placed around the infield. An innovative two rows of box seats lined the perimeter of the field. Between the lines the first grass infield in Delaware was groomed to perfection.

The new Wilmington team bested Delaware College and the Philadelphia Phillies in exhibitions and more than 4000 fans poured out of Wilmington down Market Street for the gala season opener. Within a month the team was firmly entrenched in first place with a 13-5 start.

But the enterprise was losing money from the start. The Riverview grounds just seemed to be too far out of the city for most fans, especially for a brand of ball the now sophisticated Wilmington baseball fan could recognize as decidedly inferior. On May 26 the team failed to receive its wages and broke off a trip to Brooklyn. The next day the first place team disbanded. A week later the Union League, stripped of all its preseason expectations, dissolved as well.

Minor League Baseball - The Atlantic League (1916)

Once again the lure of a town of 100,000 people without baseball proved irresistible to area sportsmen. Dr. Leon Van Horn of Philadelphia bought a Class B Atlantic League franchise for Wilmington. A nickname contest was held and the name "Diamonds" was chosen for the new team but fan response was only luke-warm.

After two dozen games the Diamonds had gone through three managers and only three players remained from Opening Day. There were many rain-outs and the other teams in the circuit - Pottsville, Paterson, Reading, Allentown and Easton - were not big draws. With the team 11-12 the players had not been paid and took possession of the gate, splitting receipts among the 16 men. Five games later the Diamonds were gone, only four days before the very shaky Atlantic League disappeared altogether.

The first Delaware town outside Wilmington to enjoy minor league baseball was Laurel. Together with five Maryland towns - Pocomoke City, Crisfield, Cambridge, Salisbury and Parksley - Laurel was a charter member of the Eastern Shore League, a "baby" Class D minor league. The longest bus ride in this lowest rung of professional baseball was a short jump of 85 miles. There were no overnight stays and all ballparks were within walking distance of the center of town.

In Laurel, a crossroads town of 4000, a tentacular stone road from the new DuPont Highway aided baseball fans from neighboring Delaware towns to the north in attending the games. The inaugural campaign for the Shore League was fraught with unpleasantries. Open betting at the games hindered attendance, especially by women and families. Attacks on umpires, always a distasteful part of early-day baseball on the Peninsula, were frequent and violent. At Crisfield a fan brutally beat an umpire while a game was in progress and there were several incidents in Laurel as well.

On the field the Laurel Chicks challenged for the lead early but were never able to get back to the break-even mark after reaching 5-5. The Chicks featured only two Delaware boys - Dorsey Donohoe and Dal Culver of Seaford - but were well-supported by the town. They won 16 of their final 25 games to finish fourth at 34-35.

In 1923 league officials took firm steps to curb its gambling and violence problems. Expansion brought the Dover Dobbins and Milford Sand Snipes into the circuit. At the state capital a new park with a grandstand for several thousand spectators was built at Ninth Street and Little Creek Road. There was a parking lot for 500 automobiles and 2000 turned out for the Dobbins' home opener.

The 1923 season started well for Dover, Laurel and Milford. The Delaware troika joined defending champion Parksley in a 4-way tie for top honors at 16-13. Play was

The Eastern Shore League did not lack for talent in the 1920s, as witnessed by Mickey Cochrane and Jimmy Foxx. League management, however, was not so skilled.

competitive throughout the league and fans were treated to good ball from the rookies who for the most part were not allowed by Eastern Shore rules to have been in the professional game before.

When Wilmington once again proved incapable of supporting pro baseball the Milford Sand Snipes bought their star players and manager. The maneuver backfired when Milford was ruled to have used several players from a higher class than Class D. The Sand Snipes forfeited nine games and disbanded on July 4.

After the holiday attendance slumped in all the Eastern Shore towns, save Dover and Salisbury. The Dobbins, led by a 20-year old future Hall-of-Famer fresh out of Boston University named Mickey Cochrane, reeled off 12 straight wins to capture the pennant at 50-23. Cochrane played under the alias "Frank King" since he was still on scholarship to the Terriers. Laurel improved to third place at 42-30. In post-season play Dover whipped Martinsburg, West Virginia of the Blue Ridge League four games to two in the "Five State Series."

The 1924 Eastern Shore League race was one of the most exciting in professional baseball history. For the first half of the season Dover dominated with a 25-14 log but the Dobbins' hitters slumped and they dropped into fourth place. With six games remaining only three games separated the top five teams.

The lone Shore League entry out of the pennant sweepstakes was Easton, under the direction of the old Philadelphia Athletics star Frank "Home Run" Baker. Easton started 2-22 despite the presence of 18-year old homeboy Jimmy Foxx behind the plate. Baker called his young catcher, "the most promising player I have ever seen." Foxx, destined to be the greatest slugger of his time behind Babe Ruth, could not pull his team from the cellar in his first year of professional ball. He finished at .296 with 10 home runs in 260 at-bats.

Dover stopped hitting altogether and Laurel came up short in the 1924 stretch drive. The Dobbins' team batting average was a microscopic .229 for the season and they connected on a league-low 43 home runs. Things were worse at Laurel; the owners were $2400 in debt and sold all its players to Salisbury as the franchise dropped out of the league.

Carrying on as Delaware's sole Eastern Shore League representative Dover struggled through a mediocre 1925 campaign but once again challenged for top honors in 1926. It was a troubled year on the Peninsula as five teams were found guilty of class violations - using players too experienced for the rookie league.

The Dobbins held to a four-game lead late in the season when they were hit with a 23-game penalty. Dover protested and the ruling was overturned, re-establishing the Dobbins in first place. But other franchises pressed the issue until Dover was stripped of 23 games again and the season ended with management still offering evidence in defense of the legality of its roster.

Disgusted with league policies Dover dropped out of the Eastern Shore League after the 1926 season. The league resisted obituaries for one more year before a lack of fans closed down professional baseball on the Delmarva Peninsula.

The Shaugnessey Playoffs

Playoffs are so woven into the fabric of sports that it feels like they naturally existed from the beginning. Not so.

Professional baseball has always been about one thing - money. Especially in the low minor leagues where short-pocketed owners could not long survive spiraling costs and sparse crowds. This was especially troubling when teams would fall hopelessly behind in the year-long pennant chase.

Enter Frank "Shag" Shaugnessy, an innovative football coach who introduced the option play at Yale University. Shaugnessy also got into a few games in the Philadelphia Athletics and Washington Senators outfields in the early 1900s. Shaughnessy managed 19 seasons in the minor leagues and in 1933 was helming the International League. it was his idea in 1933 to pit the league's top four teams against one another in a multi-game series - usually a best-of-seven to pad the coffers even further.

The Shaughnessy playoff system was embraced around minor league baseball. The National Hockey League was the first to use playoffs at the major league level and today, while Shaughnessy's name has been long forgotten, playoffs are ubiquitous in sports.

Nowadays, the best team in baseball's regular season is quickly cast aside should that success not translate into wins throughout the playoffs. But in the early years the playoffs were a novelty and it was still the regular season title that carried the most prestige. This became especially true as more and more pennant-winning teams expired in the Shaugnessey Playoff system. The Wilmington Blue Rocks, for instance, won three pennants but only once completed the season with a playoff championship.

Regular season titleists were especially vulnerable in the first round of the playoff whirl. Dover's best team, assembled in 1940, after capturing the flag with a .600 winning percentage, exited quietly in the semi-finals. Conversely, the year before a third-place Dover nine embarrassed Federalsburg, which had finished the year nearly 20 games ahead, 14-3, 12-8 and 13-1.

Increasingly these playoffs came to be regarded for what they were - money-making exhibitions. The fad faded in the 1930s and 1940s until it was revived by the proliferation of expansion teams in major league sports.

For good or ill, Shag Shaughnessy is the man responsible for the playoff system that determines sport champions.

The concept of the farm system breathed new life into the minor leagues in the 1930s. Feeder teams designed to funnel talent to the big league clubs blanketed the country. In Wilmington in 1940 the Class B Interstate League franchise became the first farm team wholly owned by Connie Mack and his Philadelphia A's. For the next 13 years the Wilmington Blue Rocks would compile one of the most enviable records in the history of minor league baseball.

For seven consecutive years Wilmington finished first or second; only twice did the Rocks miss the Interstate playoffs, reserved for the top four teams. Four times the Rocks brought the Governors Cup, awarded to the playoff winner, home to Delaware.

A newspaper contest was used to select the team nickname and over 5000 entries poured in. "Blue Rocks" was chosen after a three-day struggle with the runner-up "Colonists." The winner was 73-year old Robert Miller who remembered the famed blue granite of his youth along the Brandywine River. He received a season pass for his prize, as did Wesley Taylor who submitted "Blue Rock."

On the field the Rocks were guided by old A's star pitcher and soon to be Hall-of-Famer, Chief Bender. Seven thousand

Charles Albert "Chief" Bender was part Chippewa Indian. He won 212 big league games and was the first manager of the Wilmington Blue Rocks.

fans jammed Wilmington Park for the first game with Trenton and watched the Blue Rocks triumph 3-1 behind a six-hitter by Philadelphia's Sam Lowry.

For the first half of the 140-game season the Rocks struggled. In the first 50 games Bender auditioned 50 players for the blue and white. With Wilmington mired in fourth place at 29-28 Bender was replaced. Under new skipper Charlie Berry the Blue Rocks ran off nine straight wins and spurted to second place at the finish, although they were quickly eliminated by Lancaster in the playoffs.

Centerfielder Elmer Valo won the 1940 batting title at .364. He returned the next year before graduating to Philadelphia and becoming the best player ever produced for the A's by the Blue Rocks. But the biggest success in Wilmington was at the gate. The Blue Rocks established a new Class B attendance record in 1940 with 145,643.

The 1941 edition of the Rocks started strongly, building a three-game lead at 30-14 before injuries slowed the team. Despite a final mark of 64-62 Wilmington finished fifth, one spot out of postseason play. The 1942 race boiled down to only the Blue Rocks and the Hagerstown Owls, with the rest of the league 11 games back.

In August the Rocks reeled off 13 straight wins, including a minor league record five consecutive shutouts. The regular season ended with Wilmington 1/2 game short of the pennant when their final game was rained out. But the Blue Rocks' starting pitching overwhelmed their opponents in the playoffs for the Governors Cup. Allentown fell three games to one in the semi-finals bringing the expected match-up with Hagerstown. Certainly not helped by a team station wagon overturning on the journey between Delaware and Maryland, the Owls managed only ten runs as they were outscored by the Blue Rocks 31-10 in losing four games to one.

The World War II years were characterized by big hitting and crowd-pleasing offense - and a change of ownership. Before the 1943 season the fences at Wilmington Park were moved in considerably - especially in right field where one of the longest pokes in professional baseball was reduced from 390 feet to 320 feet. In 1944 the Rocks slugged at a .285 clip - and finished 5th in the six-team league in team batting average. Altogether there were thirty .300 hitters in the Interstate League in 1944.

Prior to the 1944 season Bob Carpenter, Jr., whose father owned the Philadelphia Phillies, completed arrangements to take control of the Blue Rocks as well. Carpenter, an ex-Duke footballer and accomplished badminton player, had been President of the Wilmington club from its inception and had purchased 50% of the team stock with his father years earlier. From this point the Wilmington Blue Rocks would be a Phillies farm team.

With the war over, Wilmington was ready for baseball. More than four thousand turned out for the season opener to see the Rocks whip 1945 champion Lancaster 17-1. And the fans didn't stop coming until a record 172,531 passed through the turnstiles. And the Rocks put on quite a show. Their final home record was 50-19 and they never lost a home series.

In mid-season Wilmington went on a 12-game winning tear to build a 6 1/2 game lead. They galloped to the Interstate League pennant by 11 full games, finishing 34 games over .500. The playoffs were a bitter disappointment, however, for the best regular season team in Rocks' history. Wilmington barely escaped Hagerstown in a seven-game semi-final before being routed in the finals. In 1947 the Blue Rocks started slowly, wallowing in last place after 33 games. But the pieces for Wilmington's most memorable team were assembling. Eighteen-year old wonder pitcher Curt Simmons came on board and the Rocks won 21 of 30. Ed Sanicki, the greatest power hitter in the history of the Interstate League hit home runs in five straight games on his way to a record 37. Sanicki, Ed Murphy and Jesse Levan all drove in 100 runs for the 1947 Rocks.

The spurt couldn't pull Wilmington all the way to first place but they swept through the playoffs to win the Governors Cup. All

Wilmington Park was constructed in three months to greet the opening of the 1940 Interstate League. The tab for the ballyard on Governor Printz Avenue at East 30th Street was $185,000. The grandstands sheltered 4,454 fans with box seats for 546. Another 1,850 could watch from the bleachers and 4,500 more could watch from outside the grandstand. It was a pitcher-friendly park with a high wall in right field that was only cleared four times in a dozen years of Interstate League play. Wilmington Park also hosted boxing matches and football games. After the Blue Rocks folded in 1952 the park stood for eleven more years before being demolished in 1963.

year attendance records fell: the single game record of 7062 was set for Simmons' debut and the league regular season mark fell with 141,125. Another 35,000 came to 30th and Governor Printz Boulevard for the playoffs. Attendance was so rabid in 1947 there were rumors that the American League St. Louis Browns might re-locate in Delaware.

1947 was the pinnacle. Afterward Wilmington continued to field strong teams with star players. There were Interstate pennants in 1948 and 1950 and Governors Cups in 1950 and 1951. Outfielder Dan Schell and pitcher Niles Jordan, who piled up 18 wins before being called up to the majors with an entire month to go, followed Sanicki (1947) and Jack Brittin (1949) as league Most Valuable Players. But fewer and fewer people were coming out to the ballpark to see them.

By 1949 the Blue Rocks were resorting to pleas in the local newspapers: "Keep Baseball in Wilmington" and "PLEASE! Support the Blue Rocks." Attendance at some games fell as low as 379. The Rocks, despite being the largest city in the league, finished 7th in attendance. Bob Carpenter proclaimed, "As long as I'm with the Phillies there will always be a Blue Rocks. I'm sure we can bring Wilmington back as a good baseball town. I'm still convinced that television murdered the club this season but I believe the novelty of TV will have worn away by next summer."

It had not. By June an angry Carpenter declared, "I'd move the club right now if there were some place to move it." He vowed that 1950 would be the final year for the Rocks. All the while his own pennant-contending Phillies were cannibalizing its tiny farm team. A Delmarva Day special train ran several times a year from Delmar to Philadelphia, making several stops through the state on its way north. A round trip train ticket and good seat at Connie Mack Stadium was only $6.35 from Delmar; $3.00 from Wilmington. Worse, it was only 60 cents for kids to see big league baseball while it cost 50 cents to get into Wilmington Park.

There were other woes as well. The Blue Rocks resorted to a free Fan Appreciation Night and got 5181 for a Monday night game. But no schedules were handed out and ticket booths to sell tickets to future games were closed. And the next night turned into "Fan Depreciation Night" when an advertised doubleheader turned out to be only a single 8:30 game and fans arriving for the 5:35 start were greeted by locked gates.

Attendance for the 1950 champion Blue Rocks was just 38,678, an average of only 774. With the Blue Rocks all but gone a Citizens Baseball Committee raised over 62,000 ticket pledges to persuade Carpenter to keep the team in Wilmington. After all the off-season hullabaloo only 2800 of an expected 6000 showed up for Opening Night 1951. By the end of the season - another championship outing for the Blue Rocks who waltzed through 8 of 9 playoff games - less than 50% of the pledges had been honored. Still, the slight increase in attendance to 43,135 was enough support for Carpenter to give the Rocks a last gasp.

It was not much of a gasp. Average attendance dropped below 500 a game. At a July 4 weekend game only 266 fans clambered around the 7000-seat stadium. In a lone highlight, on Labor Day the Blue Rocks, the most successful team in Interstate League history, won game number 1000. There would be but three more.

The ending for the Blue Rocks was nothing if not bizarre. Fighting for the final playoff spot the Rocks trailed 5-1 in the 4th inning of the second game of a Saturday night doubleheader. With a midnight curfew lurking manager Lee Riley, whose son Pat would later do some coaching of his own, attempted to stall in order to get the game replayed the next day. The umpire would tolerate none of Riley's shenanigans and forfeited the game to Allentown, ushering the Blue Rocks out of existence.

Simmons and Roberts

The two best pitchers in the history of the Blue Rocks were Curt Simmons and Robin Roberts. Both overwhelmed Class B competition and neither spent an entire year in Wilmington, each graduating directly to the parent Phillies where they starred for over a decade.

Curt Simmons was an original "bonus baby" - a high school player who sold his services to the highest bidder. A Pennsylvania schoolboy phenom, Simmons tossed two no-hitters and struck out 23 in one game in his senior season. When he whiffed 11 Phillies in an exhibition - after impressing scouts by making his own "book" on the major leaguers in batting practice - Simmons became the most coveted pitching prospect in the land. Bob Carpenter landed him for the Phillies with a signing bonus speculated wildly by the press at between $25,000 and $100,000.

Simmons joined the Blue Rocks after high school graduation in 1947 and a record Wilmington crowd of 7062 turned out for his debut. The young southpaw started nervously by walking the first two hitters but settled down to complete a 7-hit, 7-1 win, losing his shutout in the 9th inning. He struck out 11.

Simmons continued to dominate the Interstate League for the rest of the summer, winding up 13-5. In the playoff finals Simmons won two games including a crucial 14-strikeout performance in Game 6 to prime the Blue Rocks for the 1947 Governor's Cup.

Simmons started the 1948 campaign in Philadelphia but another "bonus baby" was in Wilmington to take his place. Robin Roberts was signed out of Michigan State University where his 5-4 record belied a talent that spawned a heated bidding war among major league scouts. The Phillies lured the big, shy righthander East for a reported $25,000.

Roberts was the sensation of the Phillies spring camp in 1948 and manager Ben Chapman seethed when told the fireballer was being seasoned in Wilmington. Roberts was none too pleased either but he did not sulk. He struck out 8 of the first 10 hitters he faced in the Blue Rocks' opener. Staked to a 19-run lead after a 10-run second inning Roberts dropped into cruise control and, like Simmons, lost a shutout in the 9th. On a cold, blustery April day opposing hitters were clearly in no mood to deal with Roberts' nasty stuff. Among his 17 strikeouts, one off the Interstate League record, were 8 called third strikes.

A 4-hitter followed, and a 3-hitter, and a 1-hitter. He pitched an 8-hitter over 15 innings in a 2-2 tie. Wildness finally made Robby vulnerable for one game but he fired back with a 3-hitter and 4-hitter and tied the single game strikeout mark with 18. Finally, in June the Phillies and a Hall-of-Fame career could dally in Wilmington no longer. His final Blue Rocks log: 9 wins and one loss, 96 2/3 innings pitched and only 54 hits and 29 walks. His 121 strikeouts would lead the Interstate League for another six weeks.

The day Roberts left Wilmington a third Phillies "bonus baby" arrived. Hugh Frank Radcliffe struck out 25 in his final high school game in Georgia and two weeks later he had $40,000 in the bank and a Blue Rocks uniform on his back. But lightning would not strike Carpenter and his Phillies a third time. Radcliffe left his first start in the seventh inning trailing 5-0. He finished the 1948 season with a 7-3 mark but averaged nearly a walk an inning. The next year he disappeared into the netherlands of minor league baseball. Unlike his predecessors Simmons and Roberts, Hugh Frank Radcliffe never pitched an inning in the major leagues.

Minor League Baseball - The Carolina League (1993-)

On April 16, 1993 minor league baseball came back to Delaware after its longest absence since the game was introduced to the state some 110 years earlier. More than forty years had buried past failures and disappointments before new optimistic owners. The Blue Rocks were back on the field.

This new edition played in the Single A Carolina League and was stocked by the Kansas City Royals. They gamboled in a modern multi-use $7million facility which rose from an old shipyard at the foot of Madison Street. And they won with the regularity of their Wilmington ancestors. The 1993 Blue Rocks rolled through the first half of the Carolina League Northern Division with a 44-25 record.

The Royals promoted seven Blue Rocks at the midseason break, triggering a ten-game losing skein early in the second half. Wilmington struggled home 28-39 but upset the Frederick Keys 11-0 and 3-0 in the first round of the playoffs to win the Northern Division flag.

The Blue Rocks lost in the finals, three games to one, to Winston-Salem. But it was the only disappointment in an otherwise glorious return to minor league baseball. During the year 5,400-seat Legends Stadium was 93% occupied. The home attendance of 332,132 was the 19th best among 200 minor league teams.

Their sophomore season was an even greater triumph for the Blue Rocks. They rumbled through the regular season with a Carolina League-best 94-44 record, winning both halves of the Northern Division split season. In the championship series Wilmington battered Winston-Salem in three straight games to capture the 1994 Carolina League title. The final 7-3 clincher was achieved before a stadium record crowd of 7,087.

The Blue Rocks added league titles in 1996, 1998 and 1999. Success on the field has been fleeting since but the franchise has been a staple in the community for 23 seasons and counting - twice as long as any previous Delaware professional franchise.

To date, the Blue Rocks have retired three player numbers: Johnny Damon (18), the Royals Minor League Player of the Year in 1994 who banged out 2,769 major league hits; Carlon Beltran (36), the Americna League Rookie of the Year in 1999; and Mike Sweeney (33) who swatted 215 major league home runs and was inducted into the Kansas City Royals Hall of Fame.

The Blue Rocks celebrate their 1994 Carolina League championship.

The First Delawareans Make The Big Leagues

In the late 1880s the first wave of Delawareans began to make their mark in major league baseball. Most of these boys were local pitchers as big league teams were always on the look-out for new arms - any one of which could dominate a league in a day when a good starting pitcher would throw 500 innings a season.

Ellsworth Cunningham, who was born in 1865 and grew up playing ball in Wilmington's Ninth Ward, attracted attention as a schoolboy in Moline, Illinois and was signed by the Brooklyn team of the American Association in 1887. He pitched only three games in Washington Park but re-surfaced the next year in Baltimore where he started 51 games, going 22-29.

Cunningham was a serviceable big league pitcher for the next decade until 1898 when he emerged as the National League's leading hurler. In that seminal season he won 28 games and lost only 15 for a 9th place Louisville team that suffered through a 70-81 season. That year Bert, who had walked 201 batters in 1890, developed into a control artist, surrendering little more than one free pass a game.

As a reward for his yeoman work for Louisville the 34-year old Cunningham signed a $3000 contract with Chicago in 1900 but pitched in only nine games for the Cubbies before leaving baseball with a career mark of 142-167. He went on to become the first major league umpire from Delaware, umping four years, including one in the National League before settling into a career selling typewriters in Wilmington.

Billy Day was a popular amateur pitcher around Wilmington who starred with the Americus Club before signing with the Philadelphia Phillies as a 22-year old in 1889. Day possessed a good fastball and a great drop - and a questionable idea of where either pitch was going. In his major league debut he walked ten and struck out 11. Day compiled a 1-10 log for his two years in the National League but returned to Wilmington where he was a leading local pitcher for nearly two decades.

Also in 1889 the Phillies crosstown rival, the Athletics, secured the services of another Delaware pitcher - *John McMahon*. McMahon began playing first base and pitching for the Rose Hill team of Henry Clay Village before gaining a trial with Philadelphia. The 21-year old rookie won 16 games and the *Philadelphia Record* tabbed him as one of the coming star pitchers in the country.

The reporter proved to be a good judge of talent. "Sadie" McMahon won 36 and 34 games the next two years, working over 500 innings each season and becoming baseball's highest paid pitcher earning the princely sum of $4200 a year. He went on to win 139 games in the next five years, toiling mostly for Baltimore, before his arm wore down. After retiring McMahon scouted for his old teammate John McGraw until 1925, uncovering, among many others, the slugging Hack Wilson. He remained a colorful baseball character around Wilmington for more than 50 years.

Most players were signed after building enviable local records but in the small towns of Delaware talented players sometimes went unnoticed. One day in 1892, after a game in Baltimore, colorful St. Louis Browns owner Chris Von der Ahe, the Charlie Finley of his day, was eating in a restaurant bemoaning his team's tepid play. A slender youth, "of rather countrified appearance," presented himself to the baseball magnate and asked for an engagement as a Browns pitcher. Von der Ahe was taken by the young man's coolness and tried him out the next morning. He liked what he saw and put him in against Baltimore that afternoon. *Dick Hawke* tossed a 4-hitter for the victory.

The 22-year old Hawke was well known to Delaware baseball fans, having played on nearly every local team of note for seven or eight years. Dick and his brother John comprised a formidable pitching-catching battery able to switch positions easily with no loss of effectiveness. Dick Hawke stayed in the big leagues for three years, finishing at 32-31.

Delaware Major Leaguers

Pete Cassidy (1896-1897). There is not much to Pete Cassidy's career beyond two part-time years in the 1890s as a utility infielder but the Wilmington native made baseball history off the field. His first year in 1896, as a 23-year old with Louisville, yielded an unremarkable .212 batting average but before the season could get into full swing Cassidy had suffered a wrist injury. Doctors could not determine exactly what was causing the problem.

To make a diagnosis the medics gave Cassidy an X-ray on April 7, which had just been used for medical imaging for the first time less than six months previously. They discovered a dangling piece of bone which was fixed with surgery. Today magnetic resonance imaging (MRI) is as much a part of a ballplayer's toolkit as a batting glove and Delaware's Pete Cassidy was the first to receive an X-ray.

Happy Jack Townsend (1901-1906). Jack Townsend built his reputation pitching for the town founded by his family. He left Washington College for minor league ball in Chester where he hit .401 while he compiled a 35-5 record on the mound. In 1901 "Happy Jack" joined a strong Philadelphia Phillie team featuring three Hall-of-Famers in the line-up. Townsend enjoyed a fine rookie season, winning ten and losing six for the National League runners-up.

Like most of his teammates Townsend jumped to the American League in 1902, gutting the Phillie team. Jack signed on with the Washington Senators who quickly sunk to the bottom of the championship standings. In four years toiling in the nation's capital Townsend lost 69 games against only 22 wins. When he left baseball in 1906 Townsend's 35-81 lifetime mark was the worst record of any pitcher in the 20th century with more than 100 decisions. Clearly Jack Townsend earned his nickname off the baseball field.

Harry Hoch (1908, 1914-1915). In an era when most ballplayers were hard-bitten characters, Harry Hoch was quite an anomaly - he was not only educated but even attended Dickinson Law School in the offseason. Naturally the Woodside native picked up the nickname "Schoolmaster." Hoch broke in with the Philadelphia Phillies in 1908 and won his first two games, one an 11-inning, 2-0 shutout. But he lost his next game to the Boston Braves and never pitched for the Phillies again.

He returned to the minor leagues and enjoyed several successful campaigns before earning a trial with the St. Louis Browns in 1914. In limited duty over the next two seasons Hoch was 0-6. It was time to fall back on that other career. He remained a Delaware attorney until 1962.

Hans Lobert (1903, 1905-1917). Like many players of German heritage John Bernard Lobert quickly became known as Hans. The immortal Honus Wagner was one and he called Lobert "Hans Number 2." The Wilmington-born Hans Lobert may not have been Wagner's equal on the ballfield but he wasn't far from it.

Lobert was known for his speed afoot and once set a record by circling the bases in 13 4/5 seconds. He was once even pitted against a racehorse in a sprint around the bases before a game. He sped out of Delaware almost as fast, leaving at the age of one when his father, a cabinetmaker on Justison Street, took a job in Williamsport, Pennsylvania. Lobert played parts of 14 years with five of the eight National League teams, compiling 316 stolen bases as a third baseman.

Lobert played under John McGraw with the New York Giants and later scouted for his old manager while he coached at West Point. Lobert became a lifetime baseball man and as his so-called reward he was named manager of the Philadelphia Phillies in 1941. The Phillies had finished last four years in a row and were so bad the National League considered taking steps to improve the team for the good of baseball.

"The Phils will be a fighting, aggressive club throughout the season," vowed Lobert, who was regarded as a "genial but granite-hard" leader. Maybe they were but they were also awful again. The Phillies finished with a 42-109 record in Lobert's only year at the helm. His lifetime winning percentage of .275, only a percentage point above his lifetime batting average, is the worst ever.

Press Cruthers (1913-1914. Charles Preston Cruthers of Marshallton won two baseball world championships and made it to the Baseball Hall of Fame in Cooperstown. Not bad for a playing career that spanned two seasons and covered seven games. Press Cruthers was signed out of Delaware by Connie Mack in 1913 when he was 22 years old to backup future Hall-of-Famer Eddie Collins at second base for the Philadelphia Athletics. And back up he did. The Athletics won World Series in 1913 and 1914 without Cruthers seeing action either year. He retreated from the major leagues after that and played six minor league seasons before retiring.

Cruthers moved to Kenosha, Wisconsin where he worked for the Simmons mattress company and played on the company-sponsored semi-pro team. He was also elected town clerk in Pleasant Prairie for 28 years. In between Cruthers took the reins of the Kenosha Comets of the All-American Girls Professional Baseball League in 1946. No Tom Hanks, Cruthers was described as looking and acting "like somebody's father or grandfather." The 1946 Comets stumbled to a seventh-place finish in an eight-team league with a record of 42-70. But you catch a glimpse of Press Cruthers as part of the permanent exhibit on women's professional baseball in the National Baseball Hall of Fame.

Huck Betts (1920-1925, 1932-1935) . For most of the 1920s and 1930s Delaware's sole representative in the Big Show was a slender righthanded pitcher from Millsboro named Walter "Huck" Betts. Betts pitched for Conference Academy in Dover and regularly baffled hitters on diamonds across the Peninsula. He had several downstate no-hitters on his resume when he joined the Philadelphia Phillies at the age of 23.

Betts remained with the National League club for the next six years, appearing mostly in relief. As a Phillie Betts was a marginal talent, possessor of no curve and a weak fastball. He survived on control and guile. Betts worked on developing a screwball and was tried as a starter but he continually frustrated Phillies' brass with his maddening inability to finish ballgames. Prior to the 1926 season Betts was sold to Fort Worth, champions of the Texas League.

A 29-year old pitcher with an undistinguished lifetime mark of 18-27 exiled to the minor leagues is a good bet to never be heard from again. But Betts worked his way through the bushes until 1931 when he won 22 games for St. Paul and led the Minnesotans to the Little World Series. The Boston Braves took a shot on the old Millsboro farmboy.

As a 35-year old Huck Betts found himself back in the National League. Taking a regular turn in the Braves' rotation Betts won 41 games against only 32 losses over the next three years. He had totally resurrected his career at an age when most pitchers had long since hung up their spikes. Betts lost his stuff in 1935, winning only 2 of 11 games. The next year he returned to St. Paul, his now respectable major league career over. The Delaware mound ace without a fastball or curve was still working in professional baseball into his 40s before retiring to Sussex County where he operated the Ball Theater.

Eddie Cihocki (1932-1933). One of the flashiest players ever to appear on Delaware diamonds was Eddie Cihocki. Cihocki began playing in Wilmington's top amateur league, the Twilight League, as a 15-year old shortstop in the 1920s. In 1927 Cihocki inked a Chicago Cubs' contract and began his professional baseball odyssey in Reading, Pennsylvania.

Blessed with nimble feet and a powerful arm, Cihocki's hands were so large he could hide a baseball completely in his palm. He was invited to several major league training camps until sticking with the powerful Philadelphia Athletics in 1933. When regular shortstop Eric McNair went down with an injury early in the season the 26-year old Cihocki was thrust into the starting line-up of Connie Mack's pennant contenders.

Cihocki tripled in his first major league atbat to spark an A's win but over the next month the Wilmington ace literally could not hit his weight. He was benched with an average of .144 after his 28-game trial, playing rarely the rest of the year. Following the 1933 season Cihocki was sent to Jersey City and never made the majors again.

The classic good glove,-no hit shortstop, Cihocki hit .262 for Syracuse the next year, good enough to again be picked up by the Cubs. Unable to crack a pennant-winning line-up Cihocki journeyed to Los Angeles where his defense solidified the Angels' successful drive to the Pacific Coast League League title.

Cihocki stayed with Los Angeles for three years, returning each winter to Wilmington to resume his trade as a plumber. On the West Coast Cihocki became the Angels' most popular player. His hitting improved to .286 in 1939 and he was presented the team Most Valuable Player award at "Cihocki Day."

In 1941 Cihocki was tabbed as president of the Parochial Baseball League in Delaware and he surrendered his 15-year professional career to tend to his work for the Hercules Company.

William "Bubby" Sadler (1930s). While Eddie Cihocki was the best-known native shortstop of the 1930s another Delaware shortstop was starring in professional baseball. Bubby Sadler was born in 1909 and a graduate of Howard High. He played with several Negro League teams including the Philadelphia Black Meteors, Newark Eagles and Philadelphia Stars. His greatest successes came during a five-year stint with the Bacharach Giants. After his playing days Sadler returned to Delaware City working for the state of Delaware from 1944 until his retirement in 1974.

Chip Marshall (1941). On June 14, 1941 Chip Marshall, who was born Charles Anthony Marczlewicz in Wilmington 22 years earlier, was sent in by St. Louis manager Billy Southworth to pinch run. The side was quickly retired and Marshall returned to the dugout. And that was the extent of his major leaue career.

Marshall left Delaware for the Cardinal organization in 1937. He reached the Triple A level at Rochester in the 1940s, by which time he had earned a reputation as one of the best defensive catchers ever, the owner of a spectacular throwing arm. But he couldn't hit. Marshall's four years in Rochester ended with batting marks of .217, .228, .208 and .250. His defense kept him in professional baseball for 17 years before Marshall left the field for the dugout and a minor league managing assignment.

Brandy Davis (1952-1953). Brandon Davis always knew he was going to be a lifelong baseball man. He was a good enough pitcher at Newark High School to throw a no-hitter in 1945 and even though he was signed by the Pittsburgh Pirates out of the Duke University outfield Davis began preparing for a baseball afterlife by enrolling in a baseball business management course at age 21.

The speedy Davis stole 83 bases with three teams in 1951, including a league record 69 with Bartlesville of the Kansas-Oklahoma-Missouri League. He made the Pirates the next year and was used mostly as a pinch runner in 55 games. His specialty was stealing third base and he got nine steals while going only 17-59 at the plate. Davis displayed no ability to hit in 1953 and he was soon back in the minors.

After breaking a wrist sliding in 1957 Davis began his second baseball career as a manager in the Brooklyn Dodger system. In the 1960s he scouted and managed in the minors for Houston. Afterward Davis continued as a scout into his fifth decade as a baseball man - just as he always planned.

Costen Shockley (1964-1965). Few players ever came out of Delaware with more promise than Costen Shockley. His estimated $50,000 signing bonus with the Philadelphia Phillies fresh from Georgetown High School was one of the largest of the "Bonus Baby" era of the late 1950s and early 1960s. He expected to be a pitcher but Gene Mauch made him a first baseman on his first day of spring training.

Shockley tore through the minor leagues. At Class C Twin Falls, Idaho the new prospect batted .360 and crushed 23 home runs. At Williamsport of the Eastern League in 1962 he drove in 82 runs. The next year with Chattanooga of the South Atlantic League he hit .335.

In 1964 Shockley ripped 24 home runs in half a season with Triple A Arkansas and earned a call-up to Philadelphia on July 16. Thrust into the Phillies' ill-fated pennant drive Shockley was given the first base job but played himself out of the lineup after 13 days and eight games. He stroked only 8 hits in 35 at-bats. Shockley returned to Arkansas where he finished leading the Pacific Coast League in home runs with 36.

After refusing to play winter ball following the 1964 season Shockley was shipped to the Los Angeles Angels for Bo Belinsky, known for his amorous adventures off the field and a single no-hitter on it. The left-handed slugger opened the 1965 season as the Angels regular first baseman and belted an early grand slam but by June his average plummeted below .200. On June 12 Shockley was demoted to Seattle but he refused to report, saying he had already proved he could hit minor league pitching and had vowed to make the majors in five years or quit. So he did, returning to the construction business in Georgetown.

Dave May (1967-1978). Dave May could always hit. He emerged from William Penn High School in 1962 to lead the Appalachian League in hitting with a .379 average. He added another minor league batting title, a stolen base crown and a slugging title before being promoted to the Baltimore Orioles in 1967. May was a part of one of the greatest teams ever assembled, appearing in the World Series in 1969, but a trade to the Milwaukee Brewers midway through 1970 gave the outfielder a chance to play every day.

May started for the Brewers for 4 1/2 years. His best season came in 1973 when he hit .303, slugged 25 home runs and drove home 93 runs. That year he became only the second Delawarean, after Chris Short, to appear in an All-Star game. Following a sub-par year in 1974 Dave May was the player traded to Atlanta to enable home run king Henry Aaron to finish his career back in Milwaukee.

In May's final seasons he was a part-time player, winding up as a pinch-hitter for the Pittsburgh Pirates in 1978. He returned to Delaware and played occasionally in the Delaware Semi-Pro League where his long home runs were reminders of one of the best hitters ever to come out of Delaware.

John Morris (1966-1974). The Lewes High pitcher began his major league career with a brief stay on the Phillies in 1966. Equally brief stints with the Orioles and original Seattle Pilots followed. 1970 seemed like a break-through year for the lefthander as he began the season 3-1 for the former Pilots, now the Milwaukee Brewers. Included in his wins were two complete games. But Morris contracted a debilitating kidney infection and before the year was out he was in Mexico trying to work his way back to the big leagues. Morris did pitch three more years eventually getting in 132 big league games and leaving baseball with an 11-7 mark.

Ken Szotkiewicz (1970). A hard-hitting shortstop from the playgrounds of Wilmington and Salesianum School, Ken Szotkiewicz had a professional career nearly identical to that of a previous Delaware shortstop, Eddie Cihocki. Signed out of Georgia Southern University in 1968 at the age of 21 Szotkiewicz was the Detroit Tigers' starting shortstop when the 1970 season began.

Like Cichocki, Szotkiewicz had immediate success at the plate with a key home run but after 33 games he had only nine hits in 84 plate appearances and was hitting .107. His trial as a starting shortstop judged a failure, Szotkiewicz was returned to the minor leagues, never to make the majors again. He played several more seasons, battling through two knee operations, but by 1975 Ken Szotkiewicz was out of baseball.

Renie Martin (1979-1984). Renie Martin - by way of Dover High School, the University of Richmond and Parkway of the Delaware Semi-Pro League - was a low 19th round draft pick by the Kansas City Royals in 1977 yet was pitching in the big leagues by early 1979. He saved two games for the Royals in his first week with the club, ending with five for the season.

In 1980 the 24-year old Martin joined the Kansas City rotation as a part-time starter and won 10 games for the Royals' first-ever American League champion team. In the World Series against the Philadelphia Phillies Martin was the Royals' most effective reliever, appearing in 3 games and allowing only 3 runs in 9 2/3 innings.

In 1982 Martin was traded to the San Francisco Giants where he started 25 games with limited success, working in a career-high 141 innings. His effectiveness continued to decline and he was optioned to AAA Phoenix in mid-1984. A trade to the Phillies gave his career a last gasp and he went 0-2 in nine outings, pitching occasionally to John Wockenfuss in the first ever all-Delaware battery.

Martin pitched a final Triple A season with the Omaha Royals in 1985 before retiring just 19 days shy of his five-year mark as a major league pitcher. His final mark was only 24-35 but he left baseball a career .301 hitter, 25 hits in 83 at-bats.

Chris Welsh (1981-1986). Delaware native Chris Welsh left Wilmington for Cincinnati with his family when he was 6 years old in 1961. Drafted by the New York Yankees in the 21st round of the free agent draft in 1977, Welsh was a pitcher for the San Diego Padres, Montreal Expos, Texas Rangers and Cincinnati Reds. In five years of major league service Welsh started 75 games and compiled a lifetime mark of 22-31.

Dwayne Henry (1984-1995). Dwayne Henry was born in Elkton in 1962 but moved to Delaware in time to become the first athlete to be All-State in three sports. At Middletown High School, as a fullback, he scored 162 of his team's 200 points in his senior season and gained 311 yards in one game. In basketball he was the leading scorer in Blue Hen Conference history. But his future lay in baseball. A wickedly hard thrower, he once whiffed 17 batters in a 7-inning high school game.

In pro ball Dwayne Henry became the classic diamond heartbreaker - a pitcher of immense promise never quite able to harness his talent. He teased the Texas Rangers, who looked at him as a flame-throwing closer, for most of the Eighties before they reluctantly dealt him to the Atlanta Braves. Prior to 1991 Henry had recorded 795 strikeouts in 812 pro innings. His fast ball earned him several looks at the major league level but in parts of seven big league seasons he issued 84 walks in 116 innings. A typical Henry season was 1986: 19 games, 19 innings pitched, only 14 hits, 17 strikeouts, 22 walks. Dwayne Henry would always be remembered as a great thrower who couldn't quite master pitching.

Derrick May (1990-1999). The Mays became the second father-and-son major leaguers from Delaware when Derrick was called up to the Chicago Cubs two weeks into the 1992 season. May was drafted out of Newark High School in the first round by the Cubs, the ninth player taken in the country. In his senior year at Newark May hit .462 with three home runs and 18 RBI. He progressed steadily through the minor leagues until the Cubs uncovered a minor defect in May's eyesight. His eyesight corrected May reached the big leagues in short order.

May struggled through his rookie year until establishing himself in 1993. In the Phillies home opener, before scores of friends and family, May unloaded two home runs and drove in five runs. He finished the season batting .295 with 10 home runs and 25 doubles, despite missing most of the final month with a leg injury.

Dave Williams (2001-2007). When you are born in Anchorage, Alaska and then move to Delaware it is easy to travel under the radar of big league scouts. But the Pittsburgh Pirates found Dave Williams out of Caesar Rodney High School and Delaware Technical Community College in the 17th round of the 1998 amateur draft. Still, not much was expected of the left-handed twirler until 2001 when he recorded 201 minor league strikeouts in just 181 innings. Relying on control and rarely reaching 90 miles per hour on his fastball, Williams was in the majors by the end of the year. During a six-year career as a starter he won 22 games, including 10 when he was in the Pirates rotation with fellow Riders alum Ian Snell.

Pedro Swann (2000-2003). It doesn't take long for Pedro Swann's career to elicit comparisons to Crash Davis, the fictional character played by Kevin Costner in *Bull Durham*. In the movie Davis sticks around the game to break the all-time minor league home run record. Swann, born in Wilmington and a product of Delaware State, played 17 years in the minors, piling up 189 home runs among his 1,886 hits. Heck, Swann even had a bit part playing Juan Vasquez in Costner's 1999 movie *For Love of the Game*.

Swann did a little better than Davis' 21 glorious days in "The Show." After nine seasons in the minors he made his major league debut with Atlanta in 2000, striking out in two pinch hitting appearances. Two years later he got another chance with the

Blue Jays and banged a single for his first major league hit in 12 plate appearances. In 2003, in his last short stint in the majors, Swann hit his only major league home run - off Roger Clemens. The following year he was back on minor league buses until his retirement in 2008.

Cliff Brumbaugh (2001). Cliff Brumbaugh followed a narrow path through tiny Delaware to the major leagues but the entire baseball world would open to him after that. Brumbaugh was born in Wilmington in 1974 and graduated from William Penn High School and Bob Hannah's program at the University of Delaware where the slugging outfielder was named America East Player of the Year in 1995 after hitting .442 and leading the nation in doubles. Brambaugh was then plucked by the Texas Rangers in the 13th round of the 1995 draft.

After signing, Brumbaugh batted .358 for the Hudson Valley Renegades in the short-season New York Penn League and copped the batting title and league MVP. He progressed through the Ranger system before being called up on May 30, 2001. The Delaware native failed to get a hit in ten pinch-hitting appearances and was shuttled off to the Colorado Rockies. In his first start in the National League Brumbaugh connected on a home run against the Arizona Diamondbacks for his first major league hit.

There would be only nine more before Brumbaugh was returned to the minors, playing his last major league game. But in 2003 he signed with the Hyundai Unicorns of the Korean Baseball Organization. Brumbaugh led the Unicorns to two consecutive championships, pacing the team in batting, setting Korean Series Championship records and winning a Gold Glove. All told Brumbaugh played seven seasons in the Far East, including two in Japan with the Orix Buffaloes, before ending his fifteen-year professional career with the Edmonton Capitals in Canada. There were many baseball miles on Cliff Brumbaugh after departing Delaware.

Kevin Mench (2002-2010). They called him "Shrek" because his cap size was 8 - the largest in the majors. But it could have been for the way Kevin Mench mashed baseballs. He went deep 15 times in his rookie year with the Texas Rangers in 2002 and finished 7th in Rookie of the Year voting. In 2005 he socked three home runs against the Los Angeles Angels and in 2006 Kevin Mench did what no other right-handed batter in baseball history had done - homer in seven straight games.

These feats surprised no one who saw Mench growing up on Delaware diamonds at the Independence School and St. Mark's High School. When he entered the University of Delaware he led the Blue Hens to NCAA tournament appearances in 1998 and 1999 and was named America East Player of the Year each season. In 1998 he led all collegians with 33 home runs and was named National Player of the Year.

Mench was traded by the Rangers shortly after his home run binge in 2006 and he slid into a part-time role with the Milwaukee Brewers before trying his hand at Japanese baseball for one year before officially retiring in 2012 at the age of 34.

Ian Snell (2004-2010). Ian Snell dominated batters at Caesar Rodney High School and was drafted into the Pittsburgh Pirates organization in 2000. Three years later he was the Pirates Minor League Pitcher of the Year. By 2006, at the age of 24, Snell was a mainstay of the Pittsburgh rotation, winning 14 games and striking out nearly a batter an inning. Citing Puerto Rican ancestry on his father's side, the Dover native pitched for Puerto Rico in 2009 in the World Baseball Classic. Self-inflicted pressure, however, drove Snell to announce a retirement from baseball at the age of 29 after 136 big league starts. After decompressing in his Florida home for 18 months Snell returned to baseball, pitching for an independent team in Long Island, New York.

Brett Oberholtzer (2013-). Thanks to an off-season trade in 2015, 26-year old lefthander Brett Oberholtzer arrives in Philadelphia to join a long line of Delawareans toiling for the Phillies. At William Penn High School Oberholtzer was named Louisville Slugger High School All-American. He was drafted out of Seminole Community College in Florida in the eighth round of the 2008 draft by the Atlanta Braves. He reached the majors as a pitcher with the Houston Astros in 2013 and started 24 games as a regular member of the rotation a year later.

Utility Man

"John Wockenfuss: 12-year veteran of the major leagues." At one point in his career Wockenfuss would agree those were the most unlikely words ever spoken. In 1975 the player known best for a funny-sounding name and a funnier-looking batting stance had been mired in the minor leagues for over eight years, ever since the West Virginia native concluded an all-everything career at Dickinson High School, including being a drop-kicking quarterback.

Wockenfuss signed as a pitcher with the Washington Senators organization. When he showed up for spring training and discovered pitchers only threw and never hit he promptly became an outfielder. Five forgettable years later the strong-armed Delawarean was converted into a catcher.

In December 1973 Wockenfuss was traded to the Detroit Tigers in a minor-league deal so insignificant that no printer's ink was wasted on it in the newspaper. He wallowed further in the Tiger system before getting a 13-game trial in the majors in 1974 when regular catcher Jerry Moses went down with a thumb injury. After producing only three singles and a double in 29 at-bats Wockenfuss had every reason to believe his major league baseball career was over.

That belief was hammered home in the off-season when the Tigers traded for a catcher. At the age of 26 Wockenfuss opened a pizzeria near Newark and prepared for the rapidly approaching end of his baseball days. Surprisingly, the call for Wockenfuss came again in June of 1975. To delay his departure this time Wockenfuss turned himself into the quintessential utility player. He caught, played the outfield, manned first base. Whatever was necessary to stay in the "Show."

He flashed power in his occassional plate appearance and made himself a valuable hitter against left-handed pitching. He clouted 15 home runs in 1979 and 16 more the next year. In 1982 Wockenfuss hit .301 in limited duty and added third base to his defensive resume.

In 1984, after ten years with the Tigers, the affable Wockenfuss was traded to the hometown Phillies where he finished his career as a lifetime .262 hitter with 86 home runs. Still convinced he might help a major league team Wockenfuss returned to the minor leagues for one more year in 1986, ending his playing days in the Class A Florida League. The next year Wockenfuss accepted a position as manager in the Detroit Tiger organization. He was beginning his third decade in professional baseball.

Big Leaguer for a Day

The DuPont team dominated the New Castle County League in 1909, winning 19 of 20 games. Left-hander William Crouch was the DuPont star, winning all 15 of his pitching starts and tying for the league lead in hitting at .400. The next season "Wild Bill" twirled two no-hitters early in the season and was offered a chance with the St. Louis Browns, a team on their way to 107 losses.

Crouch left for Washington where he was scheduled to face the Nationals and Walter Johnson. Straight from the amateur fields of Delaware, Crouch battled the legendary Big Train for 8 innings before the game was called of darkness at 4-4. He surrendered only six singles but allowed 8 walks. The Washington papers lauded the performance of the young hurler "plucked from the wilds of Delaware."

Still, the next day Crouch was released, told that he "needed more experience." St. Louis offered him another trial but Crouch vowed, "never again." He returned home to Marshallton and resumed his duties as a clerk for the DuPont Company. A New Castle County League rule prohibited his return to the baseball team so he hooked on with the Big Four League in Delaware County, Pennsylvania.

Later that year Crouch celebrated the arrival of his son William, Jr., who would go on to also enjoy an abbreviated three-season major league career, becoming Delaware's first father-son major league baseball duo. Bill, Jr. pitched in 50 games, made 12 starts and recorded an 8-5 record with the Dodgers, Cardinals and Phillies with a lifetime ERA of 3.47.

Oddly, although William Crouch, Sr. was a big-leaguer for little more than 24 hours and his teammates most certainly had no idea who he was, according to the *Baseball Encyclopedia*, he earned the nickname "Skip."

Bill Crouch looks like a guy who wouldn't be fazed by having to make an emergency big league start.

When Bill Couch, Jr. made the majors the Couches became the first father-son big leaguers from Delaware.

Big Shot

Delaware's first Hall-of-Famer, umpire Bill McGowan.

On a cool summer day in 1940 Bill McGowan's arthritis flared up and he missed two days of work. This would not be particularly noteworthy except that Bill McGowan had gone to work for 2532 straight games as an American League umpire - 400 games longer than Lou Gehrig's infamous streak as a player.

McGowan grew up in and around Wilmington, working in the DuPont powder yards, playing infield on the company baseball team and even doing a little sportswriting on the side. In 1912 McGowan's older brother Jack was scheduled to umpire two games, one in Wilmington and one in New Castle. Seeking to lighten his hectic day he offered his brother a chance to repay a $2 debt by taking the New Castle assignment.

So 16-year old Bill boarded a train to New Castle and worked the game as his brother Jack since neither team had ever seen either McGowan. Before he left Jack had to instruct him on how to wave his arms for out and safe. Thus was launched one of the great careers in baseball adjudication.

McGowan started working in the minor leagues in 1913 where he established a reputation for taking control of a game, despite his tender years. Fans and players alike could expect a speedy resolution to a McGowan game. Known as "the fastest-working umpire in the bushes" he once handled a 26-inning marathon in only 70 minutes.

Called "Big Shot" from his days in the powder yards, McGowan worked his way through the minor leagues for twelve years before making the major leagues as an American League umpire in 1925. At 29 McGowan was one of the youngest big league umpires in baseball history. It was quite a tribute to his skills. Baseball at the time used only three umpires - there was no 2nd base ump - and thus there were only 24 big league jobs available.

McGowan went to spring training as the umpire assigned to the mighty New York Yankees and the first player he tossed out of a game in his rookie year was none other than Babe Ruth. McGowan brought a new style of umpiring to the American League. His fast-paced management of games was copied by older umpires and his hustle to be on top of plays found favor with players and managers.

In the off-seasons McGowan toiled as a boxing promoter, an activity he was not wholly unfamiliar with, having engaged in several punching matches on the field in his minor league days. He also dabbled in scouting, uncovering Leon "Goose" Goslin, a future Hall-of Fame outfielder from Carney's Point, New Jersey, and starting him on a professional career. Later, he founded one ofthe first umpire schools near his winter home in Chevy Chase, Maryland. By 1951 his school, then in Florida, had three graduates working in the big leagues.

In 1935 McGowan was named baseball's "Outstanding Umpire" and he worked in his first World Series. He would work eight Fall Classics altogether, along with four All-Star games. Above all he considered his greatest honor being named umpire-in-chief for the first one-game playoff in American League history in 1948, since this position was based on merit and not scheduling.

By 1945 McGowan was beginning his 21st year and was dean of all umpires. He umpired through the 1954 season when a heart attack forced him to the sidelines after 30 years. He died shortly thereafter at the age of 58, eulogized by many as the greatest umpire of them all. In 1992 McGowan rightly assumed his place in the National Baseball Hall of Fame as the seventh umpire so honored.

First State Triad

After Vic Willis retired in 1910 Delaware was virtually not represented in major league baseball, save for Huck Betts, for nearly half a century. Then, in 1960 three Delaware boys popped up not only in the big leagues but on the same pitching staff. Dallas Green, who twenty years later would take the Philadelphia Phillies to their only world championship; Chris Short, a lefthander of the first rank; and Al Neiger, the first Delawarean ever named on an All-America collegiate baseball team, all hurled for the Philadelphia Phillies.

Tall and rugged, Green was out of Conrad High School where he was considered a better basketball player than a baseball player. As a junior on an undefeated 1951 Conrad team Green

played mostly in rightfield but as a pitcher worked 14 innings, striking out 15 and walking 16. Playing center on the basketball team Green was lauded for his rebounding, shooting and soft hands in the pivot.

At the University of Delaware Green averaged 12.7 points as a junior and was named all-conference in basketball. He was named captain for the upcoming senior year but that spring his 6-0 record on the mound, compiled over a 0.64 ERA, earned him a professional baseball contract. In 1956 Green was named Rookie of the Year in the Class C Pioneer League where he went 17-12. He developed a better curveball and struck out 226 but was still prone to wildness.

He continued through the Phillies system until sticking with the big club in 1960. Green's first major league win was a 3-hit shutout of the Los Angeles Dodgers but he never developed into more than a serviceable major league pitcher. Green's greatest success came when his playing days were over. He became Farm Director for the Phillies and General Manager of the Chicago Cubs. He returned to the field as only the third man to manage both the New York Yankees and the New York Mets. But what Dallas Green will always be remembered for in these parts was his teaching an underachieving band of Phillie stars how to win as manager of the 1980 World Champions.

Watching baseball in the 2000s, it is sometimes hard to remember what a good starting pitcher should do. A starter like Chris Short. For six consecutive years in the 1960s Short had an ERA over 3.00 only once. And that "down" year he won 20 games. In that period he threw 69 complete games and 20 shutouts.

Growing up in Georgetown young Short showed early promise as a pitcher. He was a starting pitcher for Lewes High in the 9th, 10th and 11th grades before prepping for a year at Bordentown Military Academy in New Jersey. At Bordentown the 6'3" Short struck out 147 and walked only 12 in 83 innings. He won ten games and lost only one, that because the catcher had trouble

holding many of Short's wicked deliveries.

Short signed with the Phillies over 12 other clubs. His assent to the majors was a rapid one and by 1960 the 22-year old lefthander was counted on for the Phillies rotation. Pitching for a horrendous ballclub did nothing to speed Short's development but by the mid-1960s he was the only southpaw in the National League who could be mentioned in the same breath as Sandy Koufax.

In a span of five years Short won 17, 18, 20, 9 and 19 games. In the year he won only nine games his ERA was 2.39. Although slowed by injuries after 1968 Short spent parts of 14 seasons with the Phillies, more than any other pitcher save Robin Roberts. In 1969 Phillie fans chose Short as the team's all-time lefthanded pitcher. He appeared in two All-Star games, the first Delawarean to do so.

In the second week of the 1969 season Short crippled his back and missed the remainder of the season. He never complained about his back after his return in 1970 but he went only 20-36 in his last four years after the surgery. Still, Short finished with a log of 135 wins against 132 losses and a lifetime ERA of 3.43 in 2325 innings.

The last member of the Delaware triumvirate to join the Phillies was Al Neiger, certainly the most improbable of the trio. As a Wilmington High School senior only three years earlier Neiger's pitching log was a singularly unimpressive 1-6. He blossomed at the University of Delaware where he went 9-3 his final year. He allowed only 80 baserunners in 103 innings and in a 1-hitter against Swarthmore Neiger struck out 21 and walked only one.

Neiger's stay with the Phillies was a brief one. He appeared in only six games in relief during 66 days in the big leagues. The lefthander was sent back to Chattanooga before the 1961 season and after an 11-9 year Neiger was sold to the Los Angeles Angels. He never pitched in the majors again.

Basketball

The American Basketball League (1901-02)

Delaware came slowly to basketball. For years the game was caged in YMCA fitness classes and dusky gymnasiums. Most Delawareans had never seen a game of what was popularly known as "indoor football."

In 1901 Wilmington found itself with a franchise in the fledgling American Basketball League, battling with teams from all the big eastern cities. Games were played once a week in the Pyle Cycle Academy at 10th and Market streets. In the first home game Wilmington slipped behind Chester 6-5 at the end of the 20-minute first half but ground out a 12-10 win. The several hundred fans on hand went home happy but many still weren't sure what they were watching.

By the third home game, however, 1500 fans cheered the blue and white to their third straight win in the Pyle Academy cage. The League shaved down to five teams and Wilmington was the best of the survivors, emerging on top with a 20-7-1 mark. The attack featured the league's top scorer in Jack Reynolds who poured in nine points a game. In post-season play Wilmington tangled with Bristol, winner of the National Basketball League, for national supremacy. In two tightly played games the Delawareans lost the United States Championship 39-27 and 30-27.

The next year Wilmington stood in third place with a 14-12 log when the league disbanded with four games to play. Delaware was out of professional basketball but nevermore would basketball be out of Delaware.

The Tri-State Basketball League (1930-31)

The evolution of basketball was a slow, halting process. Play was rough and quality arenas scarce and the game attracted little of the fans' sporting dollar at the professional level. For years struggling professional leagues peppered the country.

In 1930 the Tri-State Basketball League formed with Wilmington's Jack McGowan at the helm. The circuit boasted teams in Trenton, Bridgeton, Reading, Germantown, Philadelphia and Wilmington. The Wilmington Chicks were guided by Tommy Barlow, a Trenton native known to his Delaware admirers as "Caveman Tommy."

McGowan was 34 years by this time and had played for at least ten pro teams on the East since 1912 - many simultaneously. He stood an imposing - for the time - 6'1" and weighed a burly 195 pounds. Caveman Tommy was the highest paid cager in the game for much of the 1920s - pulling down as much as $45 a game. His tenacious defense, rebounding and just enough scoring would earn Barlow admission into the Naismith Basketball Hall of Fame in 1981. He retired in

1932 after an apparently brutal game in Wilmington.

The early basketball games were hardly fan favorites. The Chicks dumped Reading in their home opener 41-36, but 66 fouls were called in the game. Wilmington scored only eight field goals to Reading's six as the bulk of the scoring came from the parade to the foul line. In a 24-16 loss to Trenton the next week Barlow's Blue and Gold scored only three baskets.

McGowan struggled to hold the Tri-State League together as Trenton and Germantown disbanded. When Philadelphia deserted he was able to re-establish the franchise in Chester but when Reading left the Tri-State staggered on with just three teams.

The Chicks jumped to a 5-0 start among the survivors in the second half of the split season and were slated to meet Bridgeton, the winner of the first half, in a 5-game row for the Tri-State Championship. The battle went the full five games with no game decided by more than 6 points. In the final, played before 2200 at the National Guard Armory at 10th & Market, the Chicks built an early 7-point lead and froze the Tri-State title 22-16.

It would be the only Tri-State Championship. The next year the Tri-State League and the Eastern League were absorbed into the American League to become the strongest basketball league in America. The champion Chicks disbanded and most of the players quickly filled rosters in the new league.

The American Basketball League (1931-32)

For two years the Wilmington Cardinals played ignominiously through the Eastern Basketball League. Performing mostly in front of family and friends in the Salesianum School gymnasium, the Cardinals seldom escaped the basement of the professional circuit.

With the consolidation of area pro leagues into the American Basketball League in 1931 the Cardinals were now part of the top basketball league in the country. Assembled by Bill Sweeney, the Cardinals were more than competitive, dribbling to a 5-1 start and even annexing a 30-28 win over legendary Eddie Gottlieb's South Philadelphia Hebrew Association, the SPHAs.

The Cardinals closed out the first half of the 1931-32 season in third place at 8-7 and challenged for the early lead in the second session before settling into third again. But the team was not drawing well and the owners tried local Delaware players to hype the gate. Thus reinforced, the Cardinals lost their final four games which did nothing to inspire attendance.

For the 1932-33 season the Cardinals surrendered their franchise to a strong local five, St. Mary's. St. Mary's tried a blend of hired pros and local stars but in the first six games Delawareans Mike McCall and Jack Warner never got off the pine. The discouraged owners discovered they couldn't compete for high salaried players at this level of ball and professional basketball passed quietly out of Delaware once again.

The American Basketball League (1941-49)

In 1941 Bob Carpenter landed a franchise in the American Basketball League, then the reigning basketball league in America. Carpenter rented the State Armory at 10th and Du Pont streets, hoping to squeeze in 3000 fans. He built bleachers for 2700 and scattered chairs for another 640 around the court. The Blue Bombers also installed the first glass blackboards in Delaware.

The city of Wilmington was ready for the return of professional basketball. Over 1000 fans attended a Blue Bomber drill and scrimmage. A season ticket for 20 Wednesday night home games cost $16; otherwise a general admission ticket was 65 cents.

The Bombers were orchestrated on the court by diminutive ex-New York Celtic coach Barney Sedran. In the home opener Wilmington ran off 17 straight points for a 20-3 lead on their way to drubbing Eddie Gottlieb's defending champion Philadelphia SPHAS 40-24. The Bombers would go on to beat the powerful SPHAS seven straight times, always to the deafening backing of a full Armory house when in Wilmington.

Playing a split season with Philadelphia, Trenton, Washington and New York the 1941-42 Blue Bombers became the first team ever to sweep both halves of the schedule. But with the advent of World War II the government reclaimed the Armory and the undisputed American Basketball League champs were left with no place to play and the franchise was abandoned for a year.

With the revival in 1943-44 the Bombers featured a strong front line of Ben Goldfaden, Ed Smith and Ben Auerbach. Wilmington rolled to a first place finish in the first half before dropping to third the next half to force a playoff. The Blue Bombers dropped the SPHAS yet another time to win the championship again.

In 1944-45 the Bombers started once again as the class of professional basketball, winning eight of their first 11 games. But because of military obligations Wilmington could not put the same team on the court two games in a row. Sedran kept a very fluid roster with captain Moe Frankel the only sure starter from night to night. The depleted Bombers fell to the archrival SPHAS in the first round of the playoffs.

After the war the Bombers constructed their team around Paul Chadick, a Wilmington native who led the Bombers into the playoffs after returning from the Marines. With Chadick's high scoring the 4th place Blue Bombers played the champion SPHAS tough but lost 69-65 and 75-72 to once again exit post-season play early.

The big games with the SPHAS found Delaware fans hanging from the rafters but the American League began deteriorating into a haven for low priced homegrown talent as other leagues paid more money to players. The Blue Bombers slumped to 15-20 in the 1946-47 season and when they again lost use of the Armory they suspended play. When the American Basketball League went out of business shortly thereafter with the formation of the National Basketball Association and the suspension became permanent.

The Eastern Basketball League (1957-58)

The Wilmington Jets played a brand of basketball befitting their modern name - up-tempo with a 24-second clock that produced scores in the hundreds. Unfortunately for the Jets they were most often on the wrong end of those high scores. The Wilmington entry in the 8-team Eastern Basketball League was a classic "doughnut team" with no one in the middle.

Nearly 1000 saw the return of professional basketball to Delaware after a decade as the Jets romped over Reading 108-96. But the Jets sagged to 2-8 and coach and general manager Jim Donegal stepped aside in favor of Charley Eckman, two-time NBA Coach of Year from the Detroit Pistons. But Eckman stayed only two games declaring, "I couldn't help this team."

Dick Koffenberger, a former P.S. du Pont High school star and designated "local" reserve on the Jets, took over the reigns to finish the season. The Jets got consistent 20-point scoring from Gerry Paulson and Kurt Englebert but could only struggle to the end of the regular season 6-22. Attendance had cascaded to barely 300 a game as the Jets played out the string. The owners vowed to keep the franchise in Delaware but the 1958-59 season opened with the Jets in Allentown.

The Eastern Basketball League (1963-1971)

In 1963 eleven local investors brought Wilmington back into the Eastern Basketball League, then in its sixteenth year of play. The EBL played on Saturdays and Sundays and fans could glimpse an occasional preview of a future NBA star or catch the odd Hall-of-Famer, like Paul Arizin, winding down a basketball career with the Camden Bullets. But what the fan got mostly from the EBL was fast-paced entertainment - a high-voltage NBA All-Star type style of ball that typically produced team scores in the 120s.

In 1966-67, for example, 11 Eastern Leaguers averaged more than 27 points. The local draw for the new Wilmington Blue Bombers was 6'6" Nate Cloud, a Conrad High School All-Stater and the best player yet to come out of the University of Delaware. Cloud scored 1187 points in his 62 Blue Hen games and was named MVP of the Middle Atlantic Conference in 1962. He failed to make the NBA after being drafted in the 4th round by the New York Knicks and became the first Blue Bomber signee. He would stay more than six years, enjoying his best season in 1967-68 when he averaged a little better than eight points a game.

Also on that inaugural Bomber team was Waite Bellamy, a sharpshooter from Florida A & M who would lead the Bombers in scoring for much of their existence, 6'9" All-American Paul Hogue of Cincinnati and guard Raymond Flynn who would go on to be mayor of Boston. Al Severance, retired from 25 years at Villanova, was tabbed as first Bomber coach but his collegiate style did not translate easily into the EBL and he was deposed after a 7-21 last place finish.

Playing in the Salesianum gym at 18th and Broom streets Bomber crowds averaged about 1400. In the off-season the Bombers drafted John Thompson and Willis Reed, neither of whom would ever suit up in Wilmington. Future coaches Jim Lynam and George Raveling failed to make the Blue Bombers. A more important off-season addition was Neil Johnston who took over coaching duties. The Blue Bombers were slow to adapt to Johnston's methods and stumbled to an 0-5 start. But by the end of the season the Bombers were the best team in the league as they fell just short of the playoffs.

The strong 1964-65 finish was a prelude to a championship season in the Blue Bombers' third year. Under Johnston Wilmington won 16 of its final 20 games to tie for the league title in 1965-66. The fans responded to the Bomber stretch run with five straight crowds of over 2000 and for the playoffs there were turn-away crowds at the Salesianum gym.

In their first playoff series the Bombers dumped the Trenton Colonials two games to one behind the three-point bombs of Fred Crawford who tallied 36 in each of the last two games. The finals against Wilkes-Barre also went a full three games with the Bombers erasing a 43-30 second period deficit in the rubber game to win 114-104 before a standing room home crowd of 2417. Waite Bellamy pumped in 21 to lead five Bombers with 17 or more. After the championship season Johnston moved on and left the team to his hand-picked successor, forward Barney Cable.

In 1966-67 the Blue Bombers put their finest team ever on the court. Crawford and Bellamy were deadly marksmen and future NBA star Bobby Weiss orchestrated the attack from point guard. With Weiss commanding a blistering fast break the Bombers several times scored more than 150 points and routinely put eight players in double figures. Weiss set an EBL record with 24 assists in one game. Wilmington easily captured the Eastern Division flag with a 21-7 record. But before the season closed the Bombers sold Weiss to the Philadelphia 76ers and Crawford to the Knicks.

With two stars gone for the playoffs Bellamy stepped up his game. In the opening rounds he led Bomber blitzes of New Haven 136-119 and 155-130 and of Hartford 141-117 and 155-138. In the finals against the Scranton Miners Bellamy reached an all-time Bomber single game high of 46 in a 119-116 win. Wilmington finally lost a playoff game in a 149-142 loss at Scranton and the teams exchanged home wins before the deciding game in Wilmington. The Bombers won the title by crushing the Miners 143-100 as Bellamy went for 53 points and added 11 rebounds. He finished the nine playoff games with 330 points.

But the Bombers great success on the court was not matched by enthusiasm at the box office. Crowds of 2000 became as rare as a charging foul in the Sallies gym. Attendance at Blue Bombers games was reduced to a wildly partisan core of about 1000. Only 517 were on hand for the first 1966-67 playoff game and despite their great title run only 1217 turned out for the final game. In 1967-68 the Bombers won their first 13 home games, often to crowds as small as 600.

In 1968-69 the Bombers once again went to the finals but off court needed to initiate a ticket drive to stay in Wilmington. Bomber attendance continued to dive in 1969-70 despite charging only $2.50, scarcely more than a high school game. Sunday games were switched to afternoons as Wilmington again went to the league finals before losing. By 1970-71 the financial situation had become dire for Bomber management.

General Manager Joe Horwitz moved the franchise to a new gym at St. Mark's High School in search of new fans. In a desperate attempt to pare the league's highest payroll - at $100 to $200 per game - he asked Bellamy, Maurice McHartley and John Savage to accept pay cuts. When

The end was nigh for the Blue Bombers as this schedule loomed.

they refused Horwitz had no choice but to drop his three stars. He dressed only eight players instead of the normal 12, including player-coach Frank Corace.

The three players eventually returned but the Bombers were rife with dissension by this time. Players wouldn't speak to each other or ride in the same car to away games. Wilmington still sported the best talent in the league but the players didn't care and the once-proud Blue Bombers crumbled to last place at 11-17. The last game was played before only 225 diehards.

It was the final season for the Blue Bombers. Horwitz claimed losses of over $100,000 and bemoaned the lack of corporate support for his team, calling Wilmington "almost like a bush town" as he left. The same certainly couldn't be said of his Blue Bombers who amassed two championships and four trips to the EBL finals in their 8-year run.

Waite Bellamy

From beginning to end there was always Bellamy. Number 9 rising up on the left side to swish another jumper. In eight years with the Blue Bombers Waite Bellamy scored more than 4500 points, always among the league leaders.

A 6'4", 200-pound guard, Bellamy was drafted in 1963 by the St. Louis Hawks. He hobbled through summer camp trying to hide a broken foot but the injury finally sidelined him and he was forgotten by the NBA. Bellamy worked out a deal with Scranton of the EBL but before he could play a game for the Miners he was shanghaied by Bill Kauffman who was organizing a new team in Wilmington.

Bellamy spent his early years with the Blue Bombers as an instant-offense sixth man. He averaged nearly 40 points per game in the 1966-67 playoffs. The next year he finished third in the league in scoring and in 1969-70 he won his only scoring title with 29.6 points per game. That year Bellamy was the Eastern League Most Valuable Player.

Still, the NBA did not come calling. While Bellamy watched other teammates - including Bobby Weiss, Fred Crawford, Jim Caldwell, Tom Hoover, Maurice McHartley and George Sutor - graduate to the major leagues he continued to make the weekend drives to Hartford and Binghamton while teaching school during the week. Perhaps he was a step slow but mostly he was never in the right place at the right time.

Instead he remained in the bushes lighting up the tiny gyms in the Eastern League and building an indelible legacy in Wilmington. So much so that the memory of the Blue Bombers and Waite Bellamy are inseparable.

The Atlantic Basketball Association (1993-1994)

Weekend professional basketball games returned to Delaware after a two-decade hiatus in 1993. The new Delaware Blue Bombers were the inspiration of coach and owner Scott Barker and his wife and general manager Carolyn. The team consisted of players ranging from recent college graduates to 35-year old career re-treads, many cut from Continental Basketball Association camps. Recruits were paid $50 to $100 for each game on the 30-game Blue Bomber schedule.

The Bombers opened before 1300 at Newark High School, an attendance which quickly settled in around 500. Like their ancestors the new Blue Bombers played a fast-paced open floor game. Delaware featured a strong 3-guard offense who combined for 64 points per game. Two of the backcourtmen, Tee Jay Jackson and Donnie Seale, became league All-Stars, along with forward Anthony Tucker. Seale, out of North Carolina State, was the league's second-leading scorer with 28 points per outing.

Delaware completed the regular season with a 12-15 record, winning their final six home games to finish 4th and make the playoffs. Their first season was extended only briefly, however, as the Blue Bombers were bounced by Allentown in the double elimination tournament in two games.

The Ref

Lou Moser is the only Delawarean ever to be on the court in an NCAA Mens National championship game. The veteran official worked the 1981 showdown between Dean Smith's North Carolina Tarheels and Bobby Knight's Indiana Hoosiers. It was the biggest of more than 1,500 games officiated in a career spanning more than three decades.

Moser was born in Philadelphia but came to Wilmington at the age of 5. He played basketball at P.S. du Pont High School, West Chester State College and Goldey College but began his officiating career as a local baseball umpire. As a basketball referee he graduated from Delaware CYO leagues to the college level while juggling his career in a newspaper circulation department.

Moser got NBA assignments as a fill-in in 1967 and worked 4 1/2 years at the professional level in both the NBA and the old American Basketball Association. Moser was a regular official in the rabid Atlantic Coast Conference for 19 years, building a reputation that culminated in his selection as an official for the 1981 Final Four at the Spectrum in Philadelphia.

DELAWARE BASKETBALL PLAYERS

Ed Koffenberger. After his senior year at Duke University in 1947 Ed Koffenberger, a former P.S. duPont cager, was named to the Helms Foundation's Basketball All-America first team. No Delawarean before or since has ever been a first-team All-American in basketball.

The 6'3" center, known for his sweeping left hook, set an all-time school record for scoring in 1946 with 317 points. The next year Koffenberger led the Conference - then known as the Southern Conference - in scoring with another record 416 points. He paced the league in rebounding as well.

In addition to his recognition as a basketball player Koffenberger was cited as an All-American in lacrosse as well, After graduation Koffenberger forsook his career as a DuPont engineer for a brief professional dalliance with the Richmond Barons. He led the Barons in scoring but shortly returned to Delaware and his engineering profession.

Terence Stansbury. On October 31, 1984 when Terence Stansbury came off the bench to score four points in a 101-100 Indiana Pacer loss to the Dallas Mavericks it was the first time a Delawarean ever scored a point in the NBA.

Stansbury grew up in Wilmington, honing his game in the West Center City Community Center. His silky outside shot earned him games with older players despite his lack of size. He moved to California for a year when he was 16 and when he came back to Delaware he had sprouted to 6'3" on his way to 6'5".

During his senior year at Newark High School Stansbury led the state in scoring with more than 26 a game and was named Player of the Year. Temple won the recruiting battle for the talented guard with a 43" vertical leap and he went on to become the Owls' all-time leading scorer with 1,811 points. In his final two seasons with Temple Stansbury missed only seven minutes of playing time.

Stansbury became the only first-round NBA draft pick from Delware when he was selected by the Dallas Mavericks as the 15th player in the 1984 draft. However, he embarked on a disastrous salary holdout on the advice of his agent. After nine days he fired his agent and signed on his own. But the damage was done. Already seriously behind in his workouts Stansbury was shipped to the Indiana Pacers before his rookie season began.

Stansbury got enough floor time to average 7.1 points but gained his greatest fame when he slammed his way to a third place finish in the All-Star Game Dunk Contest with his immortal Statue of Liberty dunk. Stansbury began 1985 as a starter but nagging injuries and inconsistent play relegated him to the end of the bench by season's end.

After a short stop in Seattle Stansbury took his explosive talent to Europe where he developed into a continental star playing for Holland and Belgium. He joined a professional team in France where he became a national sports hero, scoring more than 25 points a game and beloved for his acrobatic "smashes" - the French term for dunks. Stansbury married a Parisian woman and settled into the cosmopolitan lifestyle - the great potential he first displayed in Delaware finally realized.

A.J. English. A.J. English was a two-time All-Stater at Howard High School and the 1986 Delaware Player of the Year. He matriculated at Division II power Virginia Union where he performed well enough (33.8 ppg and 7.4 rpg) to be named to an Olympic-sponsored team that toured China. He was the only small collage player in the elite group. The 6'4 1/2" guard used the international recognition as a springboard into the NBA, playing two years as a part-time starter for the Washington Bullets. English averaged nearly 10 points a game and scored a career high 31 but after the Bullets failed to meet his salary demands before the 1993 season he too resumed his career in Europe.

Dexter Boney. Dexter Boney's #24 was the first number retired at Brandywine High School and it could not have been much of a decision. The 6'4" scoring machine was first-team All-State three years with the Bulldogs and was Delaware Player of the Year in 1988 after pouring in 30.3 points per game and pulling down 10 rebounds. Boney was the first high schooler to score over 2,000 points in a career, finishing with 2,318 and eclipsing the previous standard of 1,821 established by Wes Townsend of Selbyville.

Boney's college ball started at Hagerstown Junior College in Maryland where he averaged 31.6 points as a sophomore. He moved up to Division I at the University of Nevada Las Vegas where he scored 11.2 points per game in his two seasons.

Boney started his professional career in the Continental Basketball Association and in 1997 he was the league's Most Valuable Player with the Florida Beach Dogs which earned him an eight-game audition with the NBA's Phoenix Suns. He scored 19 points and earned a second 10-day contract before being waived and embarking on a professional playing odyssey that took him to Italy, Alaska, Israel, Venezuala, France and North Dakota.

Monick Foote. Monick Foote left the court at Sanford School in 1994 as the most honored basketball player in state history. There were three first-team All-State nods and two Gatorade State Player of the Year awards. After leading the Warriors to the school's first-ever state championship and collecting a Delaware record 1,609 points Foote was also named Gatorade National Player of the Year. At the University of Virginia Foote finished her career as the Cavaliers' 14th all-time scorer. She was a 35.3% shooter from three-point range and her seven treys in the NCAA tournament against Florida in 1995 remains a school record.

Laron Profit. A native of the South Carolina Lowcountry, Laron Profit was part of an Air Force Family and his stepfather landed at Dover Air Force Base long enough for him to star at Caesar Rodney High School and be named Gatorade Player of the Year in 1995. It was then off to the University of Maryland where the 6'5" Profit wound up his four-year career as the Terrapins' 10th all-time leading scorer and second all-time ball hawk with 252 steals. The two-time honarble mention All-American was the 38th player taken in the 1999 NBA Daft, by the Orlando Magic. Profit carved out a three-year NBA career, starting 18 games and scoring 441 points. His professional career spanned eleven years with stops in Turkey, Argentina and China before returning to the NBA as an assistant coach with the Magic.

The Best Basketball Player Ever To Play In Delaware

Walter Davis came from North Carolina to the Sanford School in 1973-74 to polish his academic skills for a year before entering the University of North Carolina. Davis had already completed four years of high school at South Mecklenburg High School where he played on two consecutive North Carolina state championship teams.

Recruited by Sanford coach Don Frazier - who had ties to the Tarheel State - the 6'6" Davis simply overwhelmed his Independent Conference opponents. He scored 603 points in the Warriors' perfect 19-0 season and could easily have poured in another several hundred had he been so inclined. As it was Davis averaged more than ten assists.

That Davis was the best player to ever step onto a Delaware high school basketball court was obvious. Still, many coaches opposed his nomination to the All-State team. Even though Davis was only 18 years old he was declared ineligible for the state tournament as a fifth-year player and many reasoned he should be excluded for post-season honors as well. In the end his 31.7 scoring average could not be ignored and Davis was named to the 1973 Delaware All-State basketball team.

Walter Davis was on a journey to the highest echelons of basketball. He starred under Dean Smith at North Carolina, won a gold medal in the 1976 Olympics, was the NBA Rookie of the Year and a long-time All-Star. And the best schoolboy basketball player ever to play in Delaware.

Early basketball could be a joyless affair.

Boxing

The Sweet Science in the Shadows

A dark, moonless night, a clearing in the Pennsylvania woods just over the state line, scores of horse-drawn hacks tethered to trees. This was the typical setting for a boxing match in Delaware in the 1800s, when prizefighting for purses was proscribed by law.

Matches were arranged and financed by backers of the fighters, who would spread the word among local sportsmen. These "sports" were secreted to the venue in the middle of the night, where a ring was laid out with gas lamps in the corners. The gamblers cared little more for the combatants than they did for the dogs and cocks that fought to the death in gambling pits in back alleys and illegal houses throughout the region.

Many of these fights were similarly brutal. In 1876 Philip Costa, who fought around Delaware under the alias "William Walker," was killed in a backwoods fight and the body dumped into the Delaware River by his seconds where it was discovered by fishermen. But the sports settled their bets.

Only fighting for a purse was outlawed. Delaware hotels and exhibition halls would stage "demonstrations of pugilism" for paying crowds between fighters who were each paid a fee, with nothing going to the winner. These exhibitions were little more than choreographed dance routines in the science of boxing. Often the two pugilists would travel together, pre-arranging the round when one or the other would go down, usually between the seventh and tenth.

The most celebrated case of illegal prizefighting in Delaware occurred on July 1, 1886 when three fighters, including noted heavyweight Sparrow Golden of Philadelphia, who was seconding for brother, were arrested on the Wilmington and Northern railroad pier. Authorities charged that tickets were being sold for $3 each and that the pugs battled for the lion's share of a $100 purse. Local "sports" staged a benefit for the three men which attracted 400 supporters. Over 60 men testified at the trial, including several

Lightweight Jack Daly was considered the finest Delaware boxer of the 19th century - willing and able to take on all comers up to heavyweights.

prominent Wilmington businessmen. The fighters were ultimately acquitted, but not before Sparrow Golden lost a thousand-dollar payday for a bout in England.

With the rise of the athletic clubs in Wilmington in the latter part of the century these exhibitions became more authentic tests of pugilistic skill. From these clubs emerged several popular fighters, including John "Midget" Glynn, a 110-pound featherweight with a rushing style, and lightweight Cornelius J. Moriarty, alias "Jack Daly."

Both fought regularly on the undercards of nationally promoted fights. Daly, born and raised around 8th & Madison in Wilmington, was considered the greatest boxer ever developed in Delaware. He fought at 122 pounds but took on all comers, including even heavyweights. Daly won the Philadelphia Association tournament in February 1892 and a month later turned pro, winning his first fight at 125 pounds in four rounds against Ben Horn in Staunton, Virginia. Daly piled up over three dozen wins during the next decade. His greatest bout was against Englishman Stanton Abbott, who Daly fought to a draw after 37 rounds and 2 1/2 hours. The Wilmington man had much the better of the fracas but the referee called off the proceedings because "neither man was in any danger of being knocked out in less than 20 more rounds." In 1898 he battered lightweight champion Kid Lavigne for 20 rounds in Cleveland but was robbed of the title when the bout was ruled a draw. It was rumored that the referee had his money on the champ.

While Daly and Glynn were well known in Delaware the boxers who were known across the country were the heavyweight champions, the first non-four-legged superstars in the sports world. John L. Sullivan, Bob Fitzsimmons and James Jeffries all fought exhibitions in Delaware.

Thousands turned out to admire the champs' physiques and skill with a punching bag. The three-round events were little more than sparring sessions but occasionally pugilistic exuberance could not be contained, as when Jeffries came to Wilmington. Reported one observer, "With a single exception the blows Jeffries administered were merely taps, designed to show how he can hit, but one poke, in the third round, was evidently more

The best Delaware fight fans could hope for from appearances by champs like John L. Sullivan were tame exhibition matches when boxing was illegal in the state.

vigorous than the champion intended, and fairly lifted his partner from the floor."

The last bare knuckle fight in Delaware was broken up by police in 1892 and concluded across the line in Landenberg. In 1901, after decades of legal and illegal boxing in the state, officials finally decided that all fighting was against Delaware law and stopped even exhibitions. The sweet science disappeared in the First State.

Boxing Becomes Legal

In 1931, after an 18-year struggle, it became legal to stage a boxing match in Delaware for prize money. The first bill to allow prizefights was voted down 19-10 in the state legislature in 1913. Two years later the House passed a bill creating an Athletic Commission to sanction boxing bouts but the movement went no further. From that point there was a boxing bill before the General Assembly nearly every year.

While the lawmakers wrangled, boxing was flourishing in Delaware. Boxing had been taught in the army in World War I and returning soldiers hungered for similar action in peacetime. Boxing fans in Wilmington could find bouts in the Pythian Castle at 908 West Street, in the Academy of Music at 10th & Delaware, at the Elam Athletic Club on Concord Pike, in the National Guard Armory at 10th & du Pont streets, and elsewhere. Every now and then law enforcement officials would raid a club and all the participants would be arrested. But there would be a good card next week somewhere.

The charades ended April 17, 1931 with the first boxing sanctioned by the state of Delaware at the Auditorium on 11th Street in Wilmington. The fighters were mostly bantamweights and lightweights who provided non-stop action for the 2003 people who paid their way in. Soon the first boxing club outside of Wilmington was being planned for the outskirts of Harrington.

Several months later big-name fighters began to appear in Delaware. The first was Primo Carnera, a massive heavyweight contender and possessor of the largest fist in boxing history. The 278-pound Carnera was matched against Armando De Carlos in the open air arena at Shellpot Park, a trolley park developed by the Wilmington

On his way to the heavyweight championship of the world Primo Carnera stopped in Wilmington to batter an overmatched opponent.

City Railway Company in Brandywine Hundred in the 1880s. Tickets went for $2.10 and $3.50 - at the height of the Depression - and the gate was an enthusiastic 1700. Carnera, sporting an 85 1/2 pound weight advantage, bludgeoned De Carlos for four minutes and eight seconds until the fight was stopped. A more common card promoted local pugs and fight fans could see up to 30 rounds of action for 50 cents.

Before legalization Wilmington had been considered one of the "hottest" boxing towns in the East with packed houses at Shellpot Park and the Elsmere Fairgrounds. But after the game became legit the crowds dwindled. In the first year one boxing club was out of business and another punch drunk. Boxing had always been available in Maryland, Pennsylvania and New Jersey and the same fellows

Delawareans had traipsed across the state line for years to see were being trotted out in Delaware with no originality, simply resuming tiresome grudges dating five years of more. The poor matches and boring mismatches were a lethal one-two to boxing in Delaware.

Route 13 became known as the "Graveyard of Boxing Hopes." Clubs along the du Pont Highway like Shellpot Park, Playland and Harrington all went under. A grand new outdoor sports arena grandly called "Olympia" opened on the Causeway, six blocks from Front Street beyond Garausche's Lane and Market Street in Wilmington. There was seating for 4200 but barely 1/3 of that showed on Olympia's opening night and most of that crowd was papered. Olympia soon joined its predecessors on the canvas.

Having created this still-born sport the General Assembly tried to keep the game afloat. A proposal was made to allow bouts up to 20 rounds, which only three states permitted at that time. A compromise sliced the plan to a pair of 10-rounders each year. By 1938 there was enough boxing, both amateur and pro, to support three outdoor summer clubs and plenty of fistic action was available for Delawareans.

These clubs and gyms began spawning fighters of some repute in the 1930s - Johnny Aiello, Al Tribuani, Lou Brooks - who could fill an arena but big paydays for promoters were rare. During World War II Delawareans were treated to exhibitions by such stars as Sugar Ray Robinson and Joe Louis but after the war the same old mismatches and tired promotions once again infected the boxing game in Wilmington.

When Freddie "Red" Cochrane, reigning world welterweight champion, stopped in Delaware during a barnstorming tour in 1945 and crunched a tomato can named Alex Doyle (New Jersey welterweight champion with a career 35-57-8 record) with a left hook in the second round the purists howled. In 1949 ex-middleweight champion Rocky Graziano, the biggest draw in boxing, came to Wilmington to battle a well-tenderized Bobby Claus (12-19-1). A turn-away crowd of 3910 at the old Auditorium was stunned to see Claus floor the Rock in the first round with a sucker punch but Graziano bounced up and pummeled the hapless journeyman.

RING Magazine, the Bible of boxing, pulled no punches with its harsh appraisal of the bout: "In digging up Claus, who had been knocked out 9 times in 18 previous starts, Graziano stretched the idea of safety a bit too far. It's this sort (bad mismatches) that have kept Wilmington, Delaware from being one of the best fistic centers on the Atlantic Seaboard (remember that Red Cochrane-Midget Doyle whatsiz in 1945). Some folks never learn."

By the next year, 1950, Claus and his trick knee had been knocked out so many times he was suspended in Pennsylvania. But he was still fighting in Delaware. In a comeback bout for native son Al Tribuani a paycheck named Manuel Rosa took a dive in the second round. When he was fined only $60 by the Delaware State Athletic Commission cynics said it was because it was such a bad dive.

Shenanigans like these were well on their way to killing boxing in Delaware when television shoveled dirt on the coffin. Since the 1950s live boxing has been a sporadic affair kept alive in the occasional card at Fournier Memorial Hall in Wilmington's Little Italy section. To date Wilmington's potential as a great boxing town has yet to be realized.

DELAWARE BOXERS

Johnny Aiello. Delaware's first boxing hero of the legal age was Johnny Aiello, a former catcher at P.S. du Pont High School. Aiello was a 118-pound perpetual motion machine of a bantamweight. By 1938 the 20-year old had been boxing three years, losing only 3 of some 60 bouts. That year he won the Eastern Golden Gloves title and reached the finals of the national amateur tournament before losing.

In 1940 Aiello, a Wilmington plumber, won the Golden Gloves again, this time in Madison Square Garden before 17,000 fans. Aiello, the veteran of more than 100 amateur bouts, turned professional but he was exposed as only a very good amateur fighter. In five months of professional ring work in 1941 as a featherweight he won seven times, lost twice and had one draw; he scored four knockouts. By 1942 he was retired in Wilmington, training aspiring boxers at St. Anthonys CYO before heading off to World War II in the U.S. Navy.

Lou Brooks. As a kid Lou Brooks did most of his fighting on the Wilmington streets. At Howard High School he was a fast halfback and track star before entering the ring. Brooks won his first amateur bout but the raw street-brawler lost his next six fights. The 175-pound Brooks observed and developed until his amateur career concluded in the 1941 Golden Gloves tournament which he won by battering his opponent through the ropes at one point.

Brooks won his first nine professional scraps, eight by knockout, when he was matched with Lee Savold at Wilmington Park. Savold was a bruising puncher who had once taken Joe Louis' best blows. Newspaper accounts estimated the gate at over 8000, promoter Bob Carpenter claimed 10,000. Whatever, it was Delaware's biggest boxing crowd ever and they saw one of the state's best ever boxing shows. Brooks entered the ring a 3-1 underdog and weathered Savold's bombs for five rounds, giving as good as he got. But in the 6th round the Wilmington light-heavyweight fell under the onslaught of Savold's withering body punches.

Brooks ended his first year as a pro with a 14-1 record. In 1942 Brooks, a crowd-pleasing wild puncher, was a headliner at the major boxing clubs in Philadelphia. Fighting at his top weight ever, 185 pounds, his opponents included many ranking heavyweights and light-heavyweights. He battled twice with Joey Maxim, the #7 ranked light-heavyweight, drawing once and losing once. At the end of

1942 Brooks was the #13 ranked heavyweight by *RING Magazine*.

His career appeared to be on the rise when in 1943 Brooks was temporarily blinded by a wayward thumb from former light-heavyweight champion Melio Bettina in the first round of a bout in the outdoor arena in Philadelphia. The fight was stopped - and so was Brooks' career. Four eye operations couldn't restore full vision and after a few bouts in Mexico and Texas he retired. His largest purse had been $6900.

Brooks turned manager and instructor and in 1956 he was named the first black boxing judge on the Delaware Boxing Commission. He was the best big man to yet come out of Delaware.

Al Tribuani. Born in Philadelphia in 1920, Al Tribuani came to Wilmington with his family shortly afterwards and rose to the greatest prominence of any Delaware fighter before him. At Bayard Junior High School Tribuani played only soccer but longed for physical contact. He soon found himself in the downtown gyms under the guidance of his older brother Ralph, a former fighter turned trainer-promoter.

The sturdy 147-pounder found even more contact in the Salesianum backfield in 1937 and 1938 before transferring to Wilmington High School in 1939. Meanwhile Tribuani was piling up ring experience, taking over 150 amateur fights and losing only three. He capped an amateur career by winning the Eastern Golden Gloves welterweight title in Madison Square Garden on the same card as Johnny Aiello. Tribuani brought the crowd to its feet with two knockouts before decisioning Bobby Claus, a National Guard machine gunner from Buffalo, in an all-out slugfest in the final.

Tribuani, also a National Guardsman, turned pro as World War II was breaking out. His early bouts were carefully picked "stiffs" as he built a 15-2 pro record before winning a unanimous 10-round decision over former lightweight champion Lou Jenkins in front of 6500 Wilmington partisans labeled him as a potential contender.

In 1943 Tribuani earned a bout with Henry Armstrong, the only fighter ever to hold the featherweight, lightweight and welterweight titles at the same time. Armstrong, the first to inspire the proclamation "pound for pound the greatest fighter alive," was attempting a comeback at the age of 30 after 17 months of retirement.

The match was made in the Philadelphia Convention Center and 12,633 fans were on hand, the largest crowd to ever see a Delaware pro. Armstrong entered the ring at 138 1/2 pounds while Tribuani tipped the scales at 146 1/4. The Wilmington fighter lost the 10-round decision as Armstrong was awarded seven rounds but the national media praised the great fight given by the "unknown." Armstrong piped up, "It was a tough fight. I was fighting a superman." The crowd had been so boisterous the fighters could not hear the bell at the end of the rounds.

Later that summer Tribuani fought twice against Al "Bummy" Davis in Philadelphia, in bouts that were classics of the era. Tribuani won both although in the rematch he

exited the ring with a cheekbone fractured in three places. "Even now all I have to do to recall my toughest fight is rub my hand across the left side of my face. The pain and memory of that June night and a great fight against a real game guy flashes quickly to mind," he remembered in 1953. For his part, Bummy Davis would die a few years later intervening in an armed robbery which sportswriter W.C. Heinz recounted in what is still considered the best sports profile ever written.

Within months Tribuani's training had shifted from Wilmington gyms to boot camp at Fort Dix. In 1944 he was an infantryman in France. In the spring of 1945, only days before the war in Europe would end, Tribuani was struck by machine gun fire, shattering his left arm. He received the Bronze Star but never regained the snap in his left jab. He turned to training other fighters in 1947.

In 1949, after being absent from the square circle since 1944, Tribuani returned to fight an exhibition with welterweight champion Sugar Ray Robinson. As a gesture for his old Golden Gloves teammate Robinson came to Wilmington for only expense money. Tribuani trained for the four-round dance as if it was a real title shot but Robinson entered the ring at Wilmington Park with protective headgear and oversized gloves. The crowd booed but the champion wasn't about to risk injury in this benefit.

Tribuani fought a few more times but his career was essentially over - just as were the glory days of Delaware boxing. The gate for the Tribuani-Robinson match was not nearly as large as promoter Bob Carpenter had expected and but a fraction of Tribuani's bouts a decade earlier. The golden era of Delaware boxing passed with Al Tribuani.

Willie Roache. Willie Roache met more name fighters than anyone in Delaware history. Although "Whistling Willie" was born in Harrington he was not taken seriously as a boxer while in Delaware. The 130-pounder honed his skills in New York and New England as he became a challenger in the featherweight division. He would continue to box for more than two decades, eventually fighting for the world championship.

By his estimate Roache won more than 200 amateur fights in the 1930s before turning pro. His best year was in 1944 when he won 21 of 24 fights, including dropping the Mexican champion Ham Wiloby in the Blue Hen Arena at Third and Scotts streets in Wilmington. That year Roache also knocked down Willie Pep, one of boxing's greatest little men, but ran out of steam in the 15-round match, his first go at the distance, and lost the bout. In December he lost the World Boxing Association's featherweight championship to Sal Bartolo in the Boston Garden.

Roache also battled former lightweight champion Ike Williams in his 80-fight pro career, matches that took him across the world. His final record was only 30-47-3 but it was compiled against the best.

Henry Milligan. It was the type of story the media finds irresistible: Princeton graduate, Ivy League man, and professional engineer sullying himself in the boxing game. And the national scribes lined up. There were pieces in *Sports Illustrated*, the *Los Angeles Times*, the *New York Times*, even *People Magazine*. And Henry Milligan lived up to the hype.

Milligan was an all-around athlete at A.I. du Pont High School where he was a two-time state wrestling champion. At Princeton he was a 10-letter winner - a .300-hitting third baseman, a cornerback and punt returner and an All-America 190-pound wrestler. As impressive as this athletic resume was, however, there was nothing in the portfolio that was going to bring Milligan lasting recognition. And Henry Milligan wanted to be a famous person.

After graduating in 1981 he shrewdly decided to try his hand at boxing where he could indulge his passion for fitness and, if he was any good at all, would be sure to attract attention as an educated, white heavyweight. And Milligan proved to be amazingly good. After just seven months and twelve amateur fights - all knockouts - Milligan reached the semi-finals of the National Golden Gloves tournament. At the Golden Gloves the 5'11", 190-pound Milligan upset the number-one ranked Michael Arms before suffering a controversial loss in the semis.

Conditioning was his forte, carrying him further than his limited natural fistic gifts could. Never did Milligan enter the ring thinking he was out-trained. By 1984 Henry Milligan was the national amateur heavyweight champion and a favorite to make the United States Olympic team. But at the Olympic Trials in Fort Worth, Texas Milligan was stopped in the second round by a little-known 17-year old slugger named Mike Tyson. His Olympic dreams shattered, Milligan announced his retirement from amateur boxing. His record of 41-6 included 31 knockouts, twenty in the first round.

Milligan expressed no interest in professional boxing but the lure of the spotlight had him back in the ring within a year. On March 20, 1985 he dropped Garland Hall at 1:55 of the first round to win his first professional fight in the Brandywine Club in Chadds Ford, Pennsylvania. He won his first eleven pro fights - again, all by knockout - before being stopped in the second round by Al Shofner at Delaware Park on May 10, 1986. Later that year Milligan sustained bloody cuts over his eyes in a loss to Frank Minton and, still unmarked and hoping to remain so, he stepped out of boxing.

But once again the lure of celebrity enticed Milligan back. This time, in 1993 at the age of 35, Milligan won two comeback fight before suffering an 8th round knockout for the IBO Cruiserweight title. Afterwards, with a 15-2-1 pro record, he announced yet another retirement, having achieved his goal of lasting fame - certainly in Delaware.

The Promoter

Raffaele Tribuani could have come straight out of central casting. He was born in the Republic of San Marino, a microstate on the Italian peninsula. The family came to Delaware when Ralph was still a kid. He was a teenage boxer and was on the undercard of the Primo Carnera heavyweight fight in Shellpot Park in 1931. The bout was canceled but the 17-year old Tribuani was enlisted as Carnera's interpreter while he was in town.

Thus began a lifelong friendship and also a lifetime in the boxing game outside the ring for Tribuani. For the next four decades, until he died from brain surgery in the 1970s, Ralph Tribuani was at the center of most things boxing on the Delmarva Peninsula.

He promoted amateur boxing cards at Wilmington's Auditorium and managed the career of his younger brother Al when he broke big. Tribuani handled the affairs of the fighters for the T & C Athletic Association, taking them to represent the city in national Golden Gloves tournaments in New York City and Chicago.

Tribuani was connected to all of the biggest boxers of the day and made matches for many of them to fight in Wilmington. After middleweight hero Rocky Graziano was suspended from fighting in New York in the wake of a bribery kerfuffle, Tribuani got him a license to fight in Delaware and revive his career.

As television eroded the interest in live boxing in the 1950s and 1960s Tribuani turned his talents to other endeavors - he promoted professional wrestling and put on rock-and-roll shows with such acts as Bill Haley and the Comets. He found work for old fighters as referees and was known to shovel money to local fighters and put on benefits to keep the fight game alive in Delaware. If Burt Young was doing homework on the inside game of boxing preparing for his role of Paulie in *Rocky* he could have done no better than tag along

Ralph Tribuani with middleweight champion Rocky Graziano.
The Wilmington promoter helped restore Graziano's boxng career
after the boxer failed to report a bribe attempt.

Dave Tiberi

In 1898 Jack Daly was denied the opportunity to become Delaware's first boxing world champion amidst a swirl of rumors that the referee was on the take. Nearly a hundred years later, as Dave Tiberi climbed out of an Atlantic City ring, Delaware still had not claimed a world champion and there were again dark rumors circulating about the integrity of boxing officials.

Dave Tiberi grew up at the back end of 14 children, including 12 boys. Six of the Tiberi brothers were involved in boxing, including Joe, who retired in 1984 with an 18-5-1 professional record. Dave turned pro in 1985 at the age of 18. Seven years later Tiberi had fashioned a solid record of 22-2-3 with seven knockouts. He was ranked as the #10 middleweight in the world by the International Boxing Federation and deserving of a title shot against champion James Toney of Ann Arbor, Michigan.

Toney entered the ring unbeaten in 28 fights, having knocked out 20 of his victims. He trained lightly for Tiberi and boasted that "he's a good, average fighter, but he's not in my league." Tiberi, although having never been knocked down, had gone only ten rounds twice. Toney was a prohibitive favorite for the 12-round, nationally televised match.

The two fighters stood in the middle of the ring and traded punches throughout the fight. At the end of the first round Tiberi was staggered by a direct hit from a left hook but for most of the night the Delaware challenger initiated the action. The bigger punches were Toney's, but Tiberi was the busier fighter. The final cards showed one judge favoring Tiberi 117-111 and two judges placing Toney ahead 115-111 and 115-112.

The split decision outraged the Taj Mahal crowd. A chorus of boos cascaded through the hall as Delaware fans carried Tiberi triumphantly from the ring. Commentator Alex Wallou, calling the fight for ABC television, incited the protests by terming it "the most disgusting decision I've ever seen."

Donald Trump proclaimed the decision "an embarrassment to Atlantic City." Delaware legislators pleaded Tiberi's case in the federal government. The maelstrom of protest over the boxing "system" threatened to overshadow Tiberi's gutty performance.

And it has been the last Tiberi boxing performance Delawareans have been able to see. Tiberi refused all lucrative offers for a rematch, insisting he would not face Toney unless he fought as champion and Toney as challenger. Standing on principle he retired to private life and community work back in Delaware.

Football

Delaware Field Club

The Delaware Field Club, Delaware's first organization for outdoor sports, started modestly on the front porch of Henry Tatnall's house on Jefferson Street in Wilmington in 1882. The Tatnalls supplied the adhesive to bond the cricket-playing talent of the city of Wilmington. The Delaware Cricket Club was formed and negotiations were quickly underway for a club grounds which were secured at Twenty-Third and West streets, far out across the Brandywine River.

Within a fortnight a cricket crease had been laid out along with courts for tennis and open spaces for croquet and other games. One game that would never be played on the new grounds was baseball, considered too boisterous and commonplace for such an exclusive club. A strong baseball nine was eventually formed from the Field Club but many of the young members played under assumed names so as to not muddy their reputations in the local business community.

The grounds at Brandywine Village were almost two miles from center city and transportation was problematic. In fact, it was non-existent. Trolley lines did not run that far out of the city and an omnibus was hired to ferry passengers out to the Cricket Club for a 5-cent round trip fare. With a capacity of but 12 the Pioneer Coach Company was busy indeed when the flag flew above the clubhouse signaling to downtown members and fans that a game was afoot.

The club was incorporated on March 23, 1885 as a stock company and changed its name to the Delaware Field Club. William Canby was elected president and stockholders formed a "Who's Who of Delaware" society: Bancroft, Bayard, Carpenter, Haskell and du Pont. From this aristocratic group would emerge Delaware's first great football team.

In 1890 the Delaware Field Club moved to a spacious new headquarters in Elsmere which was transformed into some of the finest sporting ground in the country. The seven acres, enclosed with a 12-foot fence, featured 24 tennis courts, a baseball field and a cricket field. The graceful clubhouse included a bowling alley and shuffleboard. When the Club moved to its new grounds a new sport had been added to the roster of activities: football.

With hard practice and superior precision the Delaware Field Club dominated the other novice in-state teams. They instead reached across state borders to forge rivalries with strong collegiate squads such as the Princeton University sophomores and the St. John's eleven of Baltimore. It wasn't until Halloween day 1891 that the rest of football playing Delaware caught up with the Field Club.

The lead account of the Delaware Field Club-Delaware College game that day could hardly be described as low-key: "But who will ever forget the great contest in the Newark meadows of Saturday evening October 31! Nothing like it was ever seen or heard of in Delaware before.

It inaugurated the real commencement of football playing in the state." The college boys ground out a 4-0 upset win in Pie's Meadow that day, a victory no informed observer could have anticipated. Only two years previously Delaware College had been routed 74-0 by the Field Club in its first game ever.

It was not only the first loss of the Delaware Field Club to an in-state rival but the first points ever surrendered by the Field Club. For the rematch in December of 1892 officials in Delaware City offered each club $100 to meet in that town. Both teams and their fans loaded boats and the colorful convoy of the red-and-black Delaware Field Club and the gold-and-blue Delaware College made its way down the Delaware River.

The Field Club was coming off a bitter 12-6 Thanksgiving loss to St. John's and looked to this state championship game for redemption. In a titanic struggle neither team was able to penetrate the other's defenses and the game ended in scoreless tie. It was the last big game for the Delaware Field Club. The next year the team lost several key players and disbanded. The future glory of the Delaware Field Club lay on the golf links and not the gridiron.

The Warren Athletic Club

The most famous of Delaware's 19th century football clubs, the Warren Athletic Club, was organized in April 1883 as an athletic and social club, based in a second story room of the Washington Fire Company, then located at Third and French Streets. The club was mostly comprised of members of the fire company.

Within a few years the success of the club had spawned membership applications from men across the city, over 1000 in all. It was one of the largest athletic clubs in the country. Warren men were prominent in nearly every type of athletic endeavor for the next decade but it was football where Warren fame lingered. Warren football began in 1889 and by 1893 the club was engaging the best elevens in America.

That year Warren hosted a strong St. John's club from Baltimore on Thanksgiving, losing 6-4 before 3600 frenzied enthusiasts. The next week Warren lost "only" 24-0 in sheets of rain to national champion University of Pennsylvania. Keeping the score even for ten minutes was considered the greatest achievement in Warren football history. Warren even managed to score the only touchdown of the season against Penn but the play was disallowed as a forward pass.

By 1897 Warren had lost only one game in three years against teams other than the University of Pennsylvania. Their greatest in-state rival, the YMCA, had by now abandoned football leaving the Warren orange and black as the colors of choice for Wilmington gridiron fans. The biggest games could bring out as many as 5000 supporters for the exploits of such stars as halfback George "Kitten" Prentiss,

The Warrens could handle any opposing eleven except the national champion Penn Quakers.

considered the greatest Delaware football player of the 19th century. Prentiss was a 10-second sprinter who later pitched major league baseball until dying of typhoid fever in 1902.

As popular as the Warren Athletic Club became by the end of the 1890s financial pressures were eroding the legendary organization. Their final gridiron glory came on Thanksgiving Day 1897 when the Warren management lured the United States Artillery School of Fort Monroe, Virginia to Wilmington. The U.S. Artillery was the greatest football attraction ever seen in Delaware to that time, undefeated in four years and the best team outside the so-called Big Four: Penn, Yale, Princeton and Harvard. Early in the game Prentiss scored on a five-yard run to cap a long drive and the Warrens held off the Artillerymen the rest of the way to win 4-0.

The glory days had ended but for the next fifty years, when Delawareans talked football, they compared teams to the Warren Club.

The Orange Athletic Club

The Orange Athletic Club began playing football in 1897, engaging lightweight teams around Wilmington for several seasons. With the demise of the Warrens the Orange gradually assumed the mantle of Wilmington's "premiere" eleven.

By 1905 their reputation as the best team on the South Side Park grounds was firmly established. That year the Orange completed a 5-1-1 campaign, outscoring their opponents 112-9. Those nine points were all surrendered in their only setback, a 9-0 loss to Philadelphia's Pennsylvania Railroad YMCA - a squad comprised of former college stars.

In 1906 the Orange finally got the tough schedule the team deserved. They travelled to Ohio for a game with the Massillon Tigers, an aggregation of Western collegiate all-stars. The Tigers were a prehistoric football phenomenon - far and away the best team in the country. Their owner reportedly had a standing offer of $100,000 to any team that could defeat the Tigers. The minimum admission ticket to a Tigers game in Massillon was $1.00 at a time when most clubs were barely able to collect fifty cents for their best seats.

The Orange were not the team to threaten that $100,000 guarantee. Outweighed by nearly 50 pounds per man they fought the Tigers to a standstill for the first ten minutes and came as close to driving to the Tiger end zone as any team ever had but the Delaware boys were used to 20-minute halves, not the 30 they played in Ohio. Wearing down, the Orange were crushed 77-0 but won a national reputation for their fine performance.

But the Orange had come along at the wrong time. Big-time college football was upon the land and nearby Philadelphia was a focal point for many of America's most anticipated contests. Fan support for the Orange was never great - crowds of 500 were the rule - and a money-making season was out of the question. Orange management realized the situation and only played to get enough money ahead by season's end to throw the players a banquet and give them a team photo.

By 1909, after several financially shaky seasons, even that modest goal was unobtainable. The Orange disbanded, having suffered only one defeat to a local team ever - back in 1898 to the Franklin eleven. No more would an independent football team carry Delaware's colors to distant gridirons; from this point that duty would be the special reserve of the Delaware College Blue Hens.

The Wilmington Clippers (1937-49)

At the height of the Depression, in the face of previous failures in professional boxing and baseball, minor league football came to Delaware in 1937. During the closely watched pre-season half of Wilmington was ecstatic over Lammot du Pont, Jr.'s new professional football team while the other half warily predicted doom. It turned out that both sides were right.

The independent Clippers arranged an ambitious schedule which included four National Football League teams. Du Pont and team president John De Luca put player procurement in the hands of veteran football man Dutch Slagle. Slagle's most important recruit was Walt Masters, a former University of Pennsylvania star and Washington Senators pitcher, who was expected to provide running, kicking and passing from his halfback position.

For local flavor Slagle added Joe Scannell, who was quickly dropped, and Vic Willis, Jr. Willis, a 6'6", 190-pound end out of the University of Maryland, was employed as a chemist and turned down several more lucrative offers to stay close to home. The "elongated wingman" played half the season before being released as the Clippers' last Delaware connection.

More than 4000 fans paid the highest prices ever seen for a Delaware sporting event to see the Clippers clash with the Philadelphia Eagles at Pennsy Field to kick off the 1937 season. Box seats fetched $2.50, although admission to the game could be gained for as little as 40 cents. The Wilmington faithful went home only mildly disappointed by a 14-6 loss in a defensive struggle that saw the Clippers outgunned 145 yards to 15.

Singled out for his outstanding play on the line of scrimmage was #18, a stocky warrior from Fordham named Vince Lombardi. Lombardi broke his nose in a scrimmage the following week but was back in the starting line-up for the Clippers first win, a 25-7 dismantling of the Richmond Arrows. Lombardi played the entire 1937 season with the Clippers, his only year of professional play, appearing in 10 of the 11 games and starting five before leaving Delaware for other gridiron adventures.

As the season progressed Slagle's passing attack matured and the defense

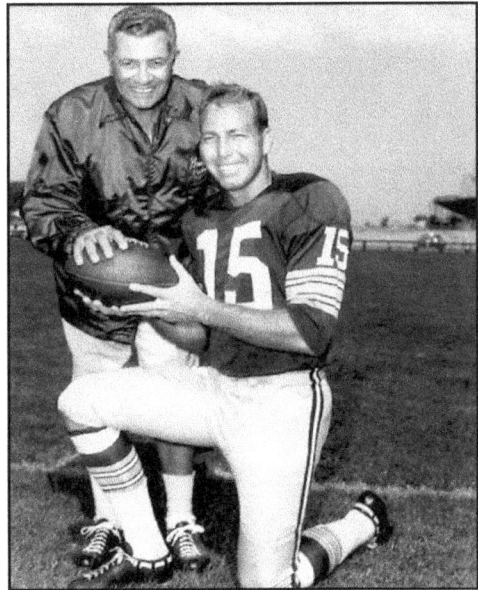

A broken nose playing with the Clippers helped Vince Lombardi, here pictured as Green Bay Packers coach with quarterback Bart Starr, decide that his football future did not lie in playing.

began dominating the Clippers' minor league opponents. Wilmington finished with 7 wins in 8 games against these teams but lost all three exhibition games against the NFL. The cost of this success was high. Slagle brought in several high-salaried ex-NFL players and despite strong fan support the Clippers lost plenty of Lammot du Pont's money.

New coach Masters forged an impressive 9-3 record for the Clippers in their second year. The "Fleet," as they were nicknamed, carried their red and blue colors to the American Association and pre-season interest for 1939 was the highest yet. A huge crowd of 5500 saw Wilmington fall 16-0 to the NFL Brooklyn Dodgers in the Friday night opener.

The passing duo of Masters and Jack Ferrante connected on a league record 9 touchdowns in 1939 as the Clippers began to perform before overflow crowds. The Clippers allowed only two touchdowns in the first six league games and finished the year tied with the Newark Bears, a farm team of the Chicago Bears, at 6-2-1. George Halas sent his star Chicago quarterback Sid Luckman to guide Newark in the championship game over the howling protests of the Clippers. More than a thousand Wilmington fans joined the 13,500 in Newark to watch the Fleet dominate the game but lose 13-6 to a late touchdown throw by Luckman. An official Clippers' protest of Luckman's appearance was overruled and the Bears were champions.

The Clippers remained strong in 1940, racing out to a 4-0-1 start, including a 13-7 revenge win over Newark. The talented Fleet outplayed the Philadelphia Eagles 16-14, the first time any American Association team had beaten an NFL team. Wilmington lost momentum after the historic win and barely stumbled into the playoffs. Once there, the Clippers stopped the Paterson Panthers 11-8 in the first round after getting a safety from the strange rule of a pass hitting the goalpost. Wilmington lost in the finals for the second year in a row, 17-7 to an old nemesis, the Jersey City Giants.

The Wilmington Clippers - known to their devoted fans as "The Fleet" - were the strongest team outside the National Football League in the early 1940s.

New coach George Venoroso installed a T-formation offense for 1941 to which the Clippers were slow to adjust. After going winless in their first four games the Fleet began to rally and scored a 28-21 win over league leader Paterson to gain the fourth and final spot in the playoffs. Many in the crowd of more than 6000 considered it the best football ever played in Wilmington.

With Venoroso's passing game now polished the Clippers ran all over the Panthers 33-0 on a wet and windy December afternoon in their first ever home playoff game. In the finals Wilmington scored all 21 points in a big third quarter to win the championship 21-13 over the Long Island Indians. Four Clippers made the All-League team - Ed Michaels at guard, Scrapper Farrell and Les Dodson in the backfield and Herschel Giddens at tackle. Three other starters from the strongest Clippers eleven yet were named to the second team.

World War II began taking a toll on the American Football Association as early as 1940. Tex Coker, Wilmington's stalwart at center had played in all 51 Clipper games before being called to National Guard duty late that year. With America at war in 1942 the American Association suspended operations. Even though the team had still never made a profit du Pont decided to continue the Clippers as an independent team.

The Fleet were the strongest football team outside the NFL in 1942. They rolled over opponents by scores like 38-0, 42-6, 59-9, 34-0, 70-0, 28-0 and 77-0. In their first three games 14 different players scored. Searching for quality opponents the Clippers engaged the New England professional champs, the Hartford Blues

and scored 7 of the first 11 times they touched the ball in a 48-7 romp.

The fans grumbled about these lopsided games and thirst for a real game was so great that fans were turned away from Wilmington Park when the Philadelphia Eagles came to town. The Clippers spotted their NFL foe three touchdowns before roaring back to tie 21-21. The Fleet threw for 182 yards, the Eagles only 30. With the caliber of opposition severely reduced the Clippers suspended operations after the 1942 season for the duration of the war.

The Clippers kicked off again in 1946 as a Washington Redskins farm team. The fans were eager but the Fleet was weak and as the losses mounted, the gate dwindled. Wilmington was outscored 184 to 57 for the year and didn't score a touchdown at home until the final game when they got a 15-yard fumble recovery to start the game.

The All-America Conference, a rival major league to the NFL, bled talent from minor league clubs like the Clippers and the team struggled on for several years with limited success. A mediocre team squeaked into the finals in 1948 but surrendered 17 second-half points to lose 24-14. In 1949 six home games attracted only 7968 fans, a far cry from the 37,566 in the championship year of 1941. The 5-5 Clippers had to win their last game to gain the playoffs where they were rudely dismissed 66-0 by Richmond.

It was the worst - and last - loss for the Wilmington Clippers. After a painful season in which his losses were estimated at $100,000, Lammot du Pont, Jr. finally pulled the plug on Delaware's all-time best professional football team before the 1950 season.

The Eastern Professional Football League (1944)

In 1944 Local 36 of the Wilmington Shipbuilders gained entry into the 8-team Eastern Professional Football League. After nearly three years of war interest was high in the new team at the outset as 3000 people turned out for a 20-20 tie with Chester. A typical crowd for the season was 1500 as the Shipbuilders, featuring local stars Bob Riley and Lou Brooks, reached the playoffs despite a 3-4-1 mark.

Wilmington won their semi-final against Camden 3-0 on a 30-yard field goal with under 2:00 remaining but conditions in the league were deteriorating. The field for the championship game at Frankford was in such bad condition several players had to be talked into suiting up. Only 250 fans were scattered around the stands to see a very bad football game. Wilmington brought home the title in its only year in existence when a bad snap on a punt led to a 2-yard drive for the only score of the game.

*Samuel H. Baynard was a watchmaker by trade but he would drift out of the jewelry business into banking as the years wound down on the 19th century.
In 1900, at the age of 49, he joined the Wilmington Board of Park Commissioners, beginning a quarter-century of work developing North Brandywine Park.
In 1912 he paid for the leveling of ground to create the Baynard Athletic Grounds.
He continued to pour money into the nascent facility: a quarter-mile cinder track and a concrete grandstand in 1921 and the acquisition of adjacent cottages to be converted into sports storage houses and locker rooms.
Since officially opening on June 24, 1922 Baynard Stadium has hosted many of the city's premier events in football, track and soccer.*

The North American Football League (1965)

In 1965 Wilmington was represented in a curious aggregation known as the North American Football League. The league's six teams were split into two geographically diverse divisions - the Northern Division included teams in Pennsylvania and Maryland as well as Delaware. The Southern Division was truly that - Mobile and Huntsville in Alabama and Lakeland, Florida. The Comets, as the Wilmington entry was known, opened the season with 21 Delaware-born players and ex-Clipper Jack Ferrante as coach.

The Comets began play before a curious band of 3410 in the 44,000-seat stadium in Mobile and scratched out a 14-14 tie despite gaining only 195 yards. Back home against the Pennsylvania Mustangs the Comets fell behind 17-0 before reviving on the arm of former North Carolina quarterback Jack Cummings to win 20-17. Wilmington won two more games before a three-game tailspin cost Ferrante his job. The Comets wound up the 1965 season 4-5-1, last in the Northern Division. It mattered not; the NAFL disbanded before the 1966 season.

The Atlantic Coast League (1966-67)

Although the NAFL folded, attendance in Wilmington had been an encouraging 19,528 for five home dates. Edward du Pont thus bought into the five-year old Atlantic Coast League on a wave of optimism in 1966.

Once again known as the Clippers, the team started in disarray. The opening game was a fiasco in Atlantic City as Wilmington forced only one punt and was outgained 527 yards to 230 in a 41-14 loss. In the next game, a 27-14 thrashing, the Clippers rushed for only 2 yards. Things were worse off the field. Two Clipper halfbacks were killed in separate auto accidents and a third back broke both legs on his day job, ending his career. Delaware football legend Tex Warrington resigned as coach, saying it just wasn't any fun.

Another home-grown legend, Ron Waller, took over and the Clippers defense toughened. They battered Rhode Island 48-7 and the loss was so disheartening the franchise folded. The Clippers climbed to 4-7 but their improvement did not catch the fancy of Wilmingtonians. Only 6700 fans turned out for six games.

The Clippers returned to Baynard Stadium in 1967 and even signed a 5-year development pact with the Philadelphia Eagles but its vital signs were weakening. Barely into their second season of play the Clippers had already run through three coaches and three general managers. The original franchise folded but the team continued under league auspices as the Renegades.

After an extended six-week road trip designed to whet expectations of Delaware football fans for their return the Renegades drew 2600 but it was far short of the 4000 expected. After another loss life supports were finally pulled on minor league football in Wilmington.

DELAWARE FOOTBALL PLAYERS

Eddie Michaels. Eddie Michaels, a star lineman at Salesianum and Villanova, was selected by the Chicago Bears in the second round of the National Football League's first-ever draft in 1936. Michaels went to work for George Halas but only stayed one season before homesickness overtook him and he asked Halas to trade him back East. Halas obliged and shipped Michaels to the Washington Redskins, with whom he defeated his former team in the 1937 NFL Championship game.

Michaels was out of the NFL the next year, back in Delaware playing and coaching for the Wilmington Clippers. He returned to the war-depleted NFL in 1943 (Michaels was classified 4-F because he was hearing impaired) and stayed with the Philadelphia Eagles through 1946. After the war Michaels went to Ottawa in the Canadian Football League where he was a two-time all-CFL performer.

In the 1950s Michaels returned to Villanova to coach, molding among others his son Ed, who was drafted by the Redskins in 1958. Young Ed didn't stick to the regular season, depriving the Michaels of the chance to be only the second father-son combination to play in the NFL.

Creighton Miller. Cleveland-born Creighton Miller came to Delaware in 1935 and became the greatest high school running back in state history in the first half of this century. After a breathtaking career at A.I. du Pont High School, Miller continued a family legacy by matriculating at Notre Dame. His father Harry had started in the Irish backfield during the Teddy Roosevelt administration, his Uncle Walter had blocked for George Gipp, his Uncle Don was one of the fabled Four Horsemen, his Uncle Ray had backed up Knute Rockne at left end and on and on. As Creighton explained it, "My father didn't ask me what college I wanted to attend. He told me what time the train was leaving for South Bend."

Despite his family legacy Miller was not immediately welcomed by Notre Dame coach Frank Leahy. The Delwarean had been diagnosed with high blood pressure and was told not to practice. Leahy considered it laziness but Miller was too good to keep off the field and made the 1941 team as a back-up halfback, gaining 183 yards in 23 carries. When Miller was rejected for militay duty because of his medical condition Leahy finally was convinced his backfield star was not shirking practice.

In 1943 Miller became only the second Notre Dame back to rush for more than 900 yards, averaged 6.17 yards per carry and was a unanimous All-American. Leahy also won his first national title. Miller was the first draft pick of the Brooklyn Dodgers but turned down an exorbitant offer of $10,000 to play pro football.

Miller already had a career path mapped out. He was a talent scout for the Cleveland Browns and an assistant coach at Yale University, where he was attending law school.

His connection with the Browns led Miller to become the first counsel for the NFL Players Association in 1960. He maintained that position for 11 years until he resigned to become a player agent.

In 1976 Miller was elected to the College Football Hall of Fame. At his induction his former Notre Dame coach Frank Leahy summed up his brief football career the best, "Creighton Miller was the best halfback I ever saw."

Tex Warrington. Caleb Van Warrington was always big. As a 12-year old growing up in Dover he weighed a robust 150 pounds and was shortly thereafter pitching semi-pro baseball for the Dover Chicks. He picked up the nickname "Tex" for his bowlegs, a characteristic of many fine athletes. Warrington attended William & Mary for three years before finishing his collegiate career at an Alabama agricultural school, today known as Auburn, in 1944.

Now a robust 6'2" and 205 pounds the 23-year old Warrington carved out an All-American season at center on offense and linebacker on defense for Auburn. He was drafted by the Boston Yankees but at the time had no desire to try pro football and began coaching at Auburn.

The Brooklyn Dodgers eventually lured Warrington into the All-America Conference for three years, including two years as their captain. Warrington then returned to a teaching career that brought him back to Delaware as a program supervisor at Ferris school in 1962.

Carl Elliott. Growing up in Laurel in the 1940s they called Carlton Batt Elliott "Stretch" because that's what all 6'4" guys were called back then. Elliott could not only reach up for passes but he was a devastating blocker from his split end postion as well. He was an All-Southern end for the Virginia Cavaliers and lined up for the Green Bay Packers when he was 24 years old in 1951. Elliott enjoyed three productive seasons in Green Bay, snaring 60 balls and scoring five touchdowns; he also returned a fumble for a tourchdown.

Leon Dombrowski. An All-State tackle at Salesianum and an all-conference guard at the University of Delaware Leon Dombrowski appeared on his way to becoming the first Blue Hen in the NFL when he played in four exhibition games for the Washington Redskins in 1960. But the 205-pound lineman was released before the season started.

He hooked on with the New York Titans for the debut season of the American Football League. He started the first two games for the Titans, later the Jets, at linebacker but tore up a knee in practice before the third game, which hastened his return to Newark to complete his degree. The Titans refused to honor Dombrowski's $8,800 contract before settling for half the value. Leon Dombrowski ended his professional career with $2,200 a game.

Tom Hall. Tom Hall was an All-State basketball and football player at Salesianum before moving on to the University of Minnesota where he starred on two Rose Bowl teams. Hall was the holder of seven Golden Gopher receiving records when he was drafted by the Detroit Lions in the 1961 draft.

In Detroit he was used as an occasional kick returner and caught only three passes in two years. Traded to the Minnesota Vikings Hall became a dependable possession receiver for Fran Tarkenton, averaging 20 catches and two touchdowns for the next three years. He was tabbed by the New Orleans Saints in the NFL expansion draft after the 1966 season and played one season as a charter Saint before wrapping up his eight-year NFL career back in Minneapolis.

John Land. John Land grew up in New York City in the 1960s where everyone played basketball. He never played football but idolized superstar running back Jim Brown so when he showed up at Delaware State he decided to try out for the football team, not knowing anything about how to block or catch. He made the team and became a 5'9", 205-pound blocking back. By his senior year he got the ball enough to gain 600 yards and score seven touchdowns. Several years of semi-professional ball followed in the Atlantic Coast League while he established his business career in Delaware. Starring for teams like the Harrisburg Capital Colts and Norfolk Neptunes and Pottstown Firebirds Land performed well enough to make the National Pro Minor League Hall of Fame After brief stints with the Philadelphia Eagles and Baltimore Colts Land signed on with the Philadelphia Bell of the World Football League in 1974 and rushed for 1,136 yards and caught passes for 646 more. Of the field he picked up a doctorate and served 19 years as a trustee at Delaware State.

Kevin Reilly. Kevin Reilly had an opportunity to watch some of football's best linebackers up close - from behind them on the depth charts. After a successful career as a two-way end on the undefeated 1968-69 Salesianum football team Reilly went on to make All-East at Villanova as a linebacker. He was drafted by the Super Bowl champion Miami Dolphins in 1973 where he tried to make the team as a back-up to Nick Buoniconti before being released in training camp.

He hooked on with the Philadelphia Eagles where he subbed for All-Pro Bill Bergey for two seasons. Slowed by injuries, Reilly was waived by the Eagles and caught on with New England for one final season, dueling with George Webster and Steve Zabel for playing time. Three years of special teams play wore down Reilly's body and forced him out of football. The highlight of his NFL career came on a 90-yard interception he brought back for a touchdown. That, and watching some excellent linebacking play.

Grant Guthrie. Grant Guthrie was the best kicker ever to come out of Delaware. He set records at Claymont High School and Florida State University before kicking for the Buffalo Bills in 1970 and 1971. His NFL career was brief but he joined the Jacksonville Sharks of the new World Football League in 1974. He set a league record with four field goals in one game but after going six games without a paycheck he left the Sharks, who folded. Guthrie then kicked game-winning field goals in the final two games for the Birmingham Americans but again they were free kicks with no paychecks forthcoming. On the field Guthrie converted 18 of 24 field goal attempts in 1974, his best kicking season ever, but the experience left him financially strapped, souring his last year in professional football.

Gary Hayman. Playing at Newark High School Gary Hayman won 33 straight games. He expected much of the same when he enrolled at Penn State with Joe Paterno. But he lost two seasons to injury and a third clearing himself of a wrongful rape charge before finally returning to the Nittany Lions in the fall of 1972. The next year Hayman was back to his winning ways. Penn State completed a perfect 12-0 season with a win over Louisiana State in the Orange Bowl.

Hayman led the nation in punt returns that year for Penn State. He also hauled in 30 passes for 525 yards. Against Maryland he returned the opening kickoff 98 yards for a touchdown. Blessed more with great acceleration than blinding speed Hayman was picked by the Buffalo Bills in the 1974 NFL draft. Converted to a running back Hayman backed up O.J. Simpson and returned kicks but a broken leg slowed his progress. After two years with the Bills there was a short stay with the Seattle Seahawks before retirement.

Conway Hayman. It took more than a half-century before Dennis Johnson became the first University of Delaware player to line up for a down in the National Football League. And when Conway Hayman became the second he had to be as surprised as anyone.

Drafted in the sixth round in 1971, the Little All-America from Newark High was among the best pro prospects to ever play for the Blue Hens. But after four years of sweating through NFL tryout camps in Washington, New England and Los Angeles Conway Hayman was back in Delaware carving out a career in the Wilmington Planning Department.

But one more training camp invitation came in 1975. And when the season opened Hayman was a regular on the Houston Oiler offensive line. For six years Hayman remained a stalwart for one of the best Oiler teams ever; twice Hayman played in the AFC Championship game. After a back injury sent Hayman to the sidelines in 1981 he returned to football as a coach for Prairie View A & M University in Texas, compiling a 5-31-1 mark in little over three years in a difficult situation.

Joe Campbell. Like Randy White before him Joe Campbell never made the Delaware All- State football team. Campbell didn't even rate Honorable Mention in his senior year in 1972 when he anchored the state champion Salesianum defensive line. College recruiters ignored Campbell as well. He followed White to the University of Maryland, almost as an afterthought on the part of the Terrapins.

Despite slipping quietly onto campus the 6'6", 250-pound defensive end lettered all four years with Maryland and made several All-American teams in his senior year. He played in bowl games all four years and was tabbed by the New Orleans Saints in the first round of the 1977 draft, the seventh player taken overall.

Campbell's inexorable climb to greatness stalled in New Orleans. Despite landing on one of the least talented teams in the NFL Campbell was unable to win a steady job. He was benched as a defensive end and was unable to make the transition to linebacker. Finally, in the middle of the 1980 season Campbell was traded from the 0-6 Saints to an Oakland Raiders team on their way to the Super Bowl.

Campbell earned a Super Bowl ring as a special teams player in the Raiders 27-10 dismantling of the Philadelphia Eagles in Super Bowl XV. But Campbell's career was on the wane. After being waived by the Raiders he played half a season with lowly Tampa Bay before winding up his career in the USFL with the New York Generals.

Tim Wilson. Tim Wilson made his NFL reputation as a blocking back, clearing holes for the likes of all-time great Earl Campbell. Ironically Wilson never blocked a single man, by his reckoning, during his three years of football at De La Warr High School. At the University of Maryland Wilson's blocking technique was so poor he was moved to offensive end. Eventually Wilson was returned to the backfield and became a ferocious blocker for future NFL runners like Louis Carter, Rickie Jennings and Steve Atkins. Wilson could move the ball as well. He gained 610 yards his senior year at College Park and led the team with 42 points.

Like Randy White, a non-Delaware All-State player who went on to a professional career Wilson was drafted into the Houston Oiler backfield in the third round of the 1977 NFL draft. In his rookie year he bulled for 431 yards on 129 carries but his notoriety came as a bruising blocker. Wilson was a prototype fullback in an offense built around a featured tailback.

Anthony Anderson. Anthony Anderson shattered Delaware state records bursting out of the McKean backfield in the mid-1970s and starred for the Temple Owls as well. He was selected by the Pittsburgh Steelers in the annual NFL draft and saw spotty action in 1979, returning 13 kickoffs. Although he didn't get in the game Anderson became the second Delawarean to claim a Super Bowl ring as a member of the victorious Steelers against the Los Angeles Rams. Dropped by the Steelers, Anderson spent part of the 1980 season with the Atlanta Falcons before resurfacing as a dependable performer in the United States Football League with the Baltimore Stars until his retirement in 1985.

Mike Meade. Mike Meade barrelled through enough defenders from the Dover Senators backfield to rush for more than 2,000 yards in both 1976 and 1977, contributing to a state championship in his senior year. In Joe Paterno's backfield at Penn State Meade job was mostly to clear space for College Hall of Famer Curt Warner. Meade was selected in the 5th round of the 1982 draft by the Green Bay Packers and started seven games the following year. He gained 201 yards and proved useful out of the backfield catching 16 passes for 110 more. Still, Meade was traded to Detroit where he saw little action with the Lions before leaving the NFL with one career touchdown.

Frank Cephous. At St. Mark's High School Cephous was a state high jump champion and a member of the Spartans 1978 football championship team. He went west and played three years, rushing for 1066 yards and gaining 300 yards receiving. Cephous spent one year with the New York Giants in 1984 returning kickoffs and gaining two yards from scrimmage on three carries.

Dan Reeder. Christiana High School product Dan Reeder wound up in the University of Delaware backfield after a stop at Boston College and was picked by the Los Angeles Raiders in the 5th round of the 1985 draft. He didn't make the silver-and-black roster but caught on with the Pittsburgh Steelers as a back-up for two years getting eight carries and gaining 28 yards.

Clarence Bailey. Clarence Bailey graduated from Milford Senior High School in 1982 and attended Wesley College before moving on to play for the Hampton University Pirates. Bailey played two years in Virginia, leading the Pirates in scoring in 1984. He averaged 19.1 yards per punt return - still a school record. He played semi-pro ball with the Chesapeake Bay Neptunes in Norfolk and signed as a free agent with Miami Dolphins in 1987, getting into three games for Don Shula and gaining 55 yards on just ten carries.

Lovett Purnell. Lovett Purnell was a three-sport star at Seaford High School, drafted by baseball's Chicago White Sox in the 54th round and second only to Delino DeShields in points scored on the Blue Jay basketball court. He chose to pursue football and caught 78 passes in two years as a West Virginia Mountaineer tight end. He was drafted by Bill Parcells and the New England Patriots in the 7th round of the 1996 draft and started every game for two years in 1997 and 1998. Targeted sparingly by Drew Bledsoe, Purnell caught only 17 passes but five were for touchdowns; he also started for the Patriots in the 1997 Super Bowl.

Jamie Duncan. Jamie Duncan was a two-time Delaware high school player of the year at linebacker for Christiana High School and the gridiron honors kept coming after he enrolled at Vanderbilt University: twice an All-American and the 1997 Southeastern Conference Defensive Player of the Year. The Tampa Bay Buccaneers snapped Duncan up in the third round and he started six games at middle linebacker in his rookie year. By his third year he was the everyday middle backer, intercepting four passes and taking one back 31 yards for a touchdown. Duncan's career ended after seven seasons and he pursued diverse business interests inlcuding a hair styling salon in his home state.

Jim Bundren. A Michigan native, Jim Bundren became an All-State performer at A. I. du Pont High School. After a year at Valley Forge Military Academy he was recruited by Clemson University and started a record 47 games for the Tigers in his four-year career. The Miami Dolphins picked Bundren in the 7th round of the 1998 NFL Draft but be did not surface until the following year with Cleveland Browns and started ten games in a two-year professional career.

Kwame Harris. Kwame Harris came to Newark from Jamaica when he was ten years old - his father opened a successful Jamaican-fusion restaurant. He favored playing the violin and piano but at over 300 pounds with speed and quickness the football field beckoned. When his career at Newark High School ended the family said the number of recruiting letters from courting colleges filled two 40-gallon trash bags. He chose Stanford University as a music major. Harris was the second-ranked offensive tackle in the 2003 NFL Draft and the San Francisco 49ers made him the 26th overall pick. Harris started 37 straight games with the 49ers but never lived up to his potential in six NFL seasons. After leaving football he came out as one of the first ex-NFL players to identify as gay. Kwame's younger borther Orien also saw spot duty in the NFL for three years.

Montell Owens. At Concord High School Montell Owens was a triple threat as a student (National Honor Society), a jazz musician (toured Europe with American Music Abroad) and on the football field where he rushed for 1,100 yards and 20 touchdowns.

Owens played his college football at the University of Maine and signed on with the Jacksonville Jaguars as an undrafted free agent in 2006. He has developed into a special teams specialist, establishing the franchise record for most career special teams tackles with 118. He only got 56 rushing attempts in his nine-year NFL career but scored three touchdowns. Twice he was named to the Pro Bowl as a special teams player and in 2011 scored twice in the game, once on a fumble recovery and once on a pass reception.

Jeff Otah. Nigerian-born Jeff Otah came to Delaware via the Bronx at the age of 13. He played only one season at William Penn High School before two years of seasoning at Valley Forge Military Academy prepared the 340-pound offensive lineman for the rigors of the Big East at the University of Pittsburgh in 2006. Two years later the Carolina Panthers drafted Otah in the first round with the 19th pick. He became an immediate starter for the Panthers but after his first two years his career was curtailed by injury.

Duron Harmon. Both of Duron Harmon's parents were graduates of Delaware State but after leading hometown Caesar Rodney High School to a state championship in 2008 the Magnolia native spurned the hometown school and went to Rutgers University instead. He had rushed for 1,126 yards for the Riders but was also the Delaware Defensive Player of the Year. Harmon concentrated on the defensive side of the ball with the Scarlet Knights. He had 129 tackles and six interceptions in his four years in East Brunswick and was taken by the New England Patriots in the third round of the 2013 NFL draft. For Bill Belichick the versatile defensive back intercepted six balls in three years, including a key pick of Joe Flacco late in the 2014 divisional playoffs to seal a game against Baltimore. A few weeks later Harmon earned a Super Bowl ring against the Seattle Seahawks.

Justin Perillo. At tiny private school Tatnall Justin Perillo figured he would be wrapping up his football career when the Hornets completed the 2009 season. He had no college recruiting interest. If anything the Delaware Basketball Player of the Year figured he had a future on the hardwood. But the University of Maine saw some Tatnall School footage and offered him a scholarship. In four years in Orono as a tight end Perillo caught 128 balls for 1,318 yards and 15 touchdowns. There were no nibbles from the pros but Perillo signed with the Green Bay Packers in 2014 and made the practice squad. In 2015 he was called into nine games and made 11 catches for 102 yards and a touchdown.

A Football Life

If Delaware ever had a mythical "Golden Boy" it was Ron Waller. An all-time high school scoring champ, an All-American running back, an All-Pro in his rookie year, married to a millionaire actress-heiress and living in southern California. What Delaware boy growing up in the 1950s didn't want to be Ron Waller?

Waller first rose to prominence on the playing fields of lower Delaware in the 1940s. By the time he graduated from Laurel High School he had hoarded 12 letters - three each in basketball, football, track and baseball. It was football, however, where Waller made his lasting fame. Ron Waller was one of the most gifted halfbacks ever to glide across a Delaware gridiron. In 1950 alone he scored a Chamberlainesque 213 points with 30 touchdowns and 33 extra points - and he often sat out the second half of games. His selection as Delaware Athlete of the Year was a no-brainer.

At the University of Maryland Waller developed into an All-Conference back averaging nine yards per carry. He also was one of the top punt returners in the nation. The Washington Redskins drafted him in the second round of the 1955 draft but traded him immediately to the Los Angeles Rams where Waller came under the tutelage of the innovative offensive tactician Sid Gillman.

In the last 1955 exhibition game Waller grabbed nine passes for 184 yards and clinched a starting backfield position in his rookie year. Taking hand-offs from Norm Van Brocklin, Waller raced to 716 yards, many on electrifying runs, to finish fourth in the league in rushing. He also averaged over 27 yards per kickoff return and was named to the Pro Bowl and UPI All-Pro teams.

His off-season was no less memorable. After a public courtship Waller married heiress and actress Marjorie Merriwether Post of the Post Cereal fortune, one of the most substantial in America. Their wedding was the highlight of the 1955 social season in Washington DC.

After an All-Pro rookie year Ron Waller married Marjorie Dye Post, an All-American swimmer at Southern California and one of the greatest open water swimmers in America.

In 1956 Waller was slowed by a shoulder injury but still gained 543 yards on an eye-popping 6.65 yards per rush and made second team All-Pro. A rib injury landed him in a backup role in 1957 and he ran for only 292 yards, still leading the league in yards per carry. But the injuries exacted their toll. The next year he was released by the Rams.

By now Waller was firmly entrenched in the California scene. He operated a plush

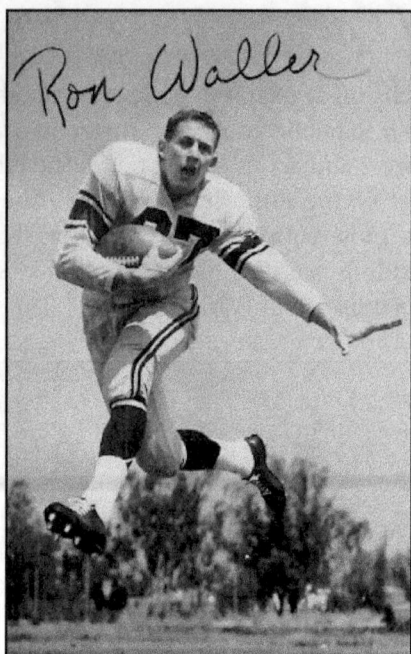

Ron Waller, as the most dynamic young runner in the NFL in the mid-1950s.

coaching. Waller resurfaced in Delaware in 1966 as a social worker and backfield coach for the Wilmington Clippers of the Atlantic Coast League. He was shortly made head coach and nursed the team, totally lacking in resources and support, through another year before it folded.

He went on to successful minor league stints with the Harrisburg Capitols, Pottstown Firebirds and Norfolk Neptunes before rejoining the NFL with the San Diego Chargers in 1973 as a special teams coach. When head coach Harland Svare was ousted in near-mutiny at mid-season Waller was elevated to head man and coaxed one win in the final six games out of the rebellion. He headed to Europe and the Intercontinental Football League saying the Charger's biggest need was a quarterback as a young future Hall-of-Famer Dan Fouts was buried on his bench.

By 1974 he was back as head coach of the Philadelphia Bell in the World Football League, one of the worst professional leagues ever devised. Waller guided the Bell through one season before he resigned in July 1975 with the tattered league in its final death throes. Waller, who once said philosophically, "I just seem to gravitate toward difficult situations," returned to California as coach and part-owner of the Southern California Rhinos of the California League.

When the United States Football League happened along in the mid-Eighties Waller was in the front office of the Kansas City Chiefs. He signed on with the USFL as Offensive Co-ordinator for the Chicago Blitz but when that league folded he turned down further NFL offers and returned to Delaware where he put his natural charm and optimism to work in a new field - politics.

bowling alley and several bar-restaurants for the California sports crowd. He fronted an exclusive catering service to the stars and raced thoroughbreds. And of course there was Hollywood. Waller produced some television shows and acted a bit, too. He did a turn on 77 Sunset Strip and in the movies had a speaking part opposite Marlon Brando and David Niven in Bedtime Story.

As his football career melted away so too did his marriage. By 1960 it was over. Waller tried his hand at promoting fights but was never able to completely extricate himself from football's grip. He began a fascinating odyssey that would touch on virtually every professional football league in the latter part of the 20th century. Waller launched a comeback in 1960 under his old coach Gilliam with the San Diego Chargers in the American Football League. There was no football left in his body and he eventually turned to

Slow and Steady

Slow. It's a word that football people always seemed to get around mentioning when they talked about Steve Watson. Which was not a particularly encouraging adjective when describing a split end. Slow. It's a word that describes how it took football people to appreciate Steve Watson's talents.

Growing up in Baltimore Watson was a superb games player. Not the least of his skills was skeet shooting, in which he was a national champion. Entering St. Mark's High School in 1972, Watson was an aspiring running back but was switched to split end where he started on back-to-back Spartan state champion teams in 1973 and 1974.

After high school only Virginia and Temple came courting the All-State end. Temple was the more ardent suitor and Watson joined the Owls where he hauled in 98 passes in four years, good for 1629 yards. Still, he was ignored on draft day, labeled by NFL scouts as "too slow." The 6'4", 195-pounder doggedly pursued his NFL dream and caught on with the Denver Broncos as a free agent in 1979. In two years of mostly special teams work Watson caught only 12 passes.

He got an opportunity to start early in 1981 when an injury felled leading receiver Rick Upchurch. In his first two games Watson grabbed 15 receptions for 321 yards. He scored five touchdowns of 29, 18, 48, 93 and 22 yards. He would go on to snare 60 balls and led the NFL in touchdowns with 13. His 1244 yards stretched all the way to the Pro Bowl in Hawaii.

Over the next five years only one NFL receiver would pile up more receiving yards than "slow" Steve Watson. From 1983 to 1986 he started 64 straight games. He was roundly praised for his exceptional hands, precise routes and the ability to make the "tough catch." Watson was the Broncos MVP on offense in 1981, 1983 and 1984 and in 1986 he became the fourth Delaware high schooler to appear in a Super Bowl.

Always one of the most popular Broncos, Watson extended his career a couple more seasons. When he was released an explanation given was that the Broncos were "heading in another offensive direction" - they were going with faster receivers.

Not necessarily better ones. Watson finished his career with 353 receptions for 6,112 yards and caught 21 more balls in the postseason. For such a slow guy his career average of 17.3 yards per catch is the 44th best in league history.

University of Delaware Football

Coaches

William McAvoy

After relying on a series of part-timers to lead its football team Delaware College made a commitment to athletics in 1908 by hiring its first permanent coach. The man tabbed for the job was William McAvoy, an All-American running back from Lafayette College. Drafted by the Pittsburgh Pirates as a baseball player, McAvoy had spent the summer patrolling the outer pastures for Rochester of the Eastern League, finishing 4th in the league in batting.

"Coach" at Delaware College was not a position assumed lightly. In addition to his duties with the football squad McAvoy guided the Blue Hen athletes in baseball, basketball and track. Under McAvoy Delaware did not magically transform into a football power. He simply did not have the material; enrollment at the college seldom topped 200 and his teams never averaged more than 165 pounds per man. Delaware officials went so far as to consider replacing football with soccer in 1913, sending McAvoy out to scout several soccer games for his evaluation.

A McAvoy team was always in shape and never quit. He operated with no funds and scholastic rules were strictly adhered to. Still Delaware enjoyed many big wins under the energetic McAvoy. He was regarded as a good motivator and popular in the coaching fraternity, able to tap the minds of many of the greatest football strategists in the country.

McAvoy led the Blue Hens until 1917 when he enlisted in Officers Training School and shipped overseas to serve as a lieutenant in World War I. After the war he returned to the sidelines with the Drexel Dragons but when his old job at Delaware opened in 1922 he was eagerly courted by his friends in Newark.

In the final game of the 1923 season McAvoy engineered one of the great upsets of the football season by drubbing national power Dickinson 21-0. As the Delaware freshmen and sophomores gathered wood, boxes and barrels for a celebratory bonfire in front of Wolf Hall, McAvoy declared himself "the happiest man in the United States."

In 1925 William McAvoy moved on to the University of Vermont. In his wake he left behind a legacy for athletic success on and off the gridiron. The annual interscholastic track and field meet McAvoy started in 1913, for instance, was drawing over 30 schools. From the point of his departure the University of Delaware would be forced to create an athletic budget to maintain the level of achievement initiated by Coach McAvoy.

Bill Murray

In 1940 Bob Carpenter, Jr. spearheaded a "new regime" at the University of Delaware, dedicated to excellence in competitive sports. The man he found to guide the fortunes of the football program was directing athletics at Winston-Salem College in Rocky Mount, North Carolina. Prior to that he was teaching school in the Blue Ridge Mountains. The *Journal Every Evening* welcomed the unheralded Bill Murray as "another in a long line of those who have made the journey to Newark in the past 12 years."

It would not be long before the former All-American halfback from Duke would excuse himself from that undistinguished procession.

Murray lost his first three games as he waited for his new charges to master the intricacies of his double-wing offensive system. Publicly he bemoaned his teams' defense and kicking. The nadir of his debut campaign came on Homecoming when Delaware was whited-out 25-0 by Ursinus in the snow. But the following week, in the first University of Delaware game played in Wilmington since 1922, the Blue Hens upended a powerful Pennsylvania Military College team 14-7 in a huge upset. Delaware would not lose for another 31 games.

As Murray began winning he bred a new sports follower in Delaware - the spoiled fan. Well-oiled routs of overmatched teams spawned cries for a tougher schedule. Less than decisive victories in the streak led to carping from disgruntled alumni about underfed wins. This from fans of a team that heretofore had notched 15 winning seasons in the past 50 years!

All the while Murray was on the defensive regarding the caliber of his football player. Most were unknown in high school; all had to come from the top half of his class. Delaware was still a small school with an enrollment of 1700 and no national reputation. Still Murray went on winning.

World War II shut down football at the University of Delaware but Murray welcomed an unprecedented 90 try-outs to spring practice in 1946. This suited Murray who was a strong advocate of single platoon football. He railed against the coming of football specialists on the offense and defense as divisive to team spirit. A large squad enabled Murray to shuffle as many as 40 players in and out of a game to keep his troops fresh.

With a team comprised entirely of returning servicemen Murray enjoyed his greatest year in 1946. More than 10,000 fans welcomed football back to the University of Delaware in Wilmington Park as the Blue Hens wiped out the cadets of PMC 25-0. After a 52-0 Homecoming win over Drexel, Delaware showed up in the Associated Press national rankings at 27th.

As the Hens reached 8-0 they climbed to 16th in the polls and Murray prepared for #19 Muhlenberg in the only battle of two Top 20 teams ever staged in Delaware. The capacity of Wilmington Park was increased from 10,000 to 14,000 for the "Battle of the Little Titans." Wilmington was the football capital of America on this day with the pressbox stuffed with national writers. There was talk of the winner being in line for a Cotton or Orange Bowl bid.

The Hens built a 13-0 lead and ground out a 20-12 win. They out-gained the Mules 330 to 185 in taking one of the greatest games ever played in Delaware. The next week the University of Delaware moved to 15th in the AP poll, ahead of such powerhouse elevens as USC, Texas and Oklahoma. They even pulled two first place votes as the best college football team in the country.

Murray accepted a bid to play in the Cigar Bowl in Tampa on January 1, one of 21 New Year's Day bowls that year, including the Cattle, the Vulcan, the Coconut and the Will Rogers Bowl. Delaware was established as a two-touchdown favorite over Rollins

After Bill Murray arrived in Newark in 1940, the University of Delaware enjoyed the services of a Hall-of-Fame football coach for the rest of the 20th century.

utilizing a double-wing attack, outscored opponents at a 337-38 clip. A host of individual records were set as well. Gerald "Doc" Doherty set a single game rushing mark with 220 yards - on only six carries. His runs were of 83, 63, 32, 18, 13 and 11 yards. He averaged more than 12 yards per carry in 1946.

The winning skein streaked into 1947 until a Gator Bowl-bound University of Maryland derailed the Blue Hens 43-19 before a record College Park crowd of 16,460. It would be the biggest crowd to watch the University of Delaware play football until Delaware Stadium would expand two decades later.

As his success in Newark grew bigger schools clamored for Murray's services. He explored the coaching job at Vanderbilt and the Athletic Director's position at the University of Minnesota before returning to Duke in 1951 trailing behind his worst season ever at 2-5-1 in 1950. He finished his tenure at Delaware 47-16-2 in eight years.

Murray rebuilt his alma mater into a premier powerhouse before becoming executive director of the American Football Coaches Association. At Duke, "Smiling Bill," as Murray was known for a slight grin built into his facial expression, went 93-51-9. In 1974, in recognition for his work at Delaware and Duke, Bill Murray was enshrined in the National Football Foundation Hall of Fame.

College of Atlanta and their 21-7 victory was one of the most impressive of the day. Navy pilot Paul Hart rushed for 113 yards and one touchdown and passed for two more to complete the scoring.

Delaware finished 19th in the 1946 final AP poll, with one writer still clinging to the belief that the Blue Hens were the top football team in the country. During the regular season the Delaware offense,

Tubby Raymond

There was a time in Tubby Raymond's career when he was in danger of becoming known as a baseball coach, not a football coach. It was true that after nine years at the University of Delaware Raymond was the winningest baseball coach in the school's history with 141 wins and only 56 losses. And it was true that he loved baseball, but Tubby Raymond was a football man. And as a well-thought-of backfield coach for the Blue Hens charting his future Raymond found potential employers thinking of his baseball achievements. So he gave up baseball.

Harold Rupert Raymond was born, raised and schooled in Michigan. He was tagged with the appellation "Tubby" as a butterball of a five-year old and was never able to fight his way out of it, although he tried. The young Raymond stopped growing at 5'8" and 167 pounds but he developed into a scrappy two-way guard in football. He was also an outstanding baseball catcher.

After a stint in the aviation cadet program during World War II Raymond enrolled at the University of Michigan. He worked his way onto the elite Wolverine football team which would win the 1947 national title but he never lettered. He was, however, a three-year starter on the baseball team and Tubby Raymond, football guy, even had an abbreviated two-year career buried deep in the New York Yankee organization.

On the recommendation of Fritz Crisler, his football coach at Michigan, Raymond got a job coaching Ann Arbor University High School in his senior year. Two years later he was in the Michigan-to-Maine-to-Delaware pipeline laid by Dave Nelson. He spent two years as line coach for the Black Bears before joining Nelson as a backfield coach at Delaware. As the leading disciple of Nelson's Winged-T offense it was not long before other schools came calling on Raymond. Iowa, Kentucky, Louisiana State, California and Oklahoma all dangled assistant coaching positions in front of Raymond. But he had long ago decided not to forsake Delaware for anything less than a head coaching job.

That opportunity arrived in 1966 with an offer to take over the football program at the University of Connecticut, a school similar in philosophy to that which Raymond loved at Delaware. Faced with losing Raymond and saddled with more and more non-coaching distractions it was the logical time for Nelson to step aside.

Under Raymond the Blue Hens climbed to even greater prominence than that achieved by Murray and Nelson. He coached for 36 years until stepping down in 2002 at the age of 75 with exactly 300 wins, measured against 119 losses and three ties. Raymond has amassed a helmetful of coaching awards and three national championships: in the polls in 1971 and 1972 (Raymond's only undefeated team at 10-0) and on the field in 1979. After moving to NCAA Division I-AA in 1980 Raymond took the Blue Hens to the playoffs 11 times, losing three times in the national semi-finals and dropping the national championship game to Eastern Kentucky in 1982, 17-14.

The old baseball coach (there were eventually 178 of those before he hung up the spikes in 1964 and three NCAA Tournament appearances) followed Murray and Nelson into the College Football Hall of Fame in 2003. His name was added to the field at Delaware Stadium.

One thing that did not come to an end with Raymond's retirement was his tradition of painting every starter in acrylics in his senior season. Raymond had painted portraits growing up and Nelson encouraged his assistants to sketch the players as a way of building team bonds. After putting down his whistle and picking up his brush, Raymond began fielding commissions in his studio and painting everyone from university officials to the neighbor's kids.

Don Miller. When Dave Nelson arrived at the University of Delaware in 1951 he was greeted by four quarterback candidates at his first practice. Nelson selected from this quartet as his quarterback a 170-pound freshman from Prospect Park, Pennsylvania who had come to Delaware mostly on his basketball ability. Don Miller would go on to start every one of the 32 games over the next four years.

Miller's completed only 58 of 123 in his rookie year but 12 tosses went for touchdowns. A bad shoulder hindered his progress in his sophomore year but Miller returned in 1953 to make third team Little All-America. In the 1953 season finale against Bucknell Miller was 14-20 for 278 yards and four touchdowns, missing a fifth when his receiver tumbled out of bounds inside the one-yard line.

Despite his talented arm Miller's greatest assets were his coachability and ball handling, where #11 was the focal point in Nelson's intricate Winged-T offense. Miller had his greatest year as a senior for the 1954 Blue Hens who lost only two games, each by a single point and romped to a win in the Refrigerator Bowl. Miller was named first team Little All-America quarterback and his 36th career touchdown pass broke the Eastern College record - on a running team.

Miller was not drafted by the NFL but he had already planned on a coaching career. He started as coach of Newark High School in 1955 and went 22-3 in his first three years, losing in-state only to William Penn by one point. In 1958 Miller's Yellowjackets won all five Blue Hen Conference games to win the state's first conference championship. After this final Delaware triumph Miller left the state for Amherst College, where he continued his now deep-rooted success.

Tom DiMuzio. Tom DiMuzio was Tubby Raymond's first great quarterback and maybe his best. A converted halfback, DiMuzio could run as well as he could pass. And he set 14 school records passing. As a senior in 1969 DiMuzio was a second team Little All-American - behind a modest talent named Terry Bradshaw. Any other year DiMuzio's grit and daring would certainly have earned him first-team status.

DiMuzio led Delaware through an uncharacteristically horrid season in his sophomore year in 1967. The Blue Hens won only twice in nine tries as DiMuzio threw just 11 times while carrying on 81 plays. The next year Delaware went 8-3 as DiMuzio took to the air. The season climaxed in Atlantic City's Boardwalk Bowl as DiMuzio threw a 9-yard scoring pass in the waning seconds to upend Indiana of Pennsylvania 31-24. It was his third touchdown strike of the day as he hit on 15 of 22 tosses for 264 yards.

In his senior year DiMuzio established a University of Delaware standard for touchdown passes in a season with 24, including a record five against Lehigh. In that game DiMuzio connected on 22 passes for 369 yards. Once again he led Delaware to a win in the Boardwalk Bowl. Although named the Most Valuable Player in the Middle Atlantic Conference, in addition to his other awards, the pros did not come calling for DiMuzio, who began his business career after leaving Newark.

Jeff Komlo. There was never any indication that Jeff Komlo would be one of the all-time Delaware quarterbacks until he actually was. A former Maryland prep star, Komlo arrived in Newark unheralded and after an undistinguished freshman year he began the 1976 season as a fourth string signal caller. Following several ineffective performances by his competition Komlo was elevated to starter, a position he would never relinquish.

Early in his career Komlo was noted mostly for his leadership skills and proclivity for the big play. He hit fewer than 50% of his passes in his sophomore and junior seasons. By his senior season the 6'2", 210-pound Komlo was a deft handler of the Wing-T at the controls of a team he would lead to the Division II national championship game.

Komlo was at his best in these 1978 playoffs, tossing for 689 yards in three games and going 21 for 35 in the Blue Hens' narrow loss to Eastern Illinois in the final game. For his career Komlo was 23-9-2 and broke every season and career passing mark at Delaware. Yet, in tribute to his consistency, he set not one single-game record.

Running a sophisticated passing attack and possessing an uncanny ability to find secondary receivers Komlo was named Delaware's second Little All-America quarterback. He went in the ninth round of the NFL draft to the Detroit Lions and made the team as a third-string quarterback. When injuries knocked out Gary Danielson and Joe Reed, Komlo became an NFL starter in his rookie season, throwing for 2238 yards and 11 touchdowns but he was plagued by 23 interceptions.

When the regulars returned the next fall Komlo was back on the bench. He threw only 69 more passes in his NFL career before winding down with the Tampa Bay Bucaneers in 1983.

Scott Brunner. As a two-year back-up to All-American Jeff Komlo, Scott Brunner enjoyed only one year as a Blue Hen starter. But that one season was the most memorable in Delaware football history. And it cemented Brunner's place in the pantheon of Delaware quarterbacks.

In his long-awaited 1979 debut Brunner completed 12 of 18 passes for 229 yards in a 34-14 opening day romp over Rhode Island. From there it was a series of highlights for Brunner and the #1 ranked Hens. A 44-yard touchdown pass with 2:28 left to Jay Hooks dispatched 1-AA Villanova 21-20; five touchdown passes tied Tom DiMuzio's record in a 47-19 win over C.W. Post; directing 602 Delaware yards against William & Mary and earning ECAC Player of the Week honors; a season-high 285 yards while upending Colgate 24-16; and, of course, the Youngstown game.

The Delaware-Youngstown State game will forever live in many a University of Delaware football fan as the greatest game ever played. Both teams were tied for the #1 Division II ranking when they tangled at Falcon Stadium in Youngstown, Ohio. The Penguins took advantage of several Delaware miscues to seemingly bury the Hens 31-7 at halftime in front of 13,142 enthusiastic partisans. But it was Youngstown making the mistakes in the second half and Brunner engineered six touchdown drives, the last starting with 2:19 to go, as Delaware outlasted the Penguins 51-45.

It was no surprise the two teams met again for the Division II Championship, this time in Albuquerque, New Mexico. Once again it was Brunner leading the Hens past an 21-7 deficit to win the national title, 38-21. Brunner finished the year with 2401 passing yards and 24 touchdown passes and was named first-team Little All-American. At 6'5" with a strong arm Brunner looked like a prototype NFL quarterback and indeed he was chosen by the New York Giants in the 6th round of the NFL draft.

At New York Brunner battled Phil Simms for several years before losing out to the future Hall-of-Famer. In his first start as a Giant in 1980 Brunner hurled touchdowns of 48 and 50 yards in a 27-21 Giant win. In part-time duty he threw for 978 yards in 1981 and in 1982 Brunner took every center snap for the Giants and threw for 2017 yards and 10 touchdowns.

The next year Brunner was again a starter and established career highs in completions with 190 and yards with 2516. But he also threw a dangerous 22 interceptions. He missed the 1984 season with a knee injury ceding the quarterback job to Simms. He tried to comeback in 1985 with the St. Louis Cardinals but his effective days as an NFL quarterback were over.

Rich Gannon. "He is the most dominant player in a football game I'ver ever seen," Tubby Raymond once said of Rich Gannon. He was certainly the most productive three-year quarterback in Delaware history, accounting for 7436 yards of total offense. The fastest of the great Delaware quarterbacks, Gannon became the first to rush for 1000 career yards from under center. And the former St. Joe's Prep star from Philadelphia averaged 37.2 yards per kick as a punter. All told Rich Gannon took 21 Blue Hen records to the NFL when he was drafted in the 4th round, the highest University of Delaware selection ever at the time, by the New England Patriots.

With all his talent Gannon was not able to take his team to the NCAA playoffs until his senior year in 1986, despite a 15-7 record his first two years. That year, after a 9-3 regular season Delaware was demolished 55-14 in the first round of the 1-AA playoffs. It was an inglorious curtain to be drawn on Gannon who threw for 5927 yards and ran for another 1509 at Delaware.

The Patriots eyed Gannon as an offensive end or defensive back but he only planned to play quarterback so he was shipped to the Minnesota Vikings where he played several years, never quite able to win a job permanently under center. Improbably that began to change in his early thirties when Gannon went to the Kansas City Chiefs as a back-up signal caller. He performed well enough to ink a free agent contract with the Oakland Raiders in 1999 and beginning at the age of 34 started every game for the silver-and-black for the next four years.

At the age of 37 Gannon threw for 4,689 yards, won the league MVP and led the Raiders to the Super Bowl against the Tampa Bay Buccaneers. Jon Gruden, who had brought Gannon to Oakland was now the coach of Tampa Bay, and his defense stymied Gannon, intercepting five passes and returning three for touchdowns in a 48-21 Buccaneer win. Injuries and age brought the curtain down on Gannon's career in 2004, after 17 years in 2004, 29,000 yards passing and 180 touchdown passes.

Andy Hall. Andy Hall was both a throwback to the Blue Hen dual threat running and passing quarterback and a pioneer in being a transferring Division I quarterback to the Delware backfield. Hall was a big-armed high school star in Cheraw, South Carolina who started his career at Georgia Tech. After two years in the Atlantic Coast Conference where he threw only 19 passes, Hall traded the Atlanta campus for Newark.

He started in 2002 and 2003 and set a school record with 28 completions in a game against Massachusetts. He also broke the school record with 234 completions and 3,474 total yards in a season. After leading the Blue Hens to the 2003 NCAA Division I-AA championship, Hall was named the Outstanding Senior Male Athlete of the Year at the University of Delaware.

The NFL came calling for Hall in the sixth round of the 2004 NFL Draft and he spent time on the Philadelphia Eagles practice squad before being assigned to Rhein Fire of the NFL Europe league. Hall drifted into the Arena Football League where he took the Austin Wranglers to the playoffs in 2008.

Joe Flacco. When sports people talk about "a cannon for an arm" Joe Flacco is the kind of guy they are talking about. The big right arm won the New Jersey native a full scholarship to the University of Pittsburgh in 2003 but it was not enough to earn him much playing time. He completed one pass for eleven yards with the Panthers and decided to transfer to lower division Delaware.

Flacco was the Blue Hen starter in 2006 and 2007, leading Delaware to a modest 13-9 record. But in a foreshadowing of what would come in his pro career Flacco seemed to save his best games for the biggest moments. He engineered a 59-52 upset of the Naval Academy by tossing for 434 yards and four touchdowns with no interceptions. In the 2007 playoffs Delaware, seeded #13, surprised top-seeded Northern Iowa and #4 seeded Southern Illinois on the road to advance to the national championship final. Flacco threw for two touchdowns in each game. Delaware fell to Appalachian State 49-21 in the title game.

Flacco's brief stay in a Blue Hen uniform produced 20 school records and the following spring the Baltimore Ravens made him the first University of Delaware player drafted in the first round. Flacco wound up starting every game as a rookie in 2008 and won two games in the playoffs as he went from Newark to NFL Rookie of the Year. In the 2012 season Flacco led the Ravens to the Super Bowl championship as he tied a postseason record with eleven touchdown passes and no interceptions. His postseason playoff record through 2015 in the NFL was 10-5, including a record seven wins on the road. And that does not include his two in Newark.

Chuck Hall

George Lacsny was the University of Delaware's Wally Pipp. Like the excellent Yankee's first baseman who got hurt and forever surrendered his job to Lou Gehrig, Lacsny was the Blue Hens' starting fullback until he was sent to the bench by a second quarter injury against Hofstra on September 21, 1968. Sophomore Chuck Hall trotted in and galloped for 127 yards in the 35-0 romp. Before he graduated three years later Chuck Hall would rush for 3,157 yards, one of a host of school records he set. The Springfield, Pennsylvania native was named a Little-American in his senior year.

Hall joined the Baltimore Colts in 1971 but a shoulder operation put him out for the season. The next year Hall was invited back to training camp but he was already in the early stages of the Hodgkins Disease that would claim his life at the age of 24. Chuck Hall became the standard against which all future Delaware runners would be measured.

Ten Historic Rivalries

Bucknell. A heated rivalry brewed between Delaware and Bucknell for most of the time the two fought in the Middle Atlantic Conference. Begun with a game in 1908 the series picked up in earnest after World War II. In 1949 the Bisons denied Delaware an undefeated season, dealing the Blue Hens a 13-7 loss in Lewisburg. Beginning in 1950 the Delaware-Bucknell clash was the traditional season-ending game for the Blue Hens. Curiously the Bisons would add the dreary exclamation mark to each of Delaware's five losing seasons during their post World War II rivalry with losses in that final game, four at Delaware Stadium.

In 1951 powerful Bucknell rolled over Delaware 33-6 in front of a home crowd whipped into a frenzy by frequent public address announcements of records repeatedly broken by one of the finest Bison teams ever. Delaware extracted revenge the next season by dumping the Bisons 13-0 in the mud at Delaware Stadium to derail a championship Bucknell season. The Blue Hens would reel off seven straight wins in the series.

The highlight came in 1962 when both teams reached their climactic final game undefeated in the Middle Atlantic Conference. The struggle for the conference title would be one familiar to Delaware fans over the years: a high-powered aerial attack against Delaware's fabled Wing-T-fueled ground game. Both Delaware and Bucknell were able to find easy going in the middle of the field but both defenses stiffened in defense of their own goals. Despite the wizardry of Bucknell quarterback Ron Giordano who, the *Evening Journal* reported, "turned in the finest individual performance against a Delaware club," Delaware was able to come away with a 9-6 classic win.

The series ended in 1985 when Delaware entered the Yankee Conference with the Blue Hens handily on top 22-11. Looking back Delaware could always gauge the success of its season by the Bucknell game. Only three times did Delaware ever lose to the Bisons during a winning campaign and never defeated them during a losing season. **Delaware 23, Bucknell 11**

Colgate. As rivalries go this one sported neither tradition nor longevity. But each time the Red Raiders flashed on the University of Delaware schedule it was the biggest game of the season for one school or the other.

In 1977 Division I Colgate was undefeated, untied and ranked #19 in the country when they stopped in Newark to primp for a postseason bowl appearance. The Blue Hens were no strangers to strong Division I teams but this Delaware squad was seemingly the weakest in a decade. The first six games resulted in three losses, a tie and a narrow two-point home decision over West Chester. Accordingly area Colgate alumni staged a "Victory Party" the Friday evening before the game.

Anxious to spotlight the high-powered Red Raiders, ranked number one in the country in total offense, ABC-TV offered to make the Delaware-Colgate game the second half of its nationally televised doubleheader - if Delaware agreed to move the game to Philadelphia. Feeling his obligation was to the students and Delaware football fans Athletic Director Dave Nelson turned down the guarantee of $175,000 to take the game off campus. The capacity crowd of 23,029 would not be disappointed.

Tentative offensive thrusts and outstanding defensive efforts carried the teams to the locker room at halftime with Delaware trailing 3-0. The Blue Hens broke through for the game's first touchdown early in the third period when Jeff Komlo found Craig Carroll alone behind the Colgate defense for a 75-yard scoring strike. From that point Delaware beat up the nationally ranked Red Raiders on both sides of the ball to grind out an epic 21-3 upset.

The next year Delaware was the contender, winging its way to a Division II playoff berth, and Colgate the pretender, suffering through a 2-7 campaign. When the two teams clashed in Newark, Delaware had its playoff berth on the line while at stake for the revenge-minded central New Yorkers was only their entire disappointing season.

The opening act was neatly played out in the first quarter as Delaware cruised to a 7-3 lead and the Hen defense yielded only 7 yards on five Colgate running plays. Then Red Raider signal caller John Marzo, a mediocre 43.7% passer, tossed away his script.

Slicing up the Blue Hen defense with a relentless medium-range passing attack Marzo tossed three scoring strikes and led the giddy Colgaters to intermission on top 23-15. To the relief of Delaware supporters the Blue Hens restored order to the game by surging ahead 31-23 before the third period wound down.

But the defense could not contain Marzo. A 28-yard touchdown pass brought Colgate within a two-point conversion of knotting the game. The attempt was turned away, however, and Delaware put away the game with a 14- play drive to push the advantage to 38-29. The unheralded Marzo never was restrained. He shredded the Blue Hen secondary for 482 yards, connecting on 31 of 51 tosses, the fourteenth best performance in NCAA history and a Delaware Stadium record. In maybe the most unbalanced offensive show of all-time the Red Raiders ran for only 16 yards.

The series was renewed only two more times, both taut Delaware victories in 1979 and 1982, before the Red Raiders dropped off the schedule. The serendipitous rivalry reached its apex twenty years later. In 2003 Colgate completed its first undefeated season since 1932 behind the running of Jamaal Branch who won the Walter Peyton Award as the best player in Division I-AA with a record 2,326 rushing yards. Runner-up was quarterback Andy Hall who ran coach K.C. Keeler's no-huddle, spread passing attack. The two teams clashed for the national championship on a snowy December night at Finely Stadium in Chattanooga, Tennessee. Colgate uncharacteristically began the game with a series of miscues and fell behind 20-0 as the Blue Hens cruised to their sixth national title in the most lopsided national final in the 26-year history of the I-AA playoffs.

The Raiders were back on the Delaware schedule in 2014 and it was a return to form in the series. Colgate dominated the game on the ground and led 25-14 heading into the final quarter at Delaware Stadium. But two fourth quarter touchdowns, including a five-yard run by quarterback Trent Hurley with 41 seconds remaining, pulled out the game for Delaware - once again.

Delaware 6, Colgate 0

Haverford. Tiny Delaware College, with so few students from which to choose, struggled on the gridiron for most of the first 40 years of its football-playing history. During that period the Blue Hens won only 38% of their games, failing to score a point in 140 of the 292 contests. With a record of such uneven quality it was difficult to develop a traditional back-and-forth rivalry with a school of equal strength.

Still, being drubbed year after year by the same school stirred the passions of the student body. No game was bigger than the Haverford scrimmage. First engaged in 1891, Delaware suffered mightily at the hands of the Main Line school for 25 years. When the Blue Hens finally took a 7-0 decision in 1917 school was dismissed the following Monday so students could properly savor the occasion.

For the next 12 years a real rivalry actually grew up between the two schools. During that time Delaware won 7 of the 12 games played, including a 19-7 upset in 1928 by a Blue Hen team that had been shut out six times in seven games to that point. Again, President Walter Hullihen declared the following Monday a school holiday.

But just as things were getting interesting Delaware ran off three straight wins in 1930-32 and Haverford dropped regrettably off the Blue Hen schedule forever.

Delaware 11, Haverford 23, 3 ties

Lehigh. The most troublesome of all Delaware's traditional rivals within its own division has been the Lehigh Engineers. Although curtailed by Delaware's entrance into the Yankee Conference, the Blue Hens lead this highly competitive series, first played in 1912, 25-16.

Delaware's first ever win over Lehigh in 1951 was its most significant as it marked the debut of legendary Blue Hen coach Dave Nelson. Delaware held off the heavily favored Engineers, coming off an undefeated 1950 campaign, 7-0 to launch the Admiral's era.

Time and again, however, a great Delaware season would be stained by a loss to Lehigh. In 1955 the only setback of an 8-1 year was a home loss to the invaders from Easton. Winning teams in 1970, 1980, 1981, 1984 and 1985 were all similarly upended by the Blue Hens' most persistent nemesis.

In recent years Delaware has experienced more breathing room with the Engineers, beating Lehigh 29-22 in the 2000 I-AA playoffs and 42-20 during its run to the NCAA finals in 2010.

Delaware 30, Lehigh 17

Massachusetts. Maybe the closest one-sided series in all of football is Delaware-Massachusetts. In the 13 meetings, through 1988, between the two schools Delaware came away the victor each time, yet seven of those games were settled by less than a touchdown. On several occasions the Delaware wins have been so improbable as to invoke the muttering "miracle."

The series kicked off with a pair of routine Blue Hen wins in the late 1950s. In 1968 the mold for future clashes was fired when underdog Delaware stormed back from a 23-14 fourth quarter deficit to dump the defending Yankee Conference champions 28-23. Running back Dick Kelley powered for 217 yards and reserve QB Bob Buckley threw for one score and rushed for another to gain the win.

The 1980s featured a supernatural run of bad luck for the Minutemen. In 1980 Rick Scully found Ed Wood with a strike in the front corner of the endzone with nine seconds left to steal a 21-17 heart-stopper. In 1982 it was Massachusetts, again defending the Yankee Conference title, roaring back with two late touchdown passes to pull within 14-13 with 2:32 remaining. Disdaining the tie, the Minutemen were turned away again when their conversion pass was swatted away. The next year the Blue Hens drove the length of Delaware Field in the waning afternoon light to wrest away a 16-13 win.

In a brilliantly played game in 1985 in Amherst both teams traded advantages until

192

Delaware seized the lead behind Rich Gannon with only 55 seconds remaining. Down 27-24 the Minutemen maneuvered into position for the tying field goal from 35 yards on the final play of the game. Cornerback Matt Haudenschield flashed through the Massachusetts line to block the kick and preserved yet another Delaware victory.

Delaware joined Massachusetts in the Yankee Conference in 1986. The Blue Hens blew out the Minutemen 41-13 that first season. The next year the Hens eased out to a 34-16 lead early in the final period. Perhaps, now that they were conference rivals, Delaware would finally be giving some order to this series. Perhaps not.

Ten minutes later, following a touchdown pass, a safety, a touchdown run off a fake field goal and two two-point conversions the score was 34-34. Both teams turned the ball over down the stretch and it was the Blue Hens who worked their way into easy field goal range where Don O'Brien was able to provide the final margin by booting a 28-yard field goal.

The 1988 match-up was for supremacy of the Yankee Conference, both teams reaching the fray 3-1. Massachusetts scored in the opening moments on a 17-yard interception return to grab a 7-0 lead but their offense was ineffectual the rest of the day. With 2:39 remaining the Minutemen started on their own 33, down 10-7. Quarterback Dave Palazzi, a wearied victim of these wars since 1985, seemed to have finally unleashed his own magic in a spectacular bomb down the right sideline. But receiver Chip Mitchell was run down from behind just three feet short of the goal line. First and goal with 1:05 left.

The Minutemen would never travel that final yard. On the next play Steve Olson fumbled in a pile-up at the goal line and Delaware recovered to seal the win. Once again the Blue Hens could claim to be the better team for 60 minutes; their case for 59 minutes is a little less certain.

Delaware 26, Massachusetts 7

Pennsylvania Military College. For many years the school that the University of Delaware met on the gridiron more than any other was the Pennsylvania Military Academy, now Widener University. Off the schedule for more than 60 years now, the Pennsylvania Military College was Delaware College's most evenly matched opponent in its formative years. Begun in 1896 the series stood at seven Delaware wins, nine PMC wins and three ties through 1922. Lining up for the Cadets on that 1896 team was Cecil B. De Mille, who would later go on to bigger things in Hollywood.

Beginning in 1929 the schools met every year until 1952, save for the war years of 1943-45 when the University of Delaware cancelled its football schedule. Most of the games were tightly fought battles with the most memorable being a 19-14 Delaware win in 1942 when the Blue Hens roared back from a 14-0 halftime deficit to preserve the school's first ever undefeated, untied season.

The Delaware-Pennsylvania Military College series was notable also for its game sites. In 1932 the teams began playing indoors in Atlantic City's Boardwalk Bowl. The shore games drew the entire student bodies of the two schools and over 15,000 fans would fill the Convention Center. In 1940 Delaware played its first game in the Wilmington Ball Park, upsetting PMC 14-7. In 1952 Delaware closed its history at Wilmington Park with a 43-20 win over PMC, which ended the series with the Chester school as well.

After more than a half-century the log stood in favor of the Blue Hens, 19-18-3 when a sad announcement appeared in the pre-season University of Delaware brochure: "An important chapter in Delaware's football history will come to an end in 1953. PMC, oldest of all gridiron rivals on the schedule, has requested that the long series be concluded with this year's game. PMC trounced the Hens, 14-0, in 1896 and rolled up a big bulge in the victory column during the early years of the twentieth century. Since 1940, however, Delaware has lost only one contest and apparently has developed too much power for the willing but outclassed Cadets." Facing only a one-game deficit in the 57-year run of the Delaware-PMC rivalry the Cadets were denied an opportunity to even the score when the last scheduled game in 1953 was snowed out.

Delaware 20, Pennsylvania Military 19, 3 ties

Swarthmore. "Rivalry" might be too strong a word for what transpired in this long-running series. Swarthmore was the first school Delaware ever played, in 1890. Delaware did not win that game, nor did they prevail in any of the next 25 games in the intervening 40 years, although they did manage a tie in 1911. In 21 of those games the Blue Hens did not score a single point.

Finally, in 1930 Delaware broke through with a 13-12 win. The next year Delaware thumped Swarthmore 26-0. The series was only renewed twice more, in 1940 and 1941, with Delaware winning both games. The Blue Hens would never be able to fully redeem 40 years of complete futility.

Delaware 4, Swarthmore 23, 1 tie

Temple. Ask most prehistoric University of Delaware football fans what school was their greatest rival and you would get one answer: Temple. The Delaware-Temple series, running from 1954 to 1985, was the longest continuous annual renewal in the history of Blue Hen football. You would be hard pressed to find another rivalry like it in the annals of college football. The schools were not backyard rivals nor particularly competitive in any other sport. For much of the time one school, Temple, was expected to crush its overmatched opponent. But for several decades there was no greater college football played in the Delaware Valley than between Delaware and Temple.

The series began on October 18, 1913 when Delaware College christened its new Frazer Field by beating up the visiting Temple Owls 28-0. Before Frazer Field, donated in the name of Joseph Frazer, a young engineer who had perished building railroads in Bolivia, Delaware College didn't even boast a grandstand for football. The new seven-acre grounds were among the finest and most modern athletic facilities yet unveiled in the country and the scraggy Delaware eleven hardly seemed worthy of such magnificent environs. Averaging less than 170 pounds only ten men on the 1913 squad would garner enough playing time that season to qualify for a varsity letter. There would be only two victories that season but, forbiddingly, the Blue Hens were able to thrash the heavier, more experienced Temple eleven. Delaware again crunched the Owls 20-7 in 1914 and the series slipped into dormancy for the next 36 years.

When the two schools met again, in 1950, Temple was aspiring to major college football. The Owls defeated weak Delaware teams that season and next to level the series. When hostilities resumed in 1954 the Blue Hens embarked on an unprecedented ten-year winning streak against their more highly regarded rival. Many were lopsided embarrassments. Strangely enough, in the 1956 Temple game, the final game of the year, the University of Delaware finally went over the career .500 mark for the first time in the 62 years the Newark school had played college-only football.

After a bad start in 1957 the Blue Hens once again struggled along with more lifetime losses than wins but when they downed Temple again the football team had once and forever recorded more wins than losses. That landmark day the Delaware Stadium rout grew to 71-7 when Coach Dave Nelson began using his timeouts in the 4th quarter and asking the officials to keep the clock running to keep the score down.

After the 1970 season the rivalry changed dramatically when Temple committed totally to big time football. With relaxed admissions policies, freshman eligibility and full scholarships Temple was clearly playing a different brand of football than Delaware. While Delaware was lining up against Wittenburg and West Chester, Temple's schedule was sprinkled with Penn State and Pittsburgh. For the remaining 15 years of the series Tubby Raymond's troops were never expected - by the so-called experts, at least - to win another Temple-Delaware football game. Yet not only did Delaware take six of those contests, they dominated the Division I Owls as often as not.

In 1974, with Temple riding the nation's second-longest winning streak at 13 games, the Owls needed to manufacture a late touchdown to eke out a 21-17 win before 37,265 fans at Veterans Stadium, the most people to ever watch a University of Delaware game. Other highlights for the Owls included pinning the only losses to Delaware's national championship teams of 1971 and 1979. But for most of the final years of the long-time series the laurels belonged to the small college Blue Hens.

By the early 1980s it was clear that the greatest college football game in the area could not continue. Delaware was joining the Yankee Conference which would fill its schedule and Temple, courting the Alabamas and Miamis of the football world, could no longer afford to be embarrassed by "little" Delaware. School officials announced the final Delaware-Temple game would take place in 1985.

Coming off perhaps Delaware's most astonishing upset in the long series, a 34-19 lesson in football in 1984, Raymond had his Blue Hens drilled to perfection for the closing act in the 72-year drama. The defense stopped Heisman Trophy candidate Paul Palmer three successive times inside the two-yard line to preserve a 17-10 win before a delirious Delaware stadium crowd. The most memorable chapter in University of Delaware football was over.

The Delaware-Temple series ended with 22 Blue Hen wins in 36 games, the final five wins coming against imponderable odds. Temple coach Bruce Arians, now cut adrift from his traditional foe, expressed few regrets, "It's fine to play teams that are lower than you, but not when they treat it like life and death. You have to consider what the game means to them and to us. There are a lot of people around here who remember how it was 20 years ago, when Delaware was the biggest game we had."
Delaware 22, Temple 14

Villanova. Delaware won its first ever meeting with the Main Line school in 1895. Victory Number Two did not come until 1965. From that point until Villanova abandoned football in 1981 the Villanova game and the Temple game were the measuring rods by which Delaware fans graded a season. Only twice were both Division I foes vanquished in the same year.

With only a rare exception a Delaware-Villanova game was a close, hard-hitting affair

- more often than not characterized by explosive offenses. After 1980, when Villanova dropped football, the series favored the Wildcats 11-9-1.

Villanova re-established football in 1988 and joined the 1-AA Yankee Conference. Now reunited on the same level and in the same conference, the rivalry renewed with its former passion. Delaware won seven of the first eight games, albeit by fewer than four points five times. But Andy Talley's bunch whitewashed the Blue Hens 27-0 in 1996 and Delaware only won five of the next 20 games.

Delaware's most enduring gridiron rivalry was formalized in 2007 with the formation of the Battle of the Blue Trophy, hardware that features a football with Villanova blue on one side and Delaware blue on the other. The trophy was introduced at a highpoint for both programs - the Blue Hens went to the national finals in 2007 and 2010 and the Wildcats won the national title in 2009. To date the Blue Trophy has spent little time in Newark, only after the 2011 season when the Blue Hens recovered from a 16-13 fourth quarter deficit to triumph 26-16.

Delaware 21, Villanova 27, 1 tie

West Chester. Delaware's series with its nearest geographical neighbor started by accident in 1941 when an infestation of infantile paralysis gripping central Pennsylvania forced Juniata College to cancel its scheduled trip to Newark. The Rams of West Chester State College were hastily substituted and rode down to play the Blue Hens to a 7-7 standstill. The deadlock proved to be the only blemish in the midst of a 32-game unbeaten streak for the University of Delaware.

The Delaware-West Chester game is for the Blue Hens what the Delaware-Temple game was for the perennially harassed Owls: a no-win proposition. Delaware is expected to handle their pesky Division III rival each time the schools renew acquaintances. And for the first 50 years of the series Delaware would win handily well over 80% of the time. But each of those Rams wins would wear like a badge of honor in West Chester.

There is never a pattern to when Delaware will fail to dodge the West Chester bullet. In the early 1950s, while Delaware was running up a four-year win total of 24-10, the Blue Hens lost three times to the Rams. West Chester was coached by Glenn Killinger who built one of the strongest small college programs in history, going 144-44-11 over 25 years.

The series went into a hiatus for over a decade before being revived in 1968. Delaware thumped West Chester 15 straight times, most by overwhelming margins, before the game became extremely competitive in the mid-eighties. The Rams came out on top twice in this span, including the worst defeat ever handed a Delaware team by West Chester, 33-13 in 1988 when the Blue Hens were Yankee Conference Co- Champions.

The series that began in 1941 played out in 2012. In the new era of I-AA playoffs, wins against Division II opponents did not count for Delaware. It was blow for West Chester since even though the Rams last won in 1992 the gate receipts paid a large chunk of the school's ten yearly scholarships. As backyard squabbles go West Chester and Delaware was never one of the greats but the Blue Hens always had to be wary of their tiny neighbor to the north.

Delaware 47, West Chester 6, 1 tie

Boardwalk Bowl

In 1968 the NCAA established a series of bowl games to decide regional College Division champions. In the East the site was indoors in Convention Hall on the Atlantic City boardwalk. Coincidentally, the University of Delaware was at this time beginning to field some of the strongest teams in its history and the Blue Hens came to use the Boardwalk Bowl as their own personal whipping post.

For the inaugural Boardwalk Bowl in 1968 Delaware was expected to have little problem with Indiana State University of Pennsylvania but the game didn't play out that way. The Big Indians raced to a 21-10 lead and countered Delaware's comeback with a 32-yard field goal with only a minute left in the game to take a 24-23 lead. Following a kick-off return to their own 43 Delaware's Tom DiMuzio passed the Hens quickly to the Big Indian 11-yard line on three completions. After a running play gained two yards DiMuzio found Ron Withelder in the endzone for the game-winner.

In the 1969 Boardwalk Bowl, in DiMuzio's last game, Delaware defeated North Carolina Central 31-13 as they piled up 373 yards rushing. The 1970 Delaware team boasted five 500-yard rushers (Chuck Hall 1084, Billy Armstrong 892, Gardy Kahoe 816, Dick Kelley 581 and Jim Colbert 510) and this group ground up Morgan State in Atlantic City 35-23.

Delaware came to the 1971 Boardwalk Bowl with the leading College Division offense in the country, ripping off 516 yards per game. On defense the swarming Hens were allowing less than 60 yards rushing per contest. In the fourth Boardwalk Bowl their opponent was C.W. Post and its much-hyped quarterback Gary Wichard. The Post Toasties were 8-2; Delaware had lost only to Temple.

The game seemed almost a scrimmage for the Blue Hens. The offense rolled up 405 yards rushing and 216 passing. The defense sacked Wichard eight times and the final score was an embarrassing 72-22. With four Boardwalk Bowl wins in as many tries the undefeated 1972 Blue Hens voted not to return to the Convention Hall dirt and sod for a fifth appearance. Their much-publicized decline of the Boardwalk Bowl invitation helped prod the NCAA into setting up a playoff system for its lower divisions. Those playoffs began in 1973 with a first round game being played, where else, back at Convention Hall where, ironically, with much more at stake than merely regional supremacy, Delaware lost for the first time.

The University of Delaware won four consecutive Boardwalk Bowls inside the Atlantic City Convention Center that was once the largest free-standing building in the world.

Golf

Golf Comes To Delaware

The first golf ball struck in Delaware was hit in the vacant fields south of Lancaster Pike on Clayton Street in Wilmington, near what is today Canby Park. It was the early 1890s and America's first golf boom was underway. Golf clubs had started organizing only in the late 1880s but by 1900 there would be 982 courses across the country.

Lieutenant Governor J. Danforth Bush brought the first set of golf clubs into Delaware after a trip to Scotland. He laid out a rudimentary course to play the game. The greens of this primitive golfing field, it was reported, were "rough as an unpaved street, and the cups were made of empty tomato cans sunk into the ground."

The activity out on Clayton Street attracted the attention of several members of the Delaware Field Club, organized in 1885 to play cricket. In 1894 these members started a course on their property in Elsmere, routing holes around houses and through cinder streets. Matches were soon arranged with neighboring clubs from Philadelphia and West Chester at the Field Club Course.

These golfing grounds were used until 1901 when the Field Club leased 147 acres of William du Pont's estate on the Kennett Pike and incorporated the Wilmington Country Club. The initiation fee was the purchase of two shares of stock for $25 each. Annual dues were set at $12.

The new course was laid out by Henry Tatnall and J. Ernest Smith. The design was esteemed enough to host the 1913 United States Women's Amateur Championship. No less an authority than Bobby Jones praised the 205-yard 6th hole as one of the finest of its kind when he visited.

Wilmington Country Club remained on the site for sixty years, weathering a conflagration of the clubhouse in 1924. Play began over two new courses designed by the two leading architects of the age - Robert Trent Jones and Dick Wilson - in the early 1960s. The South Course is regarded as one of the finest layouts in the land and has hosted several national championships.

Outside of Wilmington Country Club, golf was slow to take root in Delaware, however. Pioneer golfers were ridiculed as

Early golf courses favored geometric shapes, like this rectangular sand green.

"big men chasing little white pills across the fields with big clubs." Some men of means developed private courses at their estates but the next formal club was not formed in the state until the E.I du Pont de Nemours & Company decided to start a country club on property formerly occupied by the Wilmington Gun Club.

The original nine holes were completed in 1920, using dirt tees and sand greens. Golf was little more than a secondary activity at the new club. The most popular sport was baseball - especially women's baseball - among company departments which had forged bitter diamond rivalries. By 1922 golf was popular enough to warrant the creation of a full 18-hole course and a large grey stone clubhouse, which was completed in 1924.

Wilfrid Reid, a Scottish professional who came to Delaware at the behest of the du Pont family, designed the DuPont Course. A second 18 holes was added in 1938 and a third course opened at Milford Crossroads in 1956. By 1965 the DuPont Country Club boasted four 18-hole courses and the largest private membership of any country club in the world.

The 1920s were the golden age of golf course design in the United States. After the initial boom golf actually faded for the first two decades of this century. By 1916 there were some 742 courses available - nearly 250 less than 1900. But by 1929 there would be 5,648. For more than ten years a new golf course opened on average every day.

Delaware was no different. Golf came to downstate; courses opened in Dover and Rehoboth. Newark established a course in 1922, with nine holes sculpted from a tract of 161 acres. Golf was now available in all of the major towns in Delaware.

The Early Delaware Pros

In the formative years of American golf there was only one commandment for a club pro - Be Scottish. Americans believed that all Scots could play golf; it mattered little if he actually could. Many young Scots answered the call, sailing across the Atlantic to teach America golf, even if they had to learn the game along with their eager new disciples.

Wilmington Country Club, Delaware's only club until 1920, was fortunate in its choice of early professionals - they could play a bit, too. First pro Thomas Clark was a good British player before signing on at the Kennett Pike club in 1903. His successor, Gilbert Nicholls, was one of the top tournament players in America. Born and weaned on golf in England, Nicholls came to the United States in 1897 at the age of 18. In 1902 he set an 18-hole

Englishman Gilbert Nicholls was a top American pro when he came to Wilmington Country Club.

199

scoring record in the U.S. Open. He was a two-time runner-up in the Open before settling in Wilmington in 1908.

The popular Nicholls was head pro at Wilmington for seven years, winning several national tournaments during his tenure, including the North and South Open in Pinehurst North Carolina that was just a notch below the U.S. Open in prestige in those days. In 1911 Nicholls set an all-time 72-hole scoring mark in capturing the Metropolitan Open with a 281, including an unheard of 66 in the final round. When Nicholls left Wilmington in 1914 he went to Great Neck Country Club on Long Island as the highest paid club pro in the country. He stayed 32 years

Wilfrid Reid finished fourth in the U.S. Open while pro at Wilmington CC; he designed over 50 courses, including work in Delaware.

until his retirement at the age of 69.

In turn, Nicholls was replaced by two more Brits, Wilfrid Reid and Alex Tait. Reid was a protege of golfing great Harry Vardon and compiled a fine competitive record, finishing as high as fourth in the U.S. Open in 1916 while at Wilmington Country Club. Never one to keep his golfing accomplishments under his hat it was said that his personal stationery was filled with so much detail of his golfing prowess that there was little room to write a message.

Tait stayed as head man at Wilmington for 40 years, retiring in 1961 as Delaware's last golfing link to ancient Scotland. Other Delaware clubs were similarly blessed with gifted golfers as pros in their early years. Tommy Fisher and Alec Douglas at DuPont Country Club and Rock Manor Golf Club, respectively, each stayed more than a quarter-century at their posts. At Newark Country Club head man Ed Ginther was talented enough to qualify for both the U.S. Open and the PGA.

One of the first great American-born club pros was Ed Dudley. Dudley was a Ryder Cup player when he came to Wilmington to take command of the Concord Country Club out at Painters Crossroads, then owned by Wilmington Country Club, in 1930. Dudley was a leader on the embryonic pro tour when northern club pros would travel across the South playing tournaments in the winter. On the 1931 tour, while representing Concord, Dudley led all golfers with a 71.39 scoring average, won the Los Angeles Open and the Western Open and made the Ryder Cup team again.

When Dudley left Concord in 1933 it was to return to his native Georgia for the best golf job in America - first head pro at Bobby Jones' new Augusta National Golf Club. In 1964 Ed Dudley became the 35th enshrinee in the Golf Hall of Fame.

Public Golf In Delaware

On Labor Day 1921 a small golfing ground opened by Porter's Reservoir on the north end of Wilmington. For the first time in Delaware golf could be played without belonging to a private club, by just paying a daily fee. Trolley cars brought golfers to the new Rock Manor course at the foot of McKees Hill.

A tent served as clubhouse. Experienced players were stationed around the nine holes to help newcomers. For a while play was actually free but a small fee was soon assessed to allow for course maintenance. So rapidly did the course grow in popularity that three years later Rock Manor was extended to a full 18 holes, and within another five years the course was stretched another 600 yards.

In a unique arrangement Rock Manor was owned by the city of Wilmington, administered by the Water Department and operated by the Municipal Golf and Tennis Association, a private club. Memberships were available but members could not claim preference in starting times over the daily fee player. In this way golf fees funded all construction and upkeep of the course. Rock Manor never cost Wilmington taxpayers one cent.

By 1929 nearly 30,000 rounds of golf were being played each year at Rock Manor, far more than any private course in the area. On many days more than 350 players teed off; the single day record reached 418. In 1937 Alex Findlay, a Scot living in Philadelphia who had played over 2400 courses, was hired to re-design the course with government WPA funds. Despite the Depression, Rock Manor became even more popular. "In season," reported The *Sunday Morning Star* that year, "the weekly average of players totals 1500. Saturdays, Sundays and holidays find the course loaded."

And no wonder. Rock Manor was the only public golf available to Delawareans for more than 40 years. In 1958 William du Pont Jr. donated land containing 15 holes of the old Wilmington Country Club to the city. The 108 acres were valued at more than $1,000,000, one of the greatest gifts ever given to the state for recreation. Du Pont later granted another 15 acres to insure a complete, re-designed 18-hole course at the site.

The new club was named Green Hill, a name linked to the property since 1846. The cost of a round on Delaware's oldest golfing grounds was $2.50 during the week, $3.50 on the weekends. By 1970 more than 45,000 golfers a year were enjoying the historic links at Green Hill.

In the mid-1960s New Castle County officials prepared to build the first course by a local government in nearly 50 years. Only Rock Manor, mutilated by the new I-95 highway, and Green Hill were available to serve 343,000 county residents. The site chosen was on old state prison farm at Delcastle and when it opened in 1971 it became a showcase for public golf. The three-level, 190-car parking lot was built without removing a single tree. On the course, extra large tees, broad fairways and large greens conspired to manage the burden of heavy play smoothly.

Twenty years later the three courses still handled the bulk of public course play in Delaware. Several other semi-private courses opened to the public on a limited basis but south of Smyrna only one course, Old Landing Golf Course, welcomed the daily fee player. That changed dramtically as golf boomed again the 1990s. Southern Delaware positioned itself in the golf resort market and the First State ended the 20th century with more than two dozen course open for public play.

Delaware's Golf Architects

Although some of golf's most famous architects, most notably Robert Trent Jones and Jack Nicklaus, have stamped their imprint on Delaware, the state's golfing grounds have been shaped to a remarkable degree by only two men.

Alfred Tull was born in England in 1897. His family emigrated to Canada ten years later and Tull came to this country at the age of 17. He began his career as a construction superintendent for Walter Travis, America's first golfing champion, in 1921.

Tull first came to Delaware in 1929 to work with Devereaux Emmet on Henry du Pont's personal course at Winterthur. Following Emmet's death in 1935 Tull entered private practice as a course architect. His first commission was for nine holes on Lancaster Pike for the Hercules Company.

Tull became noted for his ability to lay out individual holes and establish a circuit by walking the land and staking the holes without consulting any topographical plans. In Delaware, he would go on to design the Nemours and DuPont courses at the Du Pont Country Club, the Brandywine Country Club, the Seaford Country Club and 18 more holes at Hercules.

Edmund Ault once estimated that he had designed or remodeled one-fourth of all the courses in the Maryland and Virginia suburbs around Washington, D.C. His percentage in Delaware is even greater.

A one-time scratch golfer, Ault was an engineer by training. After several seasons apprenticing in golf architecture he entered private practice in 1946 at the age of 38. In the early 1960s Ault introduced golf throughout downstate Delaware by building courses at the Dover Air Force Base, Dover Country Club, Sussex Pines, Shawnee and Garrisons Lake in Smyrna.

Recognized for his advocacy of flexibility in course design, Ault moved upstate in the 1970s. He re-routed Green Hill, now Porky Oliver, and created Delcastle and Pike Creek Valley (Three Little Bakers). When he was through Edmund Ault was responsible for 7 of every 10 holes of public golf in the state of Delaware.

Alfred Tull designed the two main 18-hole courses at the DuPont Country Club.

The Personal Course

There are private courses and there are private courses. In the early days of Delaware golf several prominent men built small golf courses on their expansive estates. Henry Haskell and Charles Copeland laid out links at their homes of perhaps five holes. Pierre S. du Pont enjoyed golf on the grounds at Longwood.

But none matched the facilities set up by Henry F. du Pont. For decades du Pont enjoyed one of the world's best personal courses. In 1928 du Pont commissioned Devereaux Emmet, one of America's leading golf architects, to carve a golfing field from the rolling hills on his Winterthur estate. Emmet crafted an 18-hole course from ten greens and 17 tees. The full course played to 6480 yards; the front nine sporting steel markers, the home nine porcelain. Wide fairways reached 200 feet in some spots.

Like any other course, the Henry du Pont course employed a golf pro. Du Pont had met Percy Vickers in an indoor golf school in New York City and when the course was ready at Winterthur Vickers was on hand as pro and groundskeeper. Vickers, who would stay for more than thirty years, the course's entire existence, ventured that,

"There are no more than 10 golf courses in the country on the scale of Winterthur - I mean actually for golf and not a family playground."

Henry du Pont would entertain 18-20 golf guests on a weekend. In his later years he confessed to being not particularly interested in scoring but in being outside for the exercise. He played every other day into his 80s, always walking and shunning a golf car. Vickers estimated that his boss would shoot in the 90s and du Pont was good enough to join the PGA Hole-In-One Club in 1941.

In 1963 du Pont's personal course was converted into a private club, in part "to protect the Winterthur Museum from the inroads of residential building and traffic, and to add to the beautification of its contiguous gardens." The members wanted to call their club "Winterthur" but du Pont considered that confusing and suggested the name "Bidermann" after the builder of the estate.

Delaware's last personal course was not quite gone forever. Henry du Pont retained, in addition to his indoor driving range, three holes to play himself.

At his Winterthur Estate Henry du Pont enjoyed one of the finest private golf courses in the country.

Dave Douglas

About the time Porky Oliver was building his game at Rock Manor another teenager was trading course records with him. Snowball's rival was Dave Douglas, the son of Rock Manor professional Alec Douglas. In addition to their individual battles father and son teamed against Oliver and Wilmington Country Club pro Alex Tait in highly publicized matches.

Douglas, born in Philadelphia in 1918, stood 6'3" and weighed only 154 pounds. He lettered in basketball at P.S. du Pont High School. When Oliver, a sturdy 205 pounds, turned pro after high school he invited his old Rock Manor foe to partner in pro-am events. The "fat man and the thin man" made a formidable team, setting records in several tournaments.

The experience boosted Douglas' confidence. He finished as low amateur in the Philadelphia Open and the Lake Placid Open and qualified for the National Amateur in 1938. That year the 20-year old Douglas turned professional by accepting the assistant pro job at Orchard Ridge Country Club in Fort Wayne, Indiana. He was back in Delaware by 1940 when he qualified for his first United States Open, shooting an 83-78 in the same tournament Oliver was disqualified for starting his final round early.

Douglas spent 18 months of World War II on board a hospital ship. The years after the war found him giving lessons at night at Wilmington's first driving range, the Boulevard Driving Range at 40th & Governor Printz. By the end of 1947 Douglas was ready to try pro golf's winter tour.

During a practice round at the Orlando Open, his third tournament, Douglas was playing with other unknowns Vic Catelino, Ellis Taylor, who would later win eight Delaware Amateur crowns, and Otto Greiner. Sam Snead, playing behind the young foursome, was hitting into them all day and when a second shot on a par five rolled between Catelino's legs Vic suggested they allow the famous star to play through. "We will not," said a proud Douglas. "He's no better than we are."

He proved it later in the week when he fired a final round 66 to join Jimmy Demaret and Herman Kaiser in a playoff for the $2000 top prize. Although Douglas had played before virtually no gallery to that point he cooly won the playoff the next day, first tying Demaret with a 71 and then winning the sudden death playoff on the first hole with a 5-foot birdie putt.

It was an impressive beginning but he struggled in anonymity on the Tour for the next 18 months. At the Texas Open in 1949 Douglas moved into contention with rounds of 65, 72 and 66 to earn a spot in the final threesome on Sunday with leader Snead. Douglas bogeyed the first hole but made seven birdies to finish with a 65 and his second title. The unknown underdog was hoisted to the shoulders of the crowd of 7000 and swept off the 18th green to the clubhouse. It took Douglas 15 minutes to travel the 100 feet from signing so many autographs. How unknown was Dave Douglas? San Antonio papers reported that he was "practically born and raised on his father's Park Manor golf course in Delaware, Maryland."

Douglas was one of the most likable and approachable players on tour. His tall frame and elongated swing produced a consistent fade on his long shots but his fellow pros admired most his stroke-saving short game. He finished 17th on the PGA money list in 1948 but several lean years had him contemplating quitting

Dave Douglas (right) won eight PGA Tour titles but not a great deal of recognition. When he won his second tournament in San Antonio the local papers announced the he was "practically born and raised on his father's Park Manor golf course in Delaware, Maryland."

president of the PGA by his fellow players.

His performance enabled Douglas to join Oliver on the 1953 Ryder Cup team. Remarkably, the two men who grew up on the Rock Manor links together twenty years earlier were now representing America in golf's most prestigious international competition in Wentworth, England. Oliver and Douglas were paired in foursomes play and downed Peter Allis and Harry Weetman 2 and 1. Douglas tied in his singles match the next day as the United States brought the Ryder Cup home once again.

Always a streaky player Douglas began the 1954 season by not cashing a check for over two months before he won the $6200 top prize at the Houston Open and jumped to the top of the money list. He won only $6220 the rest of the year, however, and began

the tour by the start of the 1952 campaign.

He struggled through the winter tour with finishes of 27th, 33rd, 28th, 19th, 33rd and 26th and wasn't nearly making expenses when he flashed to a win at Greensboro, worth $2000. He won the Ardmore Open in Oklahoma several months later, which carried one of golf's top prizes - $5400. Playing as an unattached pro from Newark, Delaware, Douglas was the only player in field to break par for 72 holes. He finished the 1952 season as the 7th leading money winner with $15,173 and was named vice-

searching in earnest for a club job. In 1956 Douglas accepted a post at the St. Louis Country Club. Where Oliver could never tame his wanderlust for life on the PGA Tour, returning time and time again from club jobs, Douglas settled into his work in the pro shop and was content to leave behind his touring days for good.

Like Oliver before him Douglas contracted cancer and, as his former partner did, returned to Delaware for his final days. Dave Douglas died in 1978 at the age of 60.

Witness to History

In the 1950s Dave Douglas was twice witness to golfing history, attesting the scorecard for one of golf's greatest rounds and one of the game's most famous shots.

In 1951 United States Open Douglas trailed the leader Bobby Locke by a single stroke entering the 36-hole final day at Oakland Hills Golf Club in Birmingham, Michigan. Oakland Hills had recently been remodeled for the Open and players complained bitterly about its tight driving areas and heroic proportions. Douglas was paired for the last 36 holes with Ben Hogan who came off the pace to win the tournament with an astounding three-under par 67. It was only the fourth sub-par round of the week and two shots better than anyone managed that day. Many consider it the greatest round ever played in American competitive golf. Hogan himself admitted afterward that "I'm glad I brought this course, this monster, to its knees." And Dave Douglas saw every shot.

If you walk up and down the practice range at any PGA Tour stop today and ask pros what tournament they most want to win you will hear "U.S. Open" or "Masters" or maybe "the Open Championship." Jump into the wayback machine to the 1940s and 1950s, however, and ask the same question and you would just as likely hear "George S. May's All-American."

In an era when touring pros carpooled between tournaments, doubled up at cheap roadside motels and rarely played for first-place checks of more than $1,000 George S. May - the "S" stood for "Storr" but in golf circles it was considered "Sugar" - staged golf tournaments where the winner's share was larger than any other event's entire purse. Win the Tam O'Shanter and a pro golfer was assured of finishing among the leading money winners for the entire year.

In 1953 the Tam O'Shanter was the first golf tournament to be televised nationally - with a single camera rigged behind the 18th green. The American Broadcasting Corporation (ABC), in its first year on the air, slotted one hour for the live telecast. Lew Worsham, whose previous claim to fame had been denying Sam Snead a never-to-be-won U.S. Open in a playoff at St. Louis Country Club in 1947, came to the 18th hole needing a birdie three to get into a playoff with Chandler Harper for the biggest first prize in the history of golf. With ten minutes left in the broadcast, the executives at ABC could not have asked for better sports drama.

Worsham drove the ball well and selected a MacGregor double service wedge to cover the remaining 104 yards. The ball soared above the Chicago River, slipped past two trees and landed on the front of the green about forty feet short of the pin. Jimmy Demaret, who was doing commentary on the radio, picks up the story: "The ball's running toward the hole. Oh, I'll be damned. It went in."

"The Shot Heard Round The World" was worth $25,000 to Worsham. And just like that, ABC signed off from Niles, Illinois with the most dramatic finishing shot in professional golf history having been been witnessed on an estimated 646,000 television sets. And watching from the other side of the fairway was Worsham's playing partner, Dave Douglas.

Women's Professional Golf In Delaware

The LPGA McDonald's Championship was first served to area golf fans in the bucolic horse country of Chester County, Pennsylvania at White Manor Country Club in 1981. It was a superb golfing ground and organizers ran a first class event. The tournament quickly expanded into the richest payday on the women's tour. In its first six years the McDonald's Championship produced such quality champions as Jo Anne Carner, Beth Daniel, Patty Sheehan and Juli Inkster.

White Manor was rapidly losing its ability to nurture the exploding McDonald's Championship. In 1986 the tournament committee went searching for a facility with two courses to accommodate the ever-expanding - and immensely profitable - pro-am portion of championship week. Prestigious Wilmington Country Club passed on overtures from the McDonald's folks but they found a willing host across the Brandywine River at the DuPont Country Club.

The 41 1/2-acre site proved an ideal compromise. Worries about the venerable DuPont course's ability to withstand the withering assault by the lady pros proved unfounded as the subpar round was the exception, not the rule. Betsy King won the first McDonald's Kids Classic in Delaware with a six-under par 278 to claim the $75,000 first prize. She did it with a flair, birdieing three of the final four holes to pull away by two strokes.

The immaculately groomed layout won raves from the players. The next year, in 1988, 50 of the top 51 money winners came to Wilmington. Delawareans embraced the event as well and in 1989 a single-day LPGA tour record of 38,750 turned out for the final round. Over 2500 volunteers work on the event each year. The McDonald's Kid Classic became a money machine for charity, generating two million dollars annually. More than $47,000,000 was raised for the McDonald's charities, with a third staying in Delaware. The tournament was considered the largest fundraiser in the history of golfdom.

The success off the course was equalled by the play in between the ropes. The list of worthy champions lengthened - Betsy King, Akayo Okamoto and Sheehan and Daniel again. In 1994 the McDonald's Championship graduated to become one of the major championships on the women's tour.

In 1998 Se Ri Pak ignited a craze in South Korean women's golf when she arrived in the United States as a 20-year old and won the McDonald's LPGA Championship by three strokes with an 11-under par 273. A few months later she became the youngest winner ever of the U.S. Women's Open.

Pak's win began a run of Hall of Fame winners in the championship. Juli Inkster won the next two titles and Australian Karrie Webb captured the trophy in 2001. Pak won again at DuPont Country Club in 2002.

In 2003 Annika Sorenstam, the greatest female golfer of her generation, beat South Korean Grace Park on the first hole of a sudden-death playoff to win the fifth of her ten major titles. The next year in Wilmington she would win her seventh major championship.

That would also end the run of the tournament in Delaware. The next year the LPGA Championship moved to Bulle Rock in Maryland. Sorenstam won her third straight title but the tournament would never again find the same success after leaving DuPont Country Club.

Horse Racing

Dover: Fairview Park

The Delaware State Fair opened for business in 1878 and right from the start its trotting races were the best on the Delmarva Peninsula. Fairview Park, built to be one of the finest tracks in the country, was beautifully situated at the end of the railroad lines. More than 3000 people were on hand by the final day of the inaugural week-long event. The feature race that day carried a purse of $1000, the largest yet seen in Delaware. Driver stepped to victory in three of the four heats to win the grand prize in the 2:22 class.

The next year between 10,000 and 20,000 people poured into the fairgrounds and the renewal of the 2:22 class provided the finest contest ever witnessed on any race track in Delaware. The favorite Irene finished last in all five heats of the four-horse affair. May nipped Jersey in each of the first two heats but the lightly regarded Scotland thundered from behind to win the final three heats and the race.

By 1880 the Dover races, in only their third year, were far and away the class of the state. While the Wilmington Trotting Association had to cancel their meet because it couldn't fill the fast classes Driver sped across the Fairview Park oval in 2:23, the fastest race time ever in Delaware. In a special race to beat 2:19 1/2 for $1000 the little mare Trinkett, in the hands of trainer John E. Turner, took the track on a frigid October day before 5000 people. With 50 stop watches trained on her she reached the half in 1:09 and raced to the wire in 2:19 1/4 to claim the thousand dollars.

The performance thrust Trinket into the first ranks of racehorses, causing *Farmer's Magazine* to gush the following year, "The young mare Trinket has been most carefully wintered, and is now in the most splendid form and condition. If this mare does not develop into one of the great lights of the trotting turf, then all the flattering and promising indications of the past will go for naught."

Dover's reputation for fast horses was firmly established and the State Fair became an anchor of the Peninsular circuit with race tracks in Elkton, Baltimore, Wilmington and Easton. The races at Fairview Park continued throughout the 19th century, making the Delaware State Fair the longest success story in Delaware racing in the 1800s.

Record-setting driver John E. Turner guided many champions on Delaware tracks. Here he is depicted by Currier & Ives driving the grand trotter Edwin Thorne.

Dover: Dover Downs

Horse racing at Dover Downs, restricted to the bleak winter months has proven somewhat less popular than the NASCAR oval encompassing it. The first thoroughbred meet in 1969 averaged only 2,775 fans, barely half of what was expected. Attendance topped out at 3500 in 1972 but flat racing was gone from Dover Downs by 1975. Harness racing fared somewhat better. Operating in the dead of winter Dover developed a reputation as a track that put on racing without the questionable shenanigans that oft times tainted larger plants. Horsemen enjoyed the friendly atmosphere and excellent racing surface. Attendance was on par with the thoroughbreds and reduced expenses in the harness game allowed it to survive.

The small purses at Dover seldom enticed the sport's leading performers to the track on Route 13. But occasionally one would show up. Meadow Rich established a mark for older horses at Dover with a 1:58 mile in 1985 and the next year Forrest Skipper dropped by to shatter the track record in 1:54.4 on his way to Harness Horse of the Year honors.

By the 1990s Dover Downs and Harrington were operating on limited weekend schedules. They were the last harness tracks still operating in Delaware, where once, only a score of years before, there had been four. The oldest sport in Delaware was in danger of being put down.

On December 29, 1995 the Horseracing Redevelopment Act gave people legal slot machines and Dover Downs fatter purses. Much fatter purses. Before the slot machines Dover Downs would offer a desultory card of races with purses of $800, maybe $1,000. With the infusion of slot profits a ten-race program would average $150,000 in prize money for the night.

The difference on the track was immediate. Dover was flooded with the game's best horses and on November 16, 1996 the pacer Riyadh ran away from the field in a $20,000 Open mile pace to set a track record of 1:49.1. There would be no tickets cashed on Riyadh this night - the six-year old who was brought back from retiring after failing in the breeding shed was barred from the wagering.

Dover Downs became a destination stop on Monday nights when heavy hitters like Jet Log with Canadian Luc Ouelette would battle Pilgrim's Fiery with Eddie Davis. The slot money also improved homebred Delaware racing stock. Rainbow Blue, training out of Harrington by George Teague, Jr., became the first Delaware standardbred since Adios Harry a half-century before, to garner national acclaim.

In 2004 the filly won 20 of 21 races and was named Horse of the Year, one of only three fillies ever so honored. In only two of her wins was another horse even within one length of her at the finish line. Rainbow Blue posted a stakes record 1:51 mile at the Breeders Crown.

Rainbow Blue began her four-year old campaign with four wins in four outings before a tendon injury ended her career. She won 30 of her 32 lifetime races and owned two of the three fastest miles ever paced by a three-year-old filly (1:49.2 best) when she retired. Rainbow Blue would be inducted into the Harness Racing "Living Horse" Hall of Fame in 2012.

Georgetown: Georgetown Raceway

For years the Del-Mar-Va Racing Association held the franchise to harness racing in Sussex County granted by the Delaware Harness Racing Association. Each season Del-Mar-Va would thus get a share of profits from Harrington and Brandywine without ever staging a meet.

Sussex County had traditionally been an excellent breeding and training area for standardbreds so when plans were finally announced to build a harness track on Route 18 outside Georgetown there was a paddock full of investors ready to back the venture. People from the big cities come to lower Delaware every summer for the beaches so why wouldn't they come back in the winter for harness racing?

The stands were still not enclosed and there weren't any heaters and there were no lights in the parking lot and much of the $1.5 million facility was still unfinished but on November 3, 1965 winter horse racing came to Delaware. But even though the half-mile track and the parimutuel windows were about the only things ready when Pearl C, a Delaware horse, flashed across the wire in 2:11.1 to pay $8.80 in the inaugural pace, Georgetown Raceway was off to a successful first meet.

To lure horsemen in the dead of winter Ed Keller, director of racing and future Harness Racing Hall of Famer, instituted a policy of distributing the purse among all the starters - making Georgetown the first track in the United States to do so. Racing on nights and Saturday afternoons from November to February the Georgetown Raceway averaged about 2,200 in attendance and $90,000 in handle - 10% above projected levels of profitability.

Operating with the bottom-of-the-barrel dates not assigned to Brandywine and Harrington the little track continued to prosper. The drivers liked it and fans - drawn from far-away Baltimore, Washington and Philadelphia - loved their side trips down the Delmarva Peninsula. But with Dover Downs opening in 1969 Delaware could not support four harness tracks and Georgetown was fourth in this four-horse race. A spring meeting of 21 nights was tried in direct competition with Brandywine, Atlantic City Race Course and Rosecroft and Laurel in Maryland. Despite this suicide run Georgetown still averaged 1754 fans but new owner John Rollins, who also operated Brandywine and Dover Downs, gave Georgetown's remaining 1970 dates to Dover.

The abandoned facility quickly deteriorated and Rollins sold the dilapidated property to a Maryland convenience-store owner for $167,000, with the provision he not race horses there for ten years. Plans were hatched to race stock cars and even dogs but both ideas were dropped after strong opposition in the community. Eventually after nine years as a deepening eyesore the former jewel of Sussex County racing was converted into a training center and farmers market.

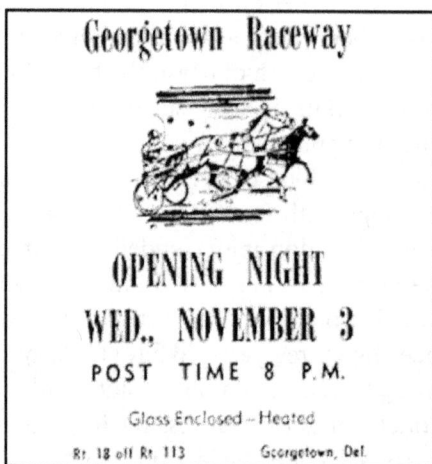

Georgetown Raceway

OPENING NIGHT
WED., NOVEMBER 3
POST TIME 8 P.M.

Glass Enclosed - Heated

Rt. 18 off Rt. 113   Georgetown, Del.

Fans were promised glass-enclosed heat but it wasn't quite ready for opening night of Georgetown Raceway in 1965.

Harrington: Harrington Raceway

Just as harness racing in Delaware was about to go the way of the hitching post in 1920 the Kent and Sussex County Fair Association formed for the purposes of "giving pleasures and diversions to the inhabitants of rural communities within the state of Delaware." One of the centerpieces for the new Fair was harness racing. Thirty acres for a track and grandstand were acquired for $6000. For the next decade these four-day meets provided the best horse racing in Delaware.

In 1946 the old Fairgrounds were spruced up a bit and Harrington hosted Delaware's first pari-mutuel night harness racing. Cards were typically eight races, run for purses of $300 and $400. The track was only wide enough to accommodate six horses so two horses broke from the second tier. Crowds estimated at 3000 turned out for Opening Night, a Monday, and didn't abate for the entire 15-night meet. Organizers hadn't imagined that kind of revenue. And the weather had been lousy.

The star driver of that first meet was Elbert J. Saunders, 72, in his 57th year at the reins. Saunders estimated he had driven horses 300,000 miles, but never on Sunday. The Sabbath was for church or "courting." He held several track records around the fair circuit and at the age of 70 drove in six heats in one day and won five. At Harrington Saunders guided Performance to the meet's best 9/16 mile

Harrington Raceway is the oldest continually operating racetrack in the state of Delaware with races on the same oval for more than 95 years. It is the last existing track to have featured both horse racing and auto racing over the same surface. On August 2, 1947 Harrington set a record for attendance at an auto race that was not approached until the construction of the modern speedway at Dover Downs. That day 36,258 fans jammed the old track to watch the big autos through plumes of dust.

time of 1:08 3/4.

In the Spring 1947 meet the handle went over $1 million at Harrington. In 1948 a $1000 stakes race was added to the program and a mobile starting gate introduced. That year each winning horse was awarded a blanket. By 1951 the average attendance was 2500 and the daily play over $60,000. That year Royal Mist set a world's record for two-year old fillies, pacing the 1/2 mile oval in 2:05.

But the Kent & Sussex Raceway in Harrington, which had been the sole nourisher of harness racing in Delaware for 34 years, was about to be pushed aside. With the coming of high-profile Brandywine Raceway in 1953 the Delaware Harness Racing Commission was obligated to award the prime racing dates where it could generate the most revenue. And that meant bustling New Castle County, not rural Kent County.

Each year Harrington was dealt increasingly worse racing dates. But the track survived and even broke attendance and handle records in the 1960s. The racing was in the century-old tradition of owners trucking their animals off the farm to test each other. With its low overhead Harrington was the only Delaware racing plant able to make a profit. But even Harrington's minimal expenses could be offset by the decline in interest in standardbred racing.

Racing was sporadic in the 1990s until the installment of the first of more than 2,000 slot machines in 1996. About 10% of all the revenue funnels straight into race purses and Harrington began offering horsemen some $135,000 a night. In 2003 the half-mile oval was given wider turns and faster times. In 2015 Wiggle It Jiggleit blazed to a track record in 1:49, one of 22 wins for the three-year old gelding in 26 tries. After pocketing $2.18 million in winnings and the Little Brown Jug, harness racing's crown jewel, Wiggle It Jiggleit became Harrington-based owner George Teague, Jr.'s second Horse of the Year.

Middletown: Gentleman's Driving Park

On May 26, 1874 the following letter appeared in *Every Evening*, "The Middletown Agricultural and Promological Association have laid out and graded their trotting course and will soon have it ready for use, and I challenge you Wilmington sports to come down with their fast nags."

Over the next decade the Middletown Fair races prospered in the Delaware horse racing community. By the the third annual meeting the Middletown races were attracting 80 entries for the three days of racing. That year more than 4000 people paid the 50-cent admission to see Sadie Bell, the popular Virginia import valued at $50,000. The first day Sadie Bell swept two heats to win a minor purse and on the final day easily won all three heats in the feature, blazing the first-half mile in the last heat in 1:06. Middletown was at the pinnacle of Delaware racing.

For the rest of its existence the Middletown races were eclipsed only by the state fair in Dover. Crowds were consistently in excess of 3000 for the annual fall meeting but the organizers found it increasingly difficult to meet expenses and closed down the Middletown fair races in 1883. Thereafter, racing was contested at the Gentleman's Driving Park on a limited scale, seldom bringing more than 250 people to the old track.

Newark: Homewood Park

Newark established what may have been the first formal race course in Delaware in 1760. In 1877, a pristine race track was constructed on the Holtzpecker farm in Newark, just outside the tiny village. It was announced by relieved observers that, "now we will know who has the fastest horse without endangering the lives of our people."

Newark sportsman and cricketeer William Homewood purchased the property and in 1882 the Homewood Trotting Park Association was organized. The half-mile track operated on a small scale for local horses. Purses were arranged for $15, $30 and $50. Crowds seldom exceeded 800 for the occasional races and the genial affairs were said to be "unattended by the objectionable features generally ascribed to such gatherings."

Stanton: Delaware Park

On July 5, 1954 there were 35,473 people basking in the sun at beautiful Delaware Park enjoying an eight-race program. It was the largest crowd ever to see horse racing in Delaware. The crowd bet $2,227,562, the most money ever wagered in one day at a state race track. And there was only daily double, win, place and show betting available - no exotic wagering options like exactas and trifectas.

Delaware Park was the most magnificent sporting palace ever built in Delaware. In the 1950s Delaware Park was on a short list with Saratoga as a place to find racing in the grand tradition. And it was one of the busiest; only eleven tracks in the country handled more than the million dollars or so bet every afternoon in Stanton.

Fifty "horse-minded people in the community," as the instigators have been described, led by William du Pont Jr., helped push through Delaware's first racing legislation on February 6, 1935. These sportsmen were not interested in making money but were just looking for a place to run their horses. That the public could come and bet a few dollars was a necessary evil. And Delaware Park has always been run as a nonprofit track.

Delaware Park opened on June 26, 1937 on 450 acres of farmland southwest of Stanton and it was spectacular. There were seats for 7,500 fans and stables for 1,226 horses. Both were filled to overflow. The plant was said to cost $1.25 million and was billed as "the lastword in safety and comfort." Over $50,000 was spent on the shrubbery alone.

The new track was in an ideal competitive position. There was no racing in Maryland or New Jersey; pari-mutuel wagering was illegal altogether in Pennsylvania and there was no night harness racing. The railroad tracks that ran right to the front gate brought fans from Washington to New York. A roundtrip ride on the Pennsylvania Railroad from Wilmington could be had for 30 cents.

There were five $10,000 stakes races on Opening Day and 18,000 people turned out to see Legal Light win the first race, galloping five furlongs in a minute. By the time the 24-day meet ended the crowds were so large du Pont started plans to double the size of the grandstand. The handle was $6,368,031 and $217,680 went into the Delaware treasury - without a penny of investment from the state.

Delaware Park was the state's entry into big league sports. The roll call of jockeys and trainers who campaigned at William du Pont's track reads like a Hall of Fame induction ceremony - Eddie Arcaro, Bill Shoemaker, Angel Cordero, Ron Turcotte, Henry Clark and so on. Delaware Park was recognized around the country for the grace and beauty of its racing. In 1953 the Kent Handicap became the first nationwide telecast to emanate from Delaware.

Once inside the three tree-lined entrances at Delaware Park it was truly the "Sport of Kings." The salad days at Delaware Park lasted about a quarter of a century. By 1960 the competition for the entertainment dollar - both inside and outside of racing - became stultifying. Brandywine Raceway, although a nighttime operation, encroached on Delaware Park's racing dates for the first time in 1960. Then Liberty Bell Park in Pennsylvania began siphoning off the lucrative Philadelphia trade.

The decline in attendance and handle continued steadily until 1982 when directors of the track announced there would be no racing in 1983. To that point Delaware Park had generated $80 million in tax revenue over its 45 years of operation. Racing was revived in time for a golden anniversary in 1987 and the track limped forward, buoyed by simulcasting and the fiduciary promise of slot machines.

When the one-armed bandits finally arrived even track officials were stunned by the impact - over $6 million a day was pumped into Delaware Park video terminals. The signature Delaware Handicap eventually became a $750,000 race. Quality thoroughbreds like Triple Crown race winners Barbaro and Afleet Alex won their maiden races in Stanton. Delaware racing was back in the big leagues.

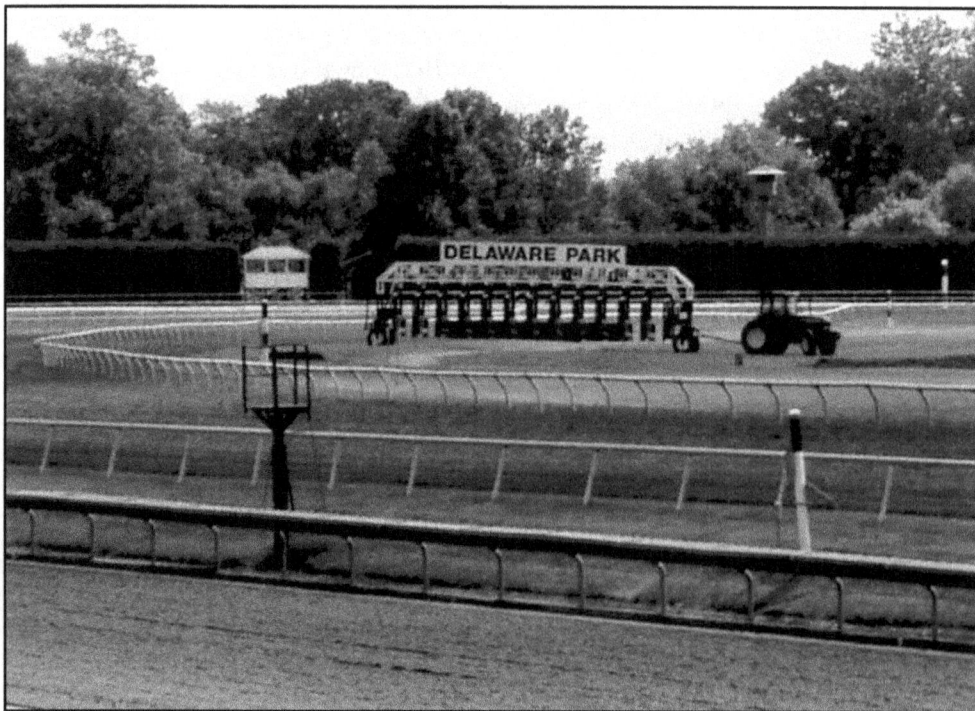

Delaware Park was the First State's first major league sporting venue.

Wilmington: Scheutzen Park

The earliest racing in Wilmington was through the city streets, often for stakes put up by the competitors. Delaware statute proscribed gambling on horse races in 1829 but street racing had become such a nuisance by 1833 that a city ordinance was issued that stipulated: "If any person shall drive or ride a horse, horses, beast or beasts of burden in running or racing with another horse, horses, beast, or beasts of burden, in any street, lane or alley of this City, every person so offending shall be guilty of a common nuisance and for every such offense shall forfeit and pay a fine of twenty dollars."

Outside the city the roadway past Hare's Corner, where Budd Doble, proprietor of the Hare's Corner Hotel would eventually build a popular track, became known as New Castle County's most notorious racing ground. Efforts to establish racing on a track in Wilmington met limited success until September 25, 1871 when Scheutzen Park opened out on the Kennett Pike.

The meets typically featured three races a day, to be contested in heats. The first horse to prevail in three heats would be declared the winner. Purses ranged from $50 to $300 with 10% of the purse required as the entry fee. Fields were set based on lifetime marks of the horses with the slowest races featuring 4:00 horses and the fastest competing in 2:30 and better classes. In addition to trotting and pacing races there were occasionally double-team and thoroughbred tests added to the program. Some horses were driven by professionals but most, especially in the slower classes, were under the reins of the owner.

The races were characterized by many

Sadie Bell, a four-year old record-holder from Virginia, was one of the most popular horses at Scheutzen Park and other Delaware tracks.

false starts and required the better part of the day to complete, if the heats could be squeezed in before nightfall at all. Although gambling was illegal, nor was it always discouraged. It was not uncommon for drivers to be set upon by disgruntled bettors after a race and often the fastest running a horse was urged to do was in flight from the grounds.

This unsavory element to the sport helped undermine the popularity of racing in Wilmington through the years. During several periods racing died out in the city totally; other years the Wilmington Trotting Association was able to present the strongest racing in Delaware. In the spring meet of 1877 the two most popular horses on the Peninsula, Delaware and Sadie Bell, tangled in a best-of-five race with each trotter winning two and a fifth race finishing in a dead heat. Later Delaware beat Sadie Bell by 150 yards when she broke as the betting favorite.

As a result of the break a $50 winner-take-all match was set up between the two horses and twice Delaware ran down Sadie Bell in the stretch to win. In the fall the two engaged again at Scheutzen Park with the same result: Delaware and Sadie Bell won two heats apiece with a dead heat. Neither of the two exhausted horses however could capture the decisive third heat and Jersey Boy won the race by winning the sixth, seventh and eight heats before an enthralled crowd of at least 2000.

In 1890, after another slack period of racing, Scheutzen Park was revived as the Wawaset Driving Park. Races were now contested on a strictly amateur basis. No purses were offered and horsemen competed only for coveted blue ribbons. Under these conditions racing at the old track flourished.

In 1902 the Delaware Horse Show Association organized to present fancy horse shows on the Wawaset grounds. As a secondary attraction a few races were staged to show the horses to best effect. So popular was the sideshow that by 1904 the horse shows were abandoned completely and the Wawaset Driving Association was formed to hold matinee races. The matinee races, run twice a week, were a staple of the Delaware sporting scene. The membership in the Driving Association grew to more than five hundred business and professional men from the Wilmington area and became a central element in the social life of Wilmington.

For more than a decade local harness racing fans enjoyed the matinees. Thousands attended and Delaware became recognized as a matinee racing center of the United States. Several nationally known horsemen graduated from the matinees to the stakes races of the Grand Circuit. But these affairs remained for amateurs only and fans would delight in the occasional entry of a horse like Prince, a bay gelding who could be seen away from the track on the streets of Wilmington pulling a milk wagon. Prince could trot the mile in 2:30 and sometimes defeated his "unemployed" competitors.

Racing for purses returned to Wawaset on July 4, 1912 as part of the program for the New Castle County Fair. Purses varied from $400 to $1000 and attracted leading horses from all the eastern hotbeds of harness racing. Intercity racing, with the pride of Wilmington horsemen on the line, was especially popular.

Wawaset, nee Scheutzen, Park was in the homestretch, however. After World War I the grand old track, nearly 50 years old, was sacrificed for the residential migration away from the city.

Wilmington: Hazel Dell Park

As part of the backlash against gambling and other unsavory goings-on around Wilmington horse tracks George Lobdell of the Lobdell Car Wheel Company built the Hazel Dell Driving Park in 1885 near his car works on the south side of Wilmington. Here gentleman drivers could come and test their fast horses. Horsemen paid a $10 subscription and were given the privilege of a first class track without the costs and drawbacks of a professional trotting course.

No premiums were offered and no betting allowed during the races. Still, 2000 turned out for the first meet at Hazel Dell and regular events consistently brought 1000 or more race fans to the track. In 1888 the first Wilmington Fair was held on the Hazel Dell grounds. The fair was a huge hit with daily crowds exceeding over 20,000 - the largest crowds ever to gather on the Peninsula.

The second Wilmington Fair in 1889 was an even more phenomenal success. Up to 40,000 people crowded into Hazel Dell on "Big Thursday," the traditional day for the week-long fairs to peak. More than 15,000 watched the trotting races that day, which now included the Brandywine Stakes for $500 and the Diamond State Stakes for $1000.

The fair continued for only three more years before it collapsed under the weight of its own popularity. More than a dozen speakeasies sprouted around the edges of the fair and the organizers were forced to place many restrictions on the exhibitors and attendees. Enough rebelled to spell doom for the great carnival.

Wilmington: Brandywine Raceway

In the fall of 1953 Brandywine Raceway became the 28th night harness track in America and the first in the Delaware Valley. Special buses were chartered to accommodate race fans in neighboring towns but track officials still weren't prepared for the onslaught of people eager to welcome Brandywine. Traffic was so congested on the feeder roads leading to the track at Concord Pike and Naamans Road that people within a mile of the track at post time didn't place a bet for two more hours. The official tally was a near-capacity 14,184 and the handle was $314,062.

The first 20-night meet featured six rich stakes in the first week which lured some of the country's leading standardbreds, including Direct Rhythm, the world's fastest living pacer. There were 13 live telecasts on WDEL-TV from Brandywine that year. When the Big B, as the track came to be affectionately known, finished racing in 1953 only Yonkers Raceway had ever enjoyed a more prosperous first year.

In 1954 Brandywine's $400,000 in purses brought the sport's best drivers to Delaware. But among Billy Haughton, Stanley Dancer and Del Miller the driving title went to Harrington's Henry Clukey with 16 wins. Later Herve Filion would win a large chunk of his most-ever career wins at Brandywine.

Over the years all the great standardbreds appeared on the Brandywine oval. Two of the first were Adios Harry and Adios Boy. Adios Harry was owned by Harrington chicken farmer J. Howard Lyons who had bought the colt for $4200. In 1954 the Delaware runner won the Little Brown

Jug, one of pacing's Triple Crown events, and in 1955 the 4-year old brown stallion set a competitive harness race record of 1:55 at Utica's Vernon Downs. For his part Adios Boy had four world records to his credit.

The half-brothers met six times before coming to Brandywine for the $15,000 Good Time Pace. Harry won all three match races and Boy won all three stakes races. Stunningly, neither would triumph on Brandywine's half-mile oval. Adios Harry broke and both he and Adios Boy finished out of the money behind 24-1 longshot Hillsota.

The next year Adios Harry returned to Brandywine and set the track record at 2:00.3, beating Meadow Rice's 2:01.1 which had been established in the first meet. Speedy Pick later lowered the track record to 2:00.1 but no horse recorded a sub-2:00 "Magic Mile" until one night in 1960 when four horses flashed under the wire in less than 2:00 in the same race. Adios Butler won the race in 1:58.4 followed by Tar Boy, Speedy Pick and O.F. Brady. No horse ever went faster on Brandywine's half-mile track.

By the end of its first decade Brandywine Raceway had established itself as one of the most beautiful and profitable racing plants anywhere - the grandstand was built facing west so patrons could enjoy the sun setting over the track. In 1966, a record 22,177 jammed the track to see Bret Hanover win his 47th race in 50 starts in a duel with Cardigan Bay. A rarity also occurred that year, on April 26, when the eight horses crossed the finish line in the exact order of their post position.

In 1970 Brandywine's original half-mile track, one of the fastest in the nation, was converted to a five-eighth mile oval. On July 3, with free admission to the grandstand, Brandywine established its all-time attendance record of 25,278. The track was still profitable but the peak years had passed. The handle had been declining since 1962 when the average play was $665,425 a night.

By the 1980s Brandywine was draining more than a million dollars a year from its owners. The great horses still turned out - Niatross, Direct Scooter and Rambling Willie - but the Atlantic City casinos were stealing the high rollers. Nightly play was less than half of its glory days of the 1960s. By the end of the decade, despite the closing of its main competition in Liberty Bell Park, losses mounted to over two million dollars a year. There would not be a 1990s for the one-time showcase of harness racing. It closed in 1990, left to stand as a weedy monolith in the residential Brandywine Hundred landscape until its destruction for a big box mall.

The annual renewal of the Battle of the Brandywine was the Delaware Valley's richest harness race, attracting the best standardbreds in America.

The Fastest Race Track In America

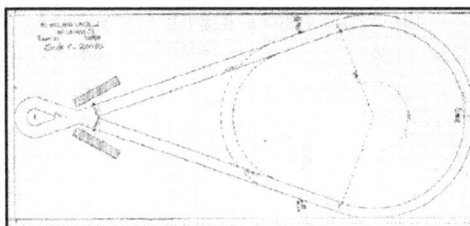

In 1890 the first so-called kite track opened in America in Independence, Iowa. The track featured a long straightaway into one long turn and another straightaway back to the finish line. With one turn instead of two the new track was graded six seconds faster than a regulation track. When Governor Leland Stanford of California opened a kite track in Stockton six world records fell in a single week.

Late in 1891 Dr. J.C. McCoy of Middletown began work on the first kite track in the eastern United States near Kirkwood, Delaware. McCoy employed 80 men for ten weeks to build his racing palace which featured stables for 190 horses and a grandstand to hold 3000 spectators. The track cost $50,000 to build, including $10,000 for an ingenious sprinkling system that could water the entire track in 1/2 minute from over one mile of 2" pipes.

The Maple Valley Trotting Association debuted the innovative track in 1892 for reporters and horsemen from Philadelphia, New York and Baltimore. The pundits quickly anointed McCoy's kite track as the swiftest surface to be found anywhere and preparations were made for a grand opening on July 4. Despite a multitude of other Independence Day events more money than 8000 race fans descended on Kirkwood. By 10:45 in the morning ticket sellers were overwhelmed.

The crowd was treated to its first world record when the trotting team of Belle Hamlin and Globe went the mile in 2:12 to break their

Doc, an Irish Setter from Canada, was the big crowd-pleaser at Kirkwood.

own record by a full second. Next onto the track was Doc, The Trotting Dog. Doc was enormously popular, earning his master Willie Ketchum more than any horse. Willie, perched in a diminutive sulky with pneumatic tires, guided the "Canine Wonder of the World" to a personal best of 48 seconds for the 1/4 mile. Adoring fans mobbed Doc, who then returned to the track and ran down a Wilmington man in a man-versus-dog sprint in front of the grandstand.

In the feature Hal Pointer trotted onto the kite track to thunderous applause in a special race against time for the world record. Hal Pointer was only able to go the mile in 2:11.3, well short of Direct's mark of 2:06, but he was only rounding into form. A month later he would shatter
the world record.

Racing at Kirkwood continued through the year, bringing a succession of personal bests for both horses and bicyclists. In 1893 McCoy prepared an even greater day of racing for July 4. He lured Mascot, the world record pacer with a 2:04 mark, to Kirkwood with an offer of $5000 for a new record. Challenging Mascot was Saladin, the Delaware champion with a world record 2:09 on a half-mile track to his credit. In the hyperbolic journalistic style of the day it was said that, "if the race had taken place in New York or Philadelphia it would attract a million spectators."

But it was the last hurrah for McCoy's celebrated kite track. With the introduction of the bicycle sulky the speed advantage of the track was no longer so apparent and the public objected to the configuration because it took the horses so far from the grandstand. Kite tracks disappeared everywhere, leaving a brief, but thrilling legacy.

Sleigh Racing In Delaware Green

In the 1800s before a winter snowfall had even ended, people began to anticipate the upcoming sleigh races through Delaware city streets. In Wilmington the raceway ran along French Street from 11th to the finish line at 2nd Street. Both sides of the street would be lined with racing fans who congregated from all parts of the area to witness the thrilling spectacle of horses and drivers flying all-out down the slippery hill to the railroad line at the foot of French Street.

The "brushes" were unofficial sport with no set of rules or formal starter. As the sleighs gathered near the starting line one horse would break and the others would un-rein in frantic pursuit. Plumes of snow exploded far into the air from the charging steeds as they raced between wildly partisan supporters. Even in the snow most horses performed at speeds estimated at 2:40 or better for a mile but many horsemen withheld their best horses due to the dangerous element of the event. Fans described the sleigh racing on French Street as the most exciting sport they had ever witnessed.

Other Delaware communities, although less geographically blessed for breakneck downhill races than Wilmington, engaged in sleigh racing. Town authorities in Milford cordoned off Northwest Front Street as a race course and diverted traffic to give the racers a clear path. In Lewes the sleigh races were held on a main street; in Townsend the course went down East Main Street. In Newark the races started at the B & O track next to the Deer Park Hotel and finished in front of the old Washington House at the railroad crossing by the present Newark Shopping Center. These brushes would attract as many as 50 to 100 horses, the best in the area, all in quest of the silver cups awarded to winners.

Winters were colder and snows heavier in Delaware a century ago which contributed to the sport's popularity. Enthusiasts often hauled snow to patch dry spots and maintained the course by sprinkling it with water. Sleigh racing remained popular in Delaware up to the 1920s when it became more of a priority to clear snow from city streets rather than groom it.

Delaware Derby Horses

Although various scions of the du Pont dynasty have been among the most prominent horse owners and breeders in the country other Delawareans, including businessmen and farmers, have sent just as many hopefuls to the post in the Kentucky Derby.

After undistinguished performances by *Gold Seeker*, 9th in 1936; and *Fairy Hill*, 11th in 1937; Delaware's first great chance for a Derby winner was Dauber in 1938, a grandson of the immortal Man O'War, owned by William du Pont and developed at the Bellevue squire's Foxcatcher Farms. Du Pont purchased *Dauber* late in his 2-year old season in 1937 for $29,000. He never liked the colt as a runner; he started slowly and finished fast as he got his legs underneath him. But Dauber was a great mudder and competitor and got to the Derby as a mid-range longshot.

True to form Dauber got off to a terrible start at Churchill Downs but by the time he reached the grandstand Delaware jockey Maurice "Moose" Peters had locked 9-1 shot Lawrin in a stretch duel. Lawrin nosed Dauber under the wire as the Delaware horse paid $12 to place and $6 to show. In the Preakness Dauber caught a muddy track at Pimlico Race Course and romped home 7 lengths the best as a 3-2 favorite. Despite the off-track Dauber raced to the finish line in 1:59.4, only three ticks off the old track's record. In the Belmont Dauber went to the post as the heavy favorite but was nosed out by an 8-1 shot Pasteurized.

Dauber suffered a bowed tendon in his ankle and was retired. Du Pont did not see him as a great sire and sold Dauber for $45,000. Six months later du Pont's acumen for horseflesh was proven out when Dauber was resold for only $29,000.

The horse that finished less than a length from the Triple Crown in 1938 produced a very mediocre crop at stud.

The 1940s saw a string of Delaware horses ship to Louisville. *Fairy Manhurst* finished 13th in 1942 and *Alexis* completed a middle-of-the pack run to 10th in 1945. In 1946 William du Pont's *Hampden* raced home an impressive third from the far outside post behind Triple Crown winner Assault. Also that year *Double J*, owned by Wilmington restaurateur James Boines and liquor dealer James Tigani, was the best 2- year old in the country. In ten starts he won six and was never out of the money. But Double J came to the 1947 Kentucky Derby overworked and wound up a fading 12th.

The Wilmington horse recovered to take four stakes races including the Garden State Stakes, Benjamin Franklin Handicap, Jersey Handicap and Trenton Handicap. He set the Garden State Park track record and retired as the all-time leading Delaware money winner with $299,810.

After Wilmington's *Greek Song* fizzled in Kentucky in 1950 the state of Delaware was thrust into the national spotlight with a Derby favorite in 1951. *Repetoire* was an overlooked colt when he was bought for only $4000 at the Saratoga Yearling Sale by Stanley Mikell, Dover businessman and councilman. Repetoire won four straight minor stakes races - the Remsen, Cherry Blossom, Experimental and Chesapeake. But when he won the Wood Memorial Derby prep at 7-1 Repetoire was suddenly the "hot horse" for Derby handicappers.

Repetoire was not a prohibitive favorite in a wide-open race. His gameness was unquestioned as all five of his wins had come by less than 3/4 of a length. But his

221

inability to distance himself from other 3-year olds in these battles cast doubt as to his true greatness.

In what was becoming a regrettable Delaware tradition Repetoire drew the far outside post - Post 21. Unable to overcome his starting gate handicap Repetoire came in 12th behind Count Turf, who emerged from the field to win the 1951 Kentucky Derby. He retired the following year as a 4-year old with lifetime earnings of $112,095.

In 1956 *Countermand* began his career only a month before the Derby and reeled off first and third place finishes at Keeneland Race Track, a 4th in the Blue Grass and a second in the Derby Trial. This crash course in preparation sent Countermand, from Brandywine Stables, off at 6-1 – despite commandeering the "Delaware Post," #17 in a field of 17. The green Countermand was overwhelmed from the start and galloped home last.

Bayard Sharp's *Trolius* led the 1959 Kentucky Derby to the half but finished last of 17 horses and never raced again. The inexperienced *Holy Land* came to Churchill Downs after three early-season wins at Gulfstream Park. In the Kentucky Derby Holy Land ran in traffic and clipped another horse's heels, spilling jockey Hector Piler and sidelining him for six months.

Arlene Daney of Wilmington shipped *Parfaitement* to Louisville in 1983. The colt had won five of six starts as a two-year old but was left far behind as a 20-1 longshot in the Derby, whipping only four foes in the 20-horse field. Two weeks later in the Preakness backers of Parfaitement could cash a winning ticket, however. Although the Delaware horse finished 8th he was coupled as an entry with winner Deputed Testamony.

John F. Porter founded the Wilmington Auto Sales in 1925 to sell Chevrolets and Buicks. The same year he started Porter Chevrolet in Newark and through the years there would be as many as 15 Porter dealerships. The third generation owner of the Porter Chevrolet Group, Rick Porter, harbored a fascination for a different type of horsepower. He had grown up attending races at Delaware Park and in 1994, at the age of 54, Porter began buying inexpensive claiming horses.

His first stakes winner was Kentucky-bred Jostle in 1999. When Rockport Harbor won all four of his races as a two-year old in 2004 he was an early-line Derby favorite but a right hind foot injury caused him to miss the 2005 race.

Hard Spun also enjoyed an undefeated two-year old season in 2006, sweeping to three victories. The big colt out of one of America's leading sires, Danzig, won two more races early in 2007 and became Porter's first Derby horse. Hard Spun went to post at 10-1 and broke on the lead under Mario Pino. After holding off the field most of the way he yielded to Street Sense in the stretch to place second. Hard Spun then finished third in the Preakness and fourth in the Belmont Stakes.

By contrast *Eight Belles* won only once in five tries in her freshman year but four straight victories in 2008 convinced trainer Larry Jones to give the filly a chance to race against the boys in the Kentucky Derby. Eight Belles ran a monster race to finish second behind Big Brown but in her gallop out after the race she broke both ankles and heartbreakingly had to be euthanized on the track.

After *Friesan Fire* finished well back in 18th place in 2009, Porter's Fox Hill Farm in Lexington, Kentucky produced a Horse of the Year in 2011 with Havre de Grace. *Normandy Invasion* ran out of the money in 4th in 2014 Porter was still without a Kentucky Derby winner - one of the few goals he has failed to achieve in racing.

DELAWARE HORSES

Harry JS. Harry JS was so intensely black he was said to sparkle as he trotted. Foaled in 1908 and named for his owner Harry J. Stoeckle, Harry JS began racing as a three year old and won five of five races when he came under the guidance of Delaware's greatest horseman, Herman R. Tyson.

Tyson orchestrated Harry JS's career on the Grand Circuit and on tracks up and down the east coast. In 1912 his ten-race mark was eight wins, one place and one show. As a six-year old he was forced to seven heats to win a race in Lexington and went the mile in 2:10 1/4 - the fastest time ever for a seventh heat.

In his final campaign in 1917 Harry JS set several world records and retired to stud acclaimed as the greatest 1/2 mile trotter ever. In 67 career races he won 35 and finished in the money 59 times. His lifetime earnings of $17,420 made him the leading trotter of his era. In all his years on the racetrack the great Harry JS was never known to break his gait. In 1925 Delaware's most beloved horse dropped dead in his stall.

Adios Harry. In 1952 J. Howard Lyons made the long drive from his farm in Greenwood to a yearling sale in Harrisburg, Pennsylvania with his eye on a potential racehorse he had scouted for bloodlines and sound confirmation. While at the sale he was convinced to also purchase a colt bred by L.T. Hempt from the immortal pacer Adios. The youngster did not look promising and even after Lyons paid only $4200 the deal did not look like a bargain when the newly named Adios Harry turned out to have a temper and kicked at anything that moved.

He did make it to the racetrack, however, while his new stablemate never did. At two Harry flashed to the win in the Bloomsburg Fair Stake and at three he captured pacing's biggest prize, the Little Brown Jug, by setting a three-heat record over the Delaware, Ohio fairgrounds oval. In 1955 Adios Harry became the fastest pacer ever when he blazed a 1:55 mile at Vernon Downs, New York. Like the four-minute human mile, the 1:55 mark was considered unobtainable for standardbreds. As it was, his record would stand for 16 years.

Adios Harry was just getting warmed up. By the time he was five years old he held 12 world pacing records and *Sports Illustrated* put him on the cover that year. When he retired in 1958 Adios Harry was the all-time money-winning pacer with $345,433.

It was always a family affair with Adios Harry. Howard did the training and his son Lucas often was in the bike. Many horsemen sniped that "Harry" could have done even better with professional connections but he had done very well, thank-you, as a family horse.

As such, Lyons decided not to sell Harry into syndication and brought him back to his Sugar Hill Farms to stand at stud. He sired 352 pacers, 26 of which ran sub-2:00 miles but none were as good as their dad. Harry lived out in the Lyons pasture until 1982 when he died at the advanced equine age of 31.

Silk Stockings. How many Delaware athletes have been profiled on *60 Minutes*? Well, none of the two-legged variety but one equine superstar once got the treatment from Morley Safer, Mike Wallace and the boys. Silk Stockings was a special performer on the track with a special cause.

Ken and Claire Mazik purchased the New York-bred Silk Stockings as a yearling for $20,000. By the time she was three years old in 1975 the daughter of Most Happy Fella had developed into the greatest harness filly of all time. That year she set eight world records, including one for the most money ever won by a filly or mare in a single season, $336,312. And the bulk of those purses went to the Au Clair School for autistic children which the Maziks operated at St. Georges. And that's what brought the camera crews from *60 Minutes* to Delaware.

Trained and driven by Pres Burris of Smyrna, Silk Stockings peaked in the middle of 1975 when she won 12 straight races. In that stretch was a 1:58 mile at the Historic Track in Goshen, New York, the fastest time there by any horse in 137 years of racing; a world record 1:57.2 on a half-mile track; and a win in the New York Off-Track Betting Classic, the richest pace ever. Later that year she clipped a 1:55.2 in Syracuse, the second fastest mile ever paced by a female horse. For the year Silk Stockings won 15 of 24 starts and was voted Pacer of the Year by the United States Trotting Association. All for the autistic children of Delaware.

Miller's Scout. It's not that hard to make a million dollars - make $20,000 a year for 50 years and you're a millionaire. That's sort of the way Miller's Scout, an unheralded pacer, became Delaware's first million dollar horse. Miller's Scout, a good horse with tremendous heart, made a living by chasing some of the sport's greatest stars in the early 1980s. Eventually all those second place checks pushed him over the million-dollar mark.

In his 2-year old season in 1978 Miller's Scout had 12 starts, winning twice and finishing second five times. He earned only $3,878. As a three-year old he finished in the money in 21 of 28 starts, winning eight times and bankrolling $46,664. It was during his 3-year old campaign that Miller's Scout, foaled and reared in Ephrata, Pennsylvania, was purchased by a Delaware consortium including Bill Brooks, veteran standardbred owner and breeder and founder of the familiar armored car business, Baird Brittingham, a one-time president of the Thoroughbred Racing Association of North America, and Alfred du Pont Dent.

In 1980, as a four-year old, Miller's Scout had his best year for wins with 12 in 32 starts. At the time his lifetime best was 1:58.1. Over the next 18 months the reliable pacer sliced his racing mark to 1:54.4 and he began touring in better company. The visits to the winner's circle were less frequent but the checks were meatier.

On October 30, 1983 Miller's Scout went to the post as a 50-1 shot in the $75,000 Blue Bonnets Challenge Pace in Montreal. The seven-year old pacer tracked Cam Fella, who was on his way to a world record 22nd consecutive victory, all the way to the wire. The $18,750 second place money raised his lifetime earnings to $1,016,026 - Delaware's first equine millionaire.

Eddie Davis

It has been a century-old tradition for Delawareans in Kent and Sussex Counties to take their best horses off their farms and test them on local harness tracks. This legacy of Delaware horsemen continues today at tracks along the East coast, even as the sport is dying in their home state.

Of the many drivers who have raced from Delaware none was ever as successful as Smyrna's Eddie Davis. Davis, born in 1944, enjoyed his best years in the early 1980s when he was a top driver at Dover Downs, Brandywine Raceway and Liberty Bell Raceway. He was also a leading trainer during this time. To date he has won over 5500 races.

Davis rated several horse to world records over the years. The highlight of his career came in 1981 when he nosed out 12-time world champion Herve Filion for the North American driving championship. Davis, the only Delawarean to ever win the title, won his 404th race on the final night of the year. Filion finished 1981 with 403 wins.

If there has been harness racing in the Delaware Valley, Eddie Davis has been the leading driver there.

Davis won the driving title for the second time in 1983, maintaining a frenetic pace to the championship. On one day he won four races at Dover Downs and six at Liberty Bell, where he set a record for most wins at a single track in one year with 333. A typical Davis day would include an afternoon of driving at Freehold in New Jersey and a fast trip to Dover for a nighttime card as he concluded a successful drive to the title.

All that commuting turned Eddie Davis into the all-time winningest driver in the Delaware Valley - he rode into the winner's circle 8,362 times.

Tic Wilcutts

John Wilcutts was so small at Caesar Rodney High School in the 1930s that he was called "Tic." After two years with the U.S. Army in the Pacific theater in World War II Wilcutts bought a discarded $700 pacer as a hobby. A horse named True Peggy took him to the winner's circle often enough that Wilcutts became a professional driver.

From those humble beginnings he became the leading driver four times at Baltimore Raceway and twice at Laurel Raceway in Maryland, once at Rockingham Park in New Hampshire, once at Liberty Bell Park in Philadelphia and five times at Brandywine Raceway. He wound up his career with 1,755 race wins and nearly $5 million in purses.

Off the track Wilcutts owned Voodoo Hanover, a broodmare who gave birth to Albatross, one of the sport's greatest champions. Wilcutts was voted into the Delaware Sports Hall of Fame in 1985.

Olympics

1908 LONDON

K.K.V. Casey - Casey won the first ever Delaware medal at the Olympics when he took the silver in the 1000-yard rifle shoot. Casey was commanding officer of Company C in the First Delaware Infantry.

George S. Dole - Dole, a Yale man, was the son of famed Wilmington minister George Henry Dole who wrestled at 133 pounds in London. Dole ripped through three straight Englishmen to reach the finals, winning through heavy home-town boos. An offensive wrestler, Dole beat Slim of England to win the gold and raise the American flag.

John W. Hessian - Hessian was a teammate of Casey's on the Olympic Rifle team, although he did not win a medal. Three of the 86-man United States team were from Delaware.

1912 AMSTERDAM

Louis Stoll - Originally from Baltimore and the Arundel Boat Club the 24-year old Stoll had been in Wilmington about a year when he made the United States 4-man crew for the 1912 Olympics.

1924 PARIS

Sid Jelinek - A Wilmington native who went to Philadelphia and crewed for the University of Pennsylvania, Jelinek won a bronze medal in the Men's Coxed Fours on the Seine River, rowing for the Bachelor's Barge Club.

Marion Zinderstein Jessup - Jessup won the silver medal in the only mixed doubles tennis ever contested in the Olympics, teaming with Vincent Richards, one of the top players of the 1920s. Originally a four-time national doubles champion from Massachusetts, Jessup was a Delaware state champion in badminton as well as tennis.

John B. Grier - Grier, a resident of Rockland and long-time captain in the Delaware National Guard, competed in the 800-meter rifle shoot in 1924. He would have easily qualified for the 1928 team as well but he was declared a professional and turned his talents to trapshooting. In 1935 he won the singles, doubles and all-around titles in Delaware and in 1936 he won the national pro title by breaking 199 of 200 targets, missing only #183. Grier won the pro singles twice, the national doubles once and the Grand American Handicap. He was an All-American shooter in 1936-37-38.

1952 HELSINKI

Frank Shakespeare - A fine all-around athlete out of Dover High School, Shakespeare concentrated on rowing at the Naval Academy after being cut from the basketball team, manning the bow oar on one of the all-time great 8-man crews. Navy won two straight Intercollegiate Rowing Association championships and 20 consecutive meets, winning the right to represent America in the Olympics. In Helsinki the Midshipmen jumped to the lead at the start and edged the Soviet crew by a length and a half to win the gold medal.

1964 TOKYO

Stan Cole - The Dover native was a water polo star at Wilson High School in Long Beach, California and at UCLA where the Bruins went 45-0 in his three All-American years on the varsity. Cole represented the United States in Tokyo, Mexico City and Munich where the water polo team won a bronze medal. He would go on to be named on the Pac-12 Conference All-Century team.

Vic Zwolak - Zwolak capped a successful collegiate racing career by finishing second in the Olympic Trials in the 3,000-meter steeplechase, becoming the first track and field Olympian from Delaware. In Tokyo Zwolak narrowly missed qualifying for the finals, finishing 4th in his preliminary heat. Zwolak ran one more competitive race before retiring, finishing second a week later in a special British Commonwealth meet in Osaka, Japan. Zwolak never stopped running and later held more than 20 state-resident age class records from aged 45 to 79.

1968 MEXICO CITY

Gardner Cox - Frank Gardner Cox, Jr. was born in Wilmington in 1920 and was educated at Philips Andover Academy and Princeton University where his exploits earned him a spot in the first class of the Intercollegiate Sailing Hall of Fame. He won several national sailing titles for the Mantoloking Yacht Club in New Jersey and represented the United States in Mexico City in the Mixed 5.5 metres class, finishing eighth in the final time the big boats competed in the Games. The U.S. Sailing Association awards the F. Gardner Cox Sportsmanship Trophy for the team that displays the highest tradition in fairness during its national regatta.

Dave Johnson - Although he didn't start swimming until his sophomore year at Archmere Academy, Johnson was a three-time All-American swimmer at Yale where he set the American record in the 400-meter individual medley. Johnson made the Olympic team as an alternate despite breaking his arm two months before the trials. In Mexico City Johnson swam preliminary heats in the 800-meter freestyle relay, qualifying the United States for its place in the finals. Twelve years later Dr. Dave Johnson returned to the Olympics - this time as a volunteer orthopedic surgeon at the Lake Placid Games.

Donnan Sharp Plumb - The Greenville-bred Plumb, 30, represented the United States as a member of the fledgling equestrian team in dressage. Plumb and her steed, the 14-year old Attache, competed in both the individual and team events, both of which were dominated by the Europeans.

Art Redden - Redden, a track and football star at Howard High and Arkansas A & M, didn't begin boxing until he was a 25-year old Marine in 1963. Within six months the 5'10", 175-pound light heavyweight qualified for the 1964 Olympic team as an alternate. Four years later Redden was a four-time Marine and All-Service champion and the leading light-heavyweight amateur in the country. He won the gold medal at the Pan-Am Games and was undefeated in the qualifying bouts for the 1968 Olympic team. In Mexico City, however, Redden lost his opening fight in a free-swinging battle with Bulgarian Georgi Stankov. Redden retired after the Olympics with a career record of 65-6, including 30 knockouts.

1972 MUNICH

Jenny Bartz - When Jenny Bartz was in the pool growing up in Delaware those who saw her thought she was destined for the Olympics. They were right but when she made the American team as a 17-year old in 1972 she was representing the Santa Clara Swim Club in California. Bartz narrowly missed the medals podium twice with 4th place finishes in the 200- and 400-metre Individual Medleys.s

Chris Dunn - Dunn, a Colgate senior from Newark High, peaked perfectly in the 1972 Olympic Trials, establishing a personal best of 7'3" to finish third in the high jump and become an Olympian. At Munich he could clear no better than 6'11 1/2", and did not qualify for the finals.

1976 MONTREAL

Steve Gregg - Gregg qualified for the Montreal games by finishing third in the 200-meter butterfly at the Olympic Trials and established himself as a gold medal favorite when he shattered the Olympic record in a qualifying heat. In the Olympic finals Gregg was in fifth place for more than 100 meters before racing down the leaders in the final 50 meters. He bettered the world record in 1:59.54 but was touched out for the gold medal by teammate Mike Bruner who won the race in 1:59.23.

1980 LAKE PLACID

Frank Masley - Just three years after getting on a sled for the first time Masley was in the Olympics. He finished 18th in the doubles with partner Ray Bateman.

1984 SARAJEVO

Frank Masley - Masley was now America's finest luger and captain of the luge team. A two-time Olympian, he was also selected to lead the American team into Olympic

Stadium holding the American flag. He competed in both singles and doubles, finishing 14th and 13th respectively.

Tom Barnes - Barnes, a Caesar Rodney graduate, helped the United States four-man bobsled Number One team to a fifth place finish, its best since 1956. Barnes, 24, took up the sport while stationed in Plattsburgh, New York in the Air Force.

1984 LOS ANGELES

Aldis Berzins - Berzins, of Latvian heritage, was born in Wilmington and went through six grades at Forwood Elementary School before his family moved to Kennett Square, Pennsylvania. Berzins played four years of volleyball at Ohio State University and made his first United States team as a 20-year old in 1977. In Los Angeles the Delaware native was an outside hitter for the gold medal winning United States volleyball team.

1988 CALGARY

Frank Masley - Masley now had competition as America's best luger but he made his third Olympics and his 12th place finish was the highest ever by an American slider.

1988 SEOUL

Terri Dendy - Dendy, a 23-year old graduate of Concord High School, qualified as one of eight women on the United States 4 x 400-meter relay team. In Seoul fewer countries than expected entered the event and there was only one heat before the finals. Dendy was not selected to run in either the semifinal qualifier or the final.

Vicki Huber - Coming out of Concord High School in 1985 as the holder of Delaware scholastic records in the 800 and 1500-meters Huber was expected to be a good collegiate runner. But in three years at Villanova she blossomed into much more than that. By the 1988 Olympics, in which she qualified in the 3,000-meters, she was the holder of five NCAA records. In Seoul she led the 3,000- meter final with less than two laps to go as she battled the world's best runners in front of 100,000 screaming fans. Huber faded to sixth place but her time of 8:37.25 was nine seconds better than her personal best and the sixth fastest women's 3,000-meter in United States history.

1996 ATLANTA

Jason Gleasman - Jason Gleasman was born in Delaware but grew up in Upstate New York where he began wrestling at the age of five. He was an outstanding wrestler at Syracuse University and was the youngest member of the United States Greco-Roman team in Atlanta. The 21-year old won his first match against Ba Yanchuan of China but lost the next two to finish 12th in the 220-pound division.

Dionna Harris - Dionna Harris got her first taste of the softball wars on the diamonds of the Stanton-Newport Little League when she was nine years old. She was a four-time

All-Conference performer at Delcastle High School and was twice an All-American infielder at Del-Tech Community College. After transferring to Temple University Harris became the Atlantic 10 conference player of the year. Following graduation she played on national and international teams for the Raybestos Brakettes of Stratford, Connecticut and in 1996 at the age of 28 Harris was the starting rightfielder for the United States in the first-ever appearance of women's softball in the Olympics. The Americans downed China in the finals to complete an 8-1 tournament and claim the gold medal.

2000 SYDNEY

Mike Neill - Mike Neill experienced his first baseball stardom in the Seaford Nanticoke Little League where he was on teams that won five state championships and went to the Senior League World Series three times. He picked up another state championship holding down first base for the Seaford Blue Jays in 1986. Another title came in the Big East with Villanova where he was Big East Player of the Year. Drafted into the Oakland A's system Neill won a pair of minor league batting crowns but only had one brief stay in the big leagues. In Sydney, Neill got the USA team rolling with a first inning home run against Cuba in the gold medal game. He also helped preserve the 4-0 win with a sliding catch in the 9th inning.

2004 ATHENS

Barb Lindquist - Barb Lindquist was born in Wilmington in 1969 but grew up in Casper, Wyoming. Whe was a national-level swimmer who failed to make the Olympic team in 1988, her only try. She tried her first triathlon in 1993 and a decade later she was the world's number one ranked women's triathlete. At Athens she placed ninth in the second time the triathlon was contested in the Olympics.

2008 BEJING

Katelyn Falgowski - Wilmington-born Katelyn Falgowski was the youngest player named to the USA U-20 field hockey team when she made the elite squad at the age of 14. She made the Women's National Team while at St. Mark's High School and then began piling up awards at the University of North Carolina. She was the youngest college player to make the Olympic Team roster in Bejing, where the Americans placed eighth.

Carrie Lingo - From her base in Sussex County, Carrie Lingo became one of the stalwarts of American field hockey. Beginning in 2002, after graduating from the University of North Carolina where she won a national championship, Lingo played in 190 international matches, including the Bejing Olympics, before retiring in 2012 as captain of the USA Women's National Field Hockey Team.

Katelyn Falgowski - Despite undergoing knee surgery for a torn anterior cruciate ligament in 2011, Falgowski was named a World All Star that year by the International Hockey Federation. She followed that up by making her second Olympic field hockey team. The Americans lost five of their six matches to finish 12th as Falgowski recorded her first shot on goal and assist in Olympic play.

Shannon Taylor - Shannon Taylor took the field hockey foundation she forged in Delaware until her sophomore year at Seaford High School to Virginia and then to Syracuse University. She took a break from coaching duties at the University of Massachusetts to compete with the U.S. National team in 2013 and then the London Olympics.

The following Olympians have trained at the Skating Club of Wilmington:

1976	Susie Kelly/Andy Stroukoff	17th in dance
1976	Alice Cook/Bill Fauver	11th in pairs
1980	Kitty Carruthers/Peter Carruthers	5th in pairs
1984	Kitty Carruthers/Peter Carruthers	Silver Medal in pairs
1984	Lea Ann Miller/Bill Fauver	10th in pairs
1984	Carol Fox/Richard Dalley	5th in dance
1984	Lisa Spitz/Scott Gregory	10th in dance
1988	Kim Seybold/Wayne Seybold	10th in pairs
1988	Suzy Semanick/Scott Gregory	6th in dance
1988	Gillion Wachsman/Todd Waggoner	5th in pairs
1992	Calla Urbanski/Rocky Marval	10th in pairs
1994	Karen Courtland/Todd Reynolds	10th in pairs
2014	Ashley Wagner	7th in Ladies Figure Skating

The following Olympians have trained at the University of Delaware Skating Club:

1998	Tara Lipinski	Gold Medal in Ladies Figure Skating
2006	Kimmie Meissner	6th in Ladies Figure Skating
2014	Felicia Zhang/Nathan Bartholmay	12th in pairs

Awards:
Delaware Athlete
of the Year

In 1950 the Wilmington Sportswriter's and Broadcaster's Association began selecting the state's outstanding sports performer for the previous year. To be eligible an athlete needed to be either a native Delawarean or to have established himself as a resident of the state.

1949 *Nick Bucci*. The 5' 8 1/2" running back led the Claymont High School Indians to a perfect season in 1949, becoming Delaware's first two-time all-state football player in the process. In addition to leading the state in scoring Bucci won the state 100-yard dash in 10.4 seconds. Also a basketball forward and a baseball outfielder for the Indians Bucci graduated with 12 letters.

1950 *Ronnie Waller*. Waller established a new state scoring record with 30 touchdowns out of the Laurel backfield. He added 33 extra points for a total of 213. In a 74-0 rout of Georgetown Waller accounted for 38 points. He ended his high school career as a three-year letterman in baseball, football, track and basketball.

1951 *Bernard Blaney*. "Bunny" Blaney established a new Delaware basketball scoring record as a junior at Newark High School and obliterated that mark in his senior year with 621 points. On the gridiron the 5'7" Blaney also led the state in scoring for the Yellowjackets. His 9.9 clocking in the 100-yard dash and 22.6 in the 200 were the fastest ever recorded in Delaware. He later attended Duke where he played football and baseball. In seven years as Durham High School football coach, he had his team in the North Carolina state playoffs seven times, reaching the final game five times and winning three championships.

1952 *Dave Douglas*. When the 1952 winter professional golf tour began Douglas was dispirited and ready to retire to a club job. He struggled in the early tournaments winding up 27th, 33rd, 28th, 19th, 33rd and 26th before breaking through for a win in the Greensboro Open. The Newark pro went on to add another win and collect $15,173 to finish 7th on the money list in 1952.

1953 *Frank Shakespeare*. The former Dover High basketball and track star entered the Naval Academy in 1949 where he began rowing in the eight-oared shell. Blessed with ideal coordination and form Shakespeare rowed in the lead-off position for one of the great crews of all-time. The Midshipmen won 20 consecutive regattas, capturing the intercollegiate title in 1952 and 1953 and bring home gold in the 1952 Helsinki Olympics.

1954 *Bob Trivits*. Trivits worked anonymously on the University of Delaware line clearing holes for the 1954 Refrigerator Bowl winners. The Stanton-born guard starred at Conrad High School before starting college at the University of Kentucky and eventually returning to Newark.

1955 *Ron Waller*. Waller became the first two-time winner of the award when he completed his college career as an All-Atlantic Coast Conference back at Maryland and made the Pro Bowl in his rookie NFL campaign.

1956 *Jerry Blackway*. Blackway was a Conrad High School football player who had been named co-captain of the 1955 squad before he was paralyzed in a swimming accident prior to the season. Not expected to survive the night when he reached the hospital Blackway courageously fought through the critical period until he was able to return home, although confined to an iron lung. The 18-year old recipient of Delaware's Outstanding Athlete award lost his battle for life on April 5, 1958, surviving his injuries a remarkable 32 months.

1957 *Jim Oddo.* Oddo emerged from the obscurity of the North Carolina State line with a 53-yard interception return against national powerhouse Duke to tie the Blue Devils 14-14 and gain the Wolfpack the Atlantic Coast Conference title. In the post-season the 5'11", 187-pound Oddo played on national television in the Blue-Gray All-Star game. The ex-Wilmington High School center garnered honorable mention All- America honors as well.

1958 *John Thropp.* Thropp grew up swimming in the C & D Canal but when he reached Salesianum in 1954 the Sallies had no swim team. He pestered the fathers into starting one and by the end of 1958 Thropp was a two-time national YMCA title holder in the 200-yard backstroke. Also in 1958 the 19-year old freshman at the University of Delaware won two Delaware interscholastic championships in the 100-yard backstroke and the 150 medley, one state outdoor crown, and the Delaware 880 and the International 220 at the Rehoboth Beach swims.

1959 *Al Neiger.* Neiger became the first Delawarean to make an All-America baseball team in 1959. He went 9-3 with the Blue Hens, allowing only 47 hits and striking out 166 in 103 innings. He tossed five straight shutouts at the beginning of the season building a scoreless streak of 55 innings. Neiger signed with the Philadelphia Phillies for $35,000 and was assigned to Class A Williamsport, whEre he continued his winning ways by taking 7 of 10 decisions.

1960 *Jack Mulvana.* Mulvana was part of a wave of five Salesianum football players who lined up for the University of Minnesota in the late 1950s. Mulvana, at 6'1" and 205 pounds, was a stalwart on the Golden Gopher line for the 1960 team that went to the Rose Bowl and won the national championship.

1961 *Tom Hall.* Another of the Delaware connection to the University of Minnesota, the athletic Hall set seven all-time Gopher receiving records. On defense he played on the line. He was drafted by the Detroit Lions.

1962 *Chris Short.* Short became the first major league baseball player to win the award when he went 11-9 for the seventh-place Phillies. But if you had asked the Milford native what his highlight of the season was chances are he would have cited the game he knocked out four base hits against the legendary Warren Spahn.

1963 *Mike Brown* and *Vic Zwolak.* The two collegians became the first co-winners of the honor. Brown, a Conrad High School product, was a Little All-American back on Delaware's first undefeated football team since 1946. Brown tallied 10 touchdowns for the 8-0 Hens and gained 838 yards in his senior season to up his three-year total to 1674. Zwolak became the first Delawarean to win NCAA track titles, racing to victory in the 3000-meter steeplechase and the cross-country run for the Villanova Wildcats. He also captured two national titles in the three-mile and cross country runs, setting records in both.

1964 *Vic Zwolak.* The Salesianum graduate repeated as Delaware Athlete of the Year when he qualified for the United States Olympic team in the steeplechase event. Earlier in the season he successfully defended his NCAA steeplechase champion, setting a national collegiate record.

1965 *Chris Short*. Short enjoyed his finest season for the Phillies in 1965, winning 18 games for a sixth-place club - five of them shutouts. Short fanned 237 batters in establishing himself as one of Philadelphia's greatest ever lefthanded pitchers.

1966 *Chris Short* and *Herb Slattery*. Short reached a pinnacle in his lustrous career when he led the improving Phillies to a fourth-place finish by winning 20 games, notching his 20th in relief on the final day of the season. He tossed four shutouts and three two-hitters. With the award Short became the first three-time winner of the award. Slattery earned All-American recognition at the University of Delaware for his outstanding play on the offensive line yet the 6'3", 245-pound two-time all-stater from Archmere Academy was quick enough to perform at defensive linebacker and even in the secondary as well.

1967 *Grant Guthrie*. A sophomore at Florida State, Guthrie booted ten field goals, including three against Alabama to help snap the Crimson Tide's 19-game winning streak. At the Gator Bowl the Claymont High School product kicked a 26-yarder in the waning minutes to tie Penn State 17-17. He was the Seminoles' leading scorer with 53 points.

1968 *Art Redden*. The 30-year old Marine sergeant slugged his way to the Olympic Games as a light-heavyweight in 1968. Along the way he swept through the Marine and inter-service championships and the Olympic trials without a defeat. But his first defeat of the year eliminated him from the medal chase in Mexico City when he fell to Georgi Stankov of Bulgaria in the Olympics' first round.

1969 *Dick Kelley*. An all-purpose back for the University of Delaware Kelley gained over 1000 all-purpose yards in 1969. He scored six touchdowns rushing and four receiving, including two as Delaware downed North Carolina Central in the Boardwalk Bowl. In his days at Newark High School Kelley earned 4 letters in track, 3 in wrestling and 3 in football.

1970 *Bill Skinner*. The 31-year old Skinner had a phenomenal season as a javelin thrower in 1970. Sidetracked by work and the military, Skinner did not pick up a javelin until the age of 23 and put off college until 28 when he accepted a scholarship to the University of Tennessee where he developed into the best collegiate tosser in the nation. In 1970 the 6'7" Skinner won the NCAA and AAU championships and represented the United States in international competition,eventually reaching a personal best of 291 feet, 9.64 inches, less than 10 feet from the world mark.

1971 *Jim Krapf*. At Tatnall Krapf was more renowned for wrestling, winning over 100 matches without a loss, than football in which he was only a second team all-state lineman. But at the University of Alabama Krapf developed into a two-year starter and in 1971 was an All-Southeastern Conference center on Bear Bryant's undefeated Crimson Tide. Krapf was drafted by the Oakland Raiders and played briefly for British Columbia in the Canadian Football League before returning to Wilmington to start in the contstruction business.

1972 *Chris Dunn*. Dunn highlighted a successful high-jumping career at Colgate University by clearing 7'3" to finish 3rd in the Olympic Trials and earn a trip to Munich. The former

Newark High athlete failed three times, however, at the qualifying height of 7' 1/2" in the Olympics but it hardly dimmed a banner year which included wins in the NCAA Indoor Championships, the Penn Relays and the Martin Luther King Games.

1973 *Gary Hayman* and *Randy White*. Hayman, a former All-State end at Newark High School, helped Penn State to a perfect 12-0 season and Orange Bowl win with over 1200 receiving and returning yards. The Nittany Lion senior pulled down 30 receptions for 525 yards and three touchdowns in 1972. White, a junior at the University of Maryland, earned first-team All-America honors at defensive tackle as the Terrapins completed an 8-4 campaign which landed them in the Peach Bowl.

1974 *Randy White*. White completed his college career at Maryland by winning every award available to a defensive player, including the Outland Trophy as the nation's outstanding lineman. The most feared defender in years, opponents constantly ran plays away from the agile and disruptive White who nonetheless figured in 147 tackles and led the team in quarterback sacks.

1975 *Judy Johnson*. Completely overlooked in Delaware during his Hall-of-Fame baseball career from 1922 to 1937 Johnson was recognized as Athlete of the Year after his induction into the National Baseball Hall of Fame and Museum at Cooperstown, New York in 1975.

1976 *Steve Gregg* and *Joe Campbell*. Steve Gregg, from Tatnall and the Wilmington Swim School, made All-America 14 times in different events at North Carolina State. In the 1976 Olympic Games at Montreal Gregg won a silver medal in the 200-meter butterfly, finishing a fraction of a second behind teammate Mike Bruner. Campbell also earned numerous All-America honors as he wound up a career at the University of Maryland where he started for three years on the defensive line. At College Park Campbell played in four bowl games (Peach, Liberty, Gator and Cotton) and two all-star games.

1977 *Randy White* and *Steve Taylor*. With the Dallas Cowboys White was switched from linebacker to defensive tackle and he promptly made the Pro Bowl at his new position. In Super Bowl XII White was named co-Most Valuable Player and could probably have gone on winning this award indefinitely. Steve Taylor was the fifth winningest pitcher in college baseball for the University of Delaware Blue Hens in 1977 with 12 wins and only one loss. The Newark High graduate twirled three shutouts and was selected in the first round of the June draft by the New York Yankees. After a brief stay with Class A Fort Lauderdale Taylor was promoted to AA West Haven where he finished out the season.

1978 *Tim Wilson*. Another University of Marylander Wilson won the award for his distinguished work in the Houston Oiler backfield. He gained 431 yards on 129 carries but was more widely known as a punishing blocker for superstar Earl Campbell.

1979 *John Wockenfuss*. The ultimate utility player, Wockenfuss had his best season ever for the Detroit Tigers in 1979. He batted .264 and slugged nine doubles, one triple and 15 home runs in only 87 games. He also chased home 46 runs in his limited duty.

1980 *Renie Martin*. The Dover native won ten games for Kansas City in helping the Royals to their first American League pennant. Martin pitched effectively in three outings against the Phillies in the 1980 World Series and was afforded a parade in Dover following the series.

1981 *The Georgetown Senior Little League Baseball Team*. The collection of 14 and 15-year olds from the tiny town of Georgetown, with a population of 2000, wrested the World Series championship away from Taiwan for the first time in nine years. The team was collectively honored as Delaware's top athletes for 1981.

1982 *Henry Milligan*. After boxing for only 15 months the 24-year old Princeton graduate was named the Athlete of the Year in recognition for his 25-2 record as a heavyweight, including two semifinal finishes in national competition. Twenty of Milligan's wins had come by knockout, 14 of them in the first round.

1983 *Chris Anderson*. The University of Virginia senior became the first amateur golfer to win the award after defending his championship in the Philadelphia Amateur and becoming only the fifth non-professional to capture the Delaware Open.

1984 *Gene Lake*. The Milford native and former Army tank driver in Germany piled up more rushing yardage at Delaware State than any player at any level of college football in 1984. Discovered in a touch football game while working as a store clerk Lake began his college career at the age of 22. After rushing for 1069 yards in 1983 Lake went for 1722 yards in 1984, including 336 in the final game against Liberty Baptist.

1985 *Terence Stansbury*. Delaware's most accomplished basketball player was honored in the middle of his second NBA season with the Indiana Pacers. Slowed by injuries which robbed him of a starting job the 6'5" shooting guard was still averaging 9.3 points in 23 minutes.

1986 *Mike Hall*. Hall became the "Strongest Man in the World" when he won the super-heavyweight International Powerlifting Federation World Championships. More impressively, in a time when virtually all the competitors weaned themselves on steroids, the 385-pound Laurel resident won the title without ever digesting a performance-enhancing drug. His world records were in the bench press (620 pounds), dead lift (800), squat (930) and total pounds (2,270). Hall had been the Junior Olympic weightlifting champion in 1971-72.

1987 *Vicki Huber*. The Villanova University junior became the first woman recipient of Athlete of the Year honors as she blossomed into one of America's premier distance runners. In 1987 Huber won NCAA titles in the 3,000-meters, both indoors and outdoors and won Big East championships in cross country and the 1,500-meters. Running the 1,600-meter anchor leg Huber also paced Villanova to a share of the world record in the indoor distance medley.

1988 *Vicki Huber*. Huber ran the second fastest 3,000-meters ever by a collegiate woman when she finished sixth in the 1988 Seoul Olympics and was recognized as the first outright winner of the Athlete of the Year award in back-to-back years. In 1990 national honors came to Huber when she was named Collegiate Female Athlete of the Year.

1989 *John Taylor*. Although his only tenuous connection with Delaware was his collegiate stint at Delaware State in the early 1980s Taylor's performance and contributions to the Super Bowl champion San Francisco 49ers were too much for voters to overlook in 1989.

1990 *Delino DeShields*. DeShields could easily have been the first high school athlete honored since the formative days of the award forty years earlier but voters waited until he became a leading candidate for the National League Rookie of the Year in 1990. Despite missing nearly a month of the season with a broken finger the Montreal Expos new second baseman hit .289 with 42 stolen bases. DeShields also belted four home runs and drove in 45 runs.

1991 *Val Whiting*. Whiting didn't know what it was like to lose the final game of a basketball season until her sophomore year in college when her Stanford Cardinal were stopped in the NCAA semifinals. In Delaware Whiting led the Ursuline Raiders to four straight state girls basketball titles. She was Delaware Player of the Year in her sophomore, junior and senior years. After averaging 30.3 points and 16.1 boards in her last season Whiting went west to Stanford where she won another championship in her freshman year. The 6'2" Whiting was averaging 18.8 points per game and leading the Pac-10 in rebounding when she won Athlete of the Year honors as a junior.

1992 *Bill Vergantino*. The Pennsylvania native left the University of Delaware career with 24 school records in tow. A starter in 47 games in four years, Vergantino threw for 6,487 yards and ran for 2,564 more in leading the Blue Hens to 34 wins and two NCAA tournament appearances. Even with the gaudy statistics more telling of his contributions was the fact that he was the only quarterback ever to captain a Tubby Raymond football team.

1993 *Derrick May*. In 1993 May had the most productive major league season ever by a Delaware hitter than anyone except, well, his father. Breaking into the Chicago Cubs' line-up after a mediocre rookie season in 1992 the former Newark High outfielder hit .295 and drove in 77 runs despite missing 34 games with an injured hamstring. He struck out only 41 times in 465 at-bats while rapping out 10 home runs and 25 doubles.

1994 *Daryl Brown*. They always have the same adjective to describe a running back like Daryl Brown: punishing. At 6'3" and 240 pounds the fullback from Landover, Maryland was certainly as big as most of the defenders trying to tackle him. While the halfbacks and quarterbacks in Tubby Raymond's Wing-T plied the edges of the field Brown plowed straight ahead like no other University of Delaware fullback ever had. By the end of 1994 Daryl Brown owned 14 school records, including most yards in a game (273, against Northeastern), most yards in a season (1,469), most yards in a career (4,587) and most career touchdowns (47).

1995 *Seth Van Neerden*. A product of Bob Mattson's Wilmington Swim School, learning disabilities hampered Seth Van Neerden's development through his school years and he quit swimming. In 1995, as a geriatric aquatic of 27, he put his past problems behind him and emerged as one of the nation's top breaststrokers. At the 1995 Pan-American Games Van Neerden won three gold medals; the 100-metres, the 200-metres and as a member of the American 4x100 medley relay team.

1996 *Dionna Harris*. Dionna Harris won most of her softball trophies as a second baseman but became an outfielder when she joined the Connecticut Brakettes of the Amateur Softball Association in 1990. She made the national team from 1993 until 1996 and was the starting rightfielder for the United States team at the 1996 Atlanta Olympics. She earned her gold medal, leading the team in batting with a .409 batting average.

1997 *Michael McCarthy* and *Jana Withrow*. Michael McCarthy grew up in the shadow of Belmont Race Track in New York and decided early on he wanted to become a jockey. But at nearly 5'10" tall he did not possess the body of the classic thoroughbred pilot. He solved that by not eating. McCarthy was known as "The Flamingo" when he rode in Florida. After kicking around racing's bush leagues for more than a decade McCarthy arrived in the Delaware Valley in 1994. He became the leading jockey at Philadelphia Park and moved to Delaware. In 1997 he set the Delaware Park record for season wins with 218, including six on one day. McCarthy retired in 2002 with six riding titles at the Stanton showplace.

Jana Withrow wrapped up her field hockey career as goalkeeper at the University of North Carolina in 1997 with her third national championship. The A.I. duPont High School athlete was a two-time All-America selection and set the school record with 46 career shutouts.

1998 *Eddie Conti* and *Kevin Mench*. At the University of Delaware wide receiver Eddie Conti put his name next to as astounding 43 school, conference and NCAA records. In 1998 he snagged 91 passes for 1,712 yards to break Jerry Rice's 1-AA record. He added a couple more records on the track team. Whereas Conti piled up his collegiate records with speed, Kevin Mench employed power. The St. Mark's graduate pounded 33 home runs to lead the University of Delaware into the NCAA baseball tournament.

1999 *Mark Eaton*. When Mark Eaton skated onto the ice on October 2, 1999 for the Philadelphia Flyers against the Ottawa Senators he became the first National Hockey League player from Delaware. He was also the first Delaware Valley skater to suit for the hometown Flyers. The defenseman out of John Dickinson High School was undrafted but enjoyed a 13-year NHL career and won a Stanley Cup with the Pittsburgh Penguins in 2009.

2000 *Mike Neill*. Mike Neill banged out 1,185 minor league hits while compiling a lifetime .307 batting average. It wasn't enough to warrant a major league career but Neill did make the United States Olympic team in 2000. He batted .219 in the Games and led the gold medal winning-American team in home runs (3) and runs scored (9).

2001 *Jamie Natalie*. Jamie Natalie grew up tumbling in Wilmington and attended A.I. duPont high School. He blossomed at Ohio State University where he was a three-time All-American gymnast and frequent national team member. At the 2000 Olympic Trials Natalie, who excelled at floor exercise, parallel bars and high bar, was a top all-around performer but was controversially left off the Olympic team in favor of athletes who excelled in a single apparatus. He came back in 2001 to lead the Buckeyes to a national title and represented the U.S. at the World University Games. Natalie won the Nissen Award as the best male collegiate gymnast in the United States.

2002 *Luke Petitgout*. Luke Petitgout wrapped up his fourth NFL season in 2002. The former Sussex Central High School and Notre Dame offensive lineman was the 19th overall pick in the 1999 NFL Draft by the New York Giants. His No. 90 high school jersey was retired that year and he chose No. 77 in the pros as a nod to the Georgetown Fire Company. Petitgout was a starter at left guard in his rookie year before finding a permanent home at left tackle. He started 110 National Football League games before his career was derailed by injuries in 2007.

2003 *Mark Romanczuk*. Before Mark Romanczuk no college baseball player not a Delaware Blue Hen had ever been named Delaware Athlete of the Year. Romanczuk was twice a Gatorade High School Player of the Year in the First State at St. Mark's and posted a 10-0 mark in his senior year with three no-hitters, a perfect game and 146 strikeouts in 66 innings. Those eye-popping numbers got the attention of the Tampa Bay Devil Rays who selected Romanczuk in the fifth round of the 2002 draft. He opted for a Stanford education and won his first 12 games as a freshman in 2003 and was one of four National Freshman of the Year selections from *Collegiate Baseball*. Romanczuk won 28 games for the Cardinal, sixth most in school history, before leaving school after being picked in the fourth round of the 2005 draft by the Arizona Diamondbacks. He retired from baseball after four minor league seasons.

2004 *Rocky Myers*. Rocky Myers of Bowers Beach was a star in the classroom and on the playing field at Caesar Rodney and Lake Forest high schools before enrolling at hometown Wesley College. He graduated Summa Cum Laude with a degree in biology and also left the Wolverines with the Gagliardi Trophy as the National Player of the Year Award for NCAA Division III college football - the only defensive back so honored. Myers won an open audition for a bit part in Mark Wahlbergs' *Invincible*, the story of walk-on Philadelphia Eagles special teamer Vince Papale, which earned him a Screen Actors Guild card and led him to move to Hollywood in pursuit of a film career.

2005 *Jackie Ciconte*. For four years as a field hockey star at the University of Maryland Jackie Ciconte, a Tatnall School graduate, was known for flying toward the net looking to pounce on a rebound for a scoring opportunity. It was only fitting that she would corral a carom and hammer home a backhanded goal to give the Terrapins a 1-0 win over Duke in the 2005 national field hockey championship game.

2006 *Ian Snell*. 2006 was a breakout year for Dover's Ian Snell when he won 14 games for a Pittsburgh Pirates team that only win 67 all season. It was the most wins for a Delaware-born hurler since the days of Chris Short four decades earlier.

2007 *Tyresa Smith* and *Carrie Lingo*. In 2007 Tyresa Smith wrapped up a basketball career at the University of Delaware in which she was the second all-time leading scorer and skilled enough on the defensive end of the court to be named the Colonial Athletic Association's Defensive Player of the Year for the second time. Those honors piled up next to her high school laurels that included a state championship at Polytech High School in Woodside. Smith was taken in the second round of the WNBA Draft by the Phoenix Mercury, the 18th player taken overall.

Carrie Lingo was a long-time member of the national women's field hockey team and the former Cape Henlopen star was named to the Atlantic Coast Conference's 50th Anniversary Team as one of the top 50 field hockey players in conference history after her standout days at the University of North Carolina.

2008 *Elena Delle Donne*. In addition to being named Delaware Athlete of the Year, Elena Delle Donne collected honors as a McDonald's All-American, the *USA Today* National Player of the Year, the Naismith Prep Player of the Year, the Gatorade National Player of the Year and the EA Sports Player of the Year. With her high school career finished, she had scored more points on a Delaware scholastic court than any player in history.

2009 *Casey Howard*. Casey Howard was a key figure in the turnaround by the University of Delaware field hockey team which flipped a 3-15 mark in 2008 into a 14-6 record and an NCAA tournament appearance in 2009. The Camden native established new Blue Hen records for goals in a game (5, against Brown), goals in a season (22), and points in a season (51).

2010 *Elena Delle Donne*. After starting her collegiate career on the volleyball team Elena Delle Donne came back to basketball and was the nation's third highest scorer with 26.7 points per game. She was both the Rookie of the Year and the Player of the Year in the Colonial Athletic Conference.

2011 *Devon Still*. In his senior year at Howard High School Devon Still was a one-man wrecking crew on the football field. He piled up 59 tackles in his senior year, 18 of them for losses. He matriculated at Penn State where he was named Big Ten Defensive Player of the Year in 2011. He was a Nittany Lions team captain and would be drafted in the second round with the 53rd pick by the Cincinnati Bengals in 2012.

2012 *Elena Delle Donne*. This was the third go-around as the state's outstanding athlete for Elena Delle Donne after she took the University of Delaware women's basketball team to unimagined places in her senior year: a 27-3 record, a 6th seed in 2013 NCAA Women's Division I Basketball Tournament and a place in the Sweet Sixteen with wins against #11 West Virginia and #3 North Carolina. Delle Donne led the nation is scoring and was then made the second overall selection in the 2013 WNBA draft by the Chicago Sky.

2013 *Paul Worrilow*. Paul Worrilow left the Delaware high school football wars at Concord High School with a Division II state title and a Defensive Player of the Year award. Neither was enough to attract any scholarship offers so he went to Coffeyville Community College in Kansas before walking on to the University of Delaware squad in 2008. He then started every game at linebacker for the next four years, making 377 career tackles, the fifth most in school history. Again he attracted no interest at the next level. Worrilow signed as a free agent with the Atlanta Falcons for the 2013 season, made the team and worked his way into the starting line-up. The undrafted lineman earned recognition on several All-Rookie teams.

2014 *Marquis Dendy* and *Christina Hillman*. Harkening back to the earliest days of voting on Delaware's top athletes, two track and field stars were recognized for their 2014 accomplishments. Marquis Dendy of Middletown and Christina Hillman of Dover both won NCAA titles. Dendy, the son of Delaware Sports Hall of Famer Terri Dendy, won both the long jump and the triple jump at the University of Florida and uncorked the world's best triple jump with a leap of 56 feet, 6 1/2 inches. At Iowa State Hillman, who owns the Delaware shot put record of 49'1", won the indoor collegiate title.

2015 *Madison Brengle*. Growing up in Dover, Madison Brengle was coached by her mother Gaby who began tossing balls to her when she was two years old. In 2001 she swept the girls 12 singles and doubles titles at the United States Tennis Association's National Open. At the age of 15 Brengle captured her first professional title as a qualifier by beating three seeds and losing only one set in route to the USTA Women's Satellite Tour of Baltimore championship. She has since won six more International Tennis Federation singles titles and six doubles championships. The 25-year old right-hander enjoyed her best season in 2015, making it to the third round of the U.S. Open and the fourth round of the Australian Open; she finished the year ranked #40 in the world.

Indices

DELAWARE SPORTSPEOPLE

(Bold) - Delaware Sports Hall of Fame Members　　　*(Italics) - Photograph*

DELAWARE TEAMS

DELAWARE VENUES

DELAWARE COMPETITIONS

DELAWARE HORSES

* 9 7 8 1 9 3 5 7 7 1 3 2 6 *